T0243427

LAST MAN DOWN

LAST MAN DOWN

USS Nautilus *and the Undersea War in the Pacific*

DAVID W. JOURDAN

Foreword by VICE ADM. ALBERT H. KONETZNI JR. (RET.)
Former Commander, Submarine Force, US Pacific Fleet
(COMSUBPAC)

LYONS
PRESS

Essex, Connecticut

An imprint of Globe Pequot, the Trade Division of
The Rowman & Littlefield Publishing Group, Inc.
4501 Forbes Blvd., Ste. 200
Lanham, MD 20706
www.rowman.com

Distributed by NATIONAL BOOK NETWORK

British Library Cataloguing in Publication Information available

Library of Congress Cataloging-in-Publication Data available

Names: Jourdan, David W., author.
Title: Last man down : USS Nautilus and the undersea war in the Pacific / David W. Jourdan.
Other titles: USS Nautilus and the undersea war in the Pacific
Description: Guilford, Connecticut : Lyons Press, [2022] | Includes bibliographical references and
index.
Identifiers: LCCN 2022014724 (print) | LCCN 2022014725 (ebook) | ISBN 9781493063956
(cloth) | ISBN 9781493063963 (ebook)
Subjects: LCSH: Nautilus (Submarine : SS-168) | World War, 1939-1945—Naval operations,
American. | World War, 1939-1945—Campaigns—Pacific Area. | Midway, Battle of, 1942. |
World War, 1939-1945—Naval operations—Submarine.
Classification: LCC D782.N38 J68 2022 (print) | LCC D782.N38 (ebook) | DDC
940.54/5160973—dc23/eng/20220329
LC record available at https://lccn.loc.gov/2022014724
LC ebook record available at https://lccn.loc.gov/2022014725

∞™ The paper used in this publication meets the minimum requirements of American National
Standard for Information Sciences—Permanence of Paper for Printed Library Materials, ANSI/
NISO Z39.48-1992.

Contents

FOREWORD

WORLD WAR II's US SUBMARINE FORCE STORY IS ONE OF DEVOTION, innovation, patriotism, and loss. As a percentage, subs garnered the most casualties recorded during the war. Much has been written of the brave men who went to sea in our submarines between 1939 and 1945.

As a career submariner, I have been closely associated with those who served in support of freedom during World War II and upholding the American Dream. I have been fortunate to know many of these heroes and I am a believer in their "can-do" spirit and aggressiveness. They were the very best that America had to offer!

Last Man Down: USS Nautilus *and the Undersea War in the Pacific* is an exceptional success. Never before has an author meshed patrol reports, bureaucratic documents, comments of crew members, and senior officer oral histories in a completely coordinated method. As I read the manuscript, I became thoroughly absorbed by the reality of what Dave Jourdan was providing the reader.

This book paints a clear picture of what our brave submariners experienced during World War II. Furthermore, it shows how proud our "old boat" crew members were of their slow, aging, and in many ways, decrepit boats!

This effort is the very best I have ever read regarding life on the "pig boats" of World War II. *Last Man Down* provides us all we need to know regarding the bravery, enthusiasm, and camaraderie that was and remains the spirit of the US Submarine Force!

Vice Adm. Albert H. Konetzni Jr. (Ret.)
Former Commander, Submarine Force,
US Pacific Fleet (COMSUBPAC)

Preface and Acknowledgments

THIS BOOK IS A TRUE STORY. ALL EVENTS PORTRAYED TOOK PLACE AS I have described them to the accuracy of the historical record. All places, dates, and times have been taken from primary sources, including ship logs, official war diaries, and contemporary reports. I have relied on a number of secondary sources to fill in details such as ship characteristics, methods of operation, strategies, and tactics. These include several history books, official US Navy histories, operating manuals, historical photographs, film, and sound recordings.

I have colored the account with material from a collection of interviews with veterans who served on USS *Nautilus* during the war, including Buzz Lee, Red Porterfield, Bob Burrell, Jerry Gross, and Pat O'Brien. Although the descriptions are vivid, and fill in much detail missing from primary sources, the accuracy of eyewitness reports is always open to question, and clearly memories have degraded with time. A few of Buzz Lee's stories, for example, could not have happened as he described them according to the timing of the primary record. In some cases, he may have confused events from different patrols, or "adopted" tales of other men's experiences. Keeping this in mind, I always relied on the primary record for particulars of time and place, but used the interviews to complete details and portray the feelings and reactions of the participants.

Family members of key *Nautilus* crew were helpful providing documents, memorabilia, and research support. Notable among them are Foy Hester Jr., son of Chief Electrician Foy Hester, and Larry Brockman, nephew of Captain William Brockman. Also, Peggy Haeger, daughter of Executive Officer Ozzie Lynch, provided copies of Lynch's 16-mm film shot on board *Nautilus*.

I have also drawn on personal experience as a US Navy submarine officer, using equipment and procedures that—in the 1970s—were surprisingly similar to World War II submarine operations. I have visited World War II Pacific battlefields on Midway, Saipan, Yap, and Tarawa. I enjoyed a tour of USS *Lionfish* (SS-298), a *Balao*-class submarine on exhibition in Fall River, Massachusetts, that patrolled Japanese waters near war's end. I consulted with diesel boat sailors from the postwar era to help validate submarine operations procedures I describe.

I have taken some liberties in describing events on *Nautilus*, including dialogue and details of operations. The latter are drawn from NAVPERS 16160, *The Fleet Type Submarine*, which was the operating manual for World War II boats. The standard terminology for diving, surfacing, launching weapons, and other common submarine evolutions was established by then and is still used today. Although I cannot be sure of the exact words used, I believe the dialogue is authentic. Again, all events—diving, surfacing, coming to periscope depth, launching a torpedo, observation angles, speeds, headings, torpedo settings, and many other details—are accurate according to contemporary logs.

I owe many thanks to those who helped me tell this story, all these years later. Jeff Morris conducted some of the original research at the National Archives in Washington, DC, beginning in 1997, and more recently Foy Hester, Tom Vinson, and Rod Blocksome who helped me capture images of every page of each day's deck log for the entire *Nautilus* war history. Jeff Palshook and Spence King connected with several *Nautilus* veterans through the organization SubVets in the late 1990s and conducted many of the interviews noted above. Those recollections were extremely valuable and inspirational. Michelle Cooper also conducted interviews and greatly supported my research. Spence, Foy, Vice Adm. George Emery (ret.), Adm. Jim Stavridis (ret.), and Vice Adm. Al Konetzni (ret.) read my draft and offered many excellent suggestions and helpful guidance.

My family has been a constant source of support and encouragement. Lynn was always eager to hear me read after every writing session, and I looked forward to those pleasant ends to long days of research and writing. Eric is an avid reader of history and I appreciate his insights.

Bethany, now a freelance graphic designer, produced and revised all my illustrations and prepared the photographs for publication. Many thanks and much love to you all.

This book continues my theme of recognizing wartime heroes of the past and the explorers and historians who uncovered details of their histories. I hope in some small measure through these contributions their sacrifices and achievements will never be forgotten.

Cape Porpoise, Maine
December 2021

PART I

INTO THE JAWS OF THE EMPIRE

THE SUN WAS SETTING OFF THE PORT BEAM AS USS *NAUTILUS* NOSED into the quiet harbor and made her way to the Sand Island pier. The scars from recent aerial bombardments were evident on Midway Atoll as the crew topside solemnly surveyed the scene before them. Twenty-four-year-old radioman Harold "Buzz" Lee was on the quarterdeck and was shocked by what he saw. "As soon as we got inside the entrance buoys, we went to quarters topside, all in a line with hats on. God almighty, Midway was a terrible thing to see. The whole island was still smoking. Next to us there were wooden buildings on Sand Island, and they were all burned."[1] The atoll was a mess—the Eastern Island power plant was destroyed; gasoline lines used for refueling planes were set afire; the command post was flattened; Sand Island oil tanks were burning, and many buildings were wrecked. Plumes of oily black smoke billowed into the sky. Remarkably, in the three days since the air attack on the naval island base, much had been repaired, including flight facilities. Thankfully, the submarine docks had escaped damage.

In the waning twilight, the submarine moored. Dockyard workers soon began refueling, rearming, and resupplying her and the other boats[2] arriving there, returning from the Midway battle. *Nautilus* would be shoving off again in less than forty-eight hours to continue her first war patrol.

---

1. Interview with Harold "Buzz" Lee, March 2005.

2. Submarines are often referred to as "boats," especially by submariners. This is thought to be a historical convention dating back to the early days of small submersible boats that were carried and launched by larger vessels.

I

Besides the submarines, the other vessels in the harbor were PT[3] boats, which had been on daily patrols around the island, watching for Japanese submarines, sighting aircraft, and picking up downed pilots. Since the bombing of Midway, which commenced on June 4, 1942, they had been engaged in a more solemn duty—burial at sea. On June 6, a parade of PT boats left the harbor and ceremonially cast eleven dead Marines and sailors to the deep; each morning, over the next several days, the grim ritual was repeated as more bodies were found in the wreckage and men died of their wounds. Buzz Lee remembered seeing the fate of fallen comrades:

> *The only other ships there were the PT boats. On them were our dead—it was the saddest thing to see—wrapped in canvas and covered with bunting. They were lined up on the decks, three or four in a row. Then the boats would leave, slowly, to sea. They'd tie a big five-inch shell between their legs for weight, then slide them off gently to the bottom of the ocean. We stood there in awe, grateful that it wasn't us.*[4]

Most of the casualties from Midway Island were pilots: twenty-two navy, two-dozen army air force, and another thirty-six Marine pilots perished in attacks on the Japanese fleet and in defense of the island. Most of them were lost at sea, downed in their flaming aircraft. Another twenty men died on the ground, a remarkably small tally considering the destruction of the facilities, including barracks, mess hall, chapel, and the dispensary.

In all, some 186 American flight crew from the carriers USS *Enterprise*, USS *Hornet*, and USS *Yorktown*, and Naval Air Station Midway were lost in defense of the island. Counting those on the ground and sailors lost in the sinking of USS *Yorktown* and the destroyer USS *Hammann*, more than four hundred US servicemen lost their lives. The Japanese suffered the destruction of four carriers and their aircraft, the heart of the Japanese air fleet, along with a heavy cruiser and other ships

---

3. Patrol Torpedo boats. Small, fast, and inexpensive, these vessels were used throughout the Pacific during the war.
4. Interview with Harold "Buzz" Lee, March 2005.

that endured damages. More than three thousand Japanese sailors died in their failed attempt to take Midway.

Nautilus suffered strikes by aircraft and several depth charge attacks during her twelve-hour encounter with the Japanese fleet on June 4. Forty-two depth charges were dropped on her, some close enough to cause damage. For the ninety-two crew members on board, every officer and enlisted man on his first war patrol, the experience was horrifying. "I thought I was going to die," remembered Lee. "I thought it was the end." There was nothing to be done, nowhere to turn, and no way to help a shipmate through the ordeal. It didn't help to see the fear in another man's eyes. "You didn't even look at anybody else. You just held on and sat there. What are you going to do? You're helpless."[5]

In spite of the horror and risk of destruction, Lt. Cdr. William Brockman, captain of *Nautilus*, skillfully and aggressively engaged the enemy, firing torpedoes at a battleship, a destroyer, and the aircraft carrier *Kaga* in the fleet. Though none of his torpedoes hit the mark—or if any did, they failed to explode—the actions of the submarine played a significant role in the outcome of the battle.[6]

The Imperial Japanese Navy was severely bloodied at Midway. The loss of four heavy aircraft carriers, all veterans of the infamous surprise attack on Pearl Harbor in December 1941, was crippling, and the destruction of more than 250 carrier-based aircraft was a serious blow. More grievous was the loss of 130 aircrew, including experienced pilots who could not be easily replaced. As the Japanese fleet retreated from the waters west of Midway, Adm. Isoroku Yamamoto, commander of the Combined Fleet, had suffered a crushing defeat, the first real setback of the war in the Pacific. However, the Japanese fleet remained one of the most powerful navies in the world, and still fielded the most formidable naval air force in history. With nine aircraft carriers and more than one thousand warplanes in operation, the Japanese considerably out gunned the American Pacific Fleet with just three carriers still afloat. A similar superiority was enjoyed by the Combined Fleet with battleships at eleven

5. Interview with Harold "Buzz" Lee, March 2005.
6. See *The Search for the Japanese Fleet: USS* Nautilus *and the Battle of Midway* (Jourdan, 2015) for the full story of the submarine's role in the battle.

to three, nearly double the number of cruisers, and more destroyers, submarines, patrol craft, sub chasers, and auxiliaries. For the time being, Admiral Yamamoto consolidated his forces in defense of his Pacific bases and the Japanese homeland. The turning point in the Pacific war had passed with the Battle of Midway. The grim and grisly work of defeating the Japanese Empire was just beginning.

The US fleet was not yet strong enough for a major naval offensive, but the Americans moved quickly to keep the initiative after the Midway victory. Although the navy could not attack on the sea, with fifty-six submarines in the Pacific theater an undersea campaign was feasible. Rear Adm. Robert English, submarine Pacific Fleet commander, took immediate steps to deploy his boats to Japanese waters. He took harsh measures with his staff and submarine commanders, dismissing all who he felt were not aggressive enough or competent enough to meet his standards. A few of the older hands who had performed well were sent stateside to commission new boats and train fresh crews. He also asked the Pacific Fleet commander, Adm. Chester Nimitz, to construct a major submarine base at Midway.

Following the battle, six boats were ordered to put in to Midway to refuel, rearm, and proceed directly to Japanese Empire waters. Among them was *Nautilus* and her aggressive and highly regarded skipper, Bill Brockman. Her destination: the Honshu coast of Japan, near the entrance to Tokyo Bay, to seek the enemy in his home waters.

Into the jaws of the empire.

CHAPTER ONE

Honshu

THERE WAS NO TIME FOR A HERO'S WELCOME AS *NAUTILUS* TIED UP TO the Midway submarine pier on Sunday evening, June 7, 1942. While Captain Brockman went ashore to deliver his interim patrol report, the crew set to work making repairs and preparations to return to sea.

On June 4, the submarine made several torpedo attacks against Japanese warships and the enemy had counterattacked with depth charges. The shock waves and concussive jarring of forty-two undersea explosions over a period of a few hours had rattled the crew and caused some damage to the vessel. Most serious was the rudder, knocked loose during the attacks. It developed a knocking noise and was binding in its bearings making it difficult to move. Other derangements included seawater leaks, a ruptured hydraulic line, and a few electrical shorts. The brunt of the work fell on the torpedomen who busied themselves moving 3,800 pound weapons around and making repairs to malfunctioning tubes. Brockman characterized the damage to the ship as "negligible," though the crew may have disagreed. His assessment was fair considering what was to come in the ensuing weeks of war patrol.

Chief Bosun's Mate Floyd "Red" Porterfield took charge. As chief of the boat, he was the senior enlisted man and worked directly with executive officer Lt. Cdr. Roy Benson to manage the crew. He also led the torpedomen during battle stations and took a particular interest in their work.

"John, let's get cracking. I want those tin pickles[1] sorted out during the midwatch. Mind we'll be refueling in the morning and the pier will be busy."

"Got it, chief," replied John Sabbe, first class torpedoman. "O'Brien's moving fish with Bacon, Galli, and Campbell. I'm working with Porter and Lewis on tube one. I told the other guys to get some sleep. I doubt they will with all the shit going on around here."

"There'll be time to sleep when we get underway. I don't want to go up against the Japs again with a FUBAR[2] tube," replied Red. "If you get it working by morning XO[3] says we can cycle people ashore for a look around. We get underway on Tuesday afternoon."

"Christ, chief, that's the day after tomorrow! We just got here! Any idea where we're going?"

"We'll find out when we get there—they don't ask my advice. Let me know soon as you have anything on tube one."

"Will do, chief."

Red Porterfield was a tall, ruddy redhead with a booming voice and language as colorful as his visage. He hailed from Quay, Oklahoma, about as far from the ocean as one could be, but had proved to be an accomplished sailor and a natural leader. Just two months earlier he had advanced to chief at barely twenty-five years of age and was named "chief of the boat."[4] Though fairly junior, he obviously had the confidence of Captain Brockman to be given such a position of responsibility. He did well enough that he was commissioned as an ensign the following year. Sailing on all but the last of *Nautilus'* fourteen war patrols, Porterfield would eventually hold every officer position except commanding officer and communicator.

John Sabbe reported on board *Nautilus* shortly before Porterfield in 1941, and the chief relied on him to manage the torpedo division. Of

---

1. Torpedoes, also referred to as "fish."

2. Fouled (or fucked) up beyond all recognition.

3. Executive Officer, second in command to the captain.

4. The chief of the boat, or COB, is the senior enlisted man on a submarine. He reports to the executive officer and helps with personnel management and morale, in addition to his technical and operational duties.

medium build, with brown hair and unremarkable features, Sabbe was a quiet, but firm leader. He was one of seven crewmen who served on all fourteen *Nautilus* war patrols, and was promoted to ensign in 1944.

"John, I want to tell you something," said Porterfield before moving on to check on other work on board.

"What is it, chief?" wondered Sabbe, fearing the worst. "Something wrong?"

"No. Not wrong. I wanted to tell you I was talking with the captain after things calmed down, after the depth charging. He told me he was surprised to see the "ready" light[5] come up so fast. He couldn't believe we had the tubes reloaded so quick. Captain was real happy with that."

"Oh, thanks, chief! I'll tell the boys. They'll be tickled to hear it."

"OK, don't get a swelled head. But keep it up. There are more Japs to shoot out there!"

"Right, chief!"

The *Nautilus* crew worked through the night, conducting a "blanket drill" (taking a nap) whenever possible. By morning much progress was evident, and a number of crewmen were allowed ashore. There being few working facilities and many signs of the Japanese bombing just a few days earlier, it was not a relaxing diversion.

One man left the boat for good—according to Lee, he "went mad" during the depth charging suffered by *Nautilus* during the battle. Interestingly, the captain's patrol report mentions that a man was transferred off the boat at Midway owing to "arthritis." The official muster roll says that Seaman First Class William Troutman was transferred to Naval Air Station Midway on June 9 "for further transfer, US Naval Hospital, Pearl Harbor, Territory of Hawaii." Arthritis seems an unusual affliction for a young seaman, and hospitalization a drastic measure. Perhaps the captain was reluctant to put the true nature of the sailor's ailment in the official report? Considering the horrors experienced by the young *Nautilus* crew, and the frightful unknown of patrols to come, it is remarkable that only one of the men failed to retain his sanity.

---

5. Interview with Floyd "Red" Porterfield, August 2006. The "ready" light illuminates in the conning tower attack center when a torpedo tube is reloaded and ready to shoot.

Captain Brockman reported to makeshift headquarters (the island command post having been wrecked by Japanese bombs) to report to Admiral English, who had rushed to Midway from his base in Pearl Harbor to meet his incoming skippers.

"Welcome, Bill, sit down!" The admiral, excited to greet his most successful commander, quickly dispensed with formalities. "Well done out there! We really licked 'em, didn't we?"

"Yes, sir, we sure did," Brockman replied, taking a seat. The thirty-seven-year-old commanding officer was an imposing figure who was big enough to play football on the offensive line at the Naval Academy, which no doubt enhanced his image. He was described by shipmate Buzz Lee as a "tough guy" and stern, commanding tremendous respect from the crew. "He had a way about him; you immediately knew that he had command." Brockman was more than a physical presence; he was also capable—he "knew what he was doing." He was demanding of his officers, and was described by his executive officer (and future admiral) Roy Benson as "a difficult man to shave, and told his own crew very little of what was going on."[6] But his most notable trait as a submarine captain was his willingness to boldly pursue the enemy. Lee said, "He was the bravest man I ever knew. He never turned away from anything."[7]

English said, "Well, you handled yourself very well. We need more aggressive captains and I want to make an example out of you. I'm putting you and your crew in for some commendations."

"Thank you, sir. The men did their jobs. And I have some good officers on board." He handed the admiral his interim patrol report, covering the actions of June 4. "Here is a narrative covering the day of the battle. I'll include that with my regular patrol report when we return, but I thought some things might be of immediate interest." He went on to detail some observations about Japanese sonars noted by his chief sonar

---

6. Letter to Jeff Palshook from Edward Beach, October 30, 2000. Beach was a junior officer under Roy Benson when he commanded USS *Trigger*. Beach went on to write the 1983 classic novel of submarine warfare in the Pacific, *Run Silent, Run Deep*.

7. Interview with Harold "Buzz" Lee, March 2005.

man, Irving (Ike) Wetmore. "Sir, I also want to add that all the officers and men were excellent. I particularly want to note Lt. Hogan, our diving officer. *Nautilus* is not an easy boat to handle, but he did an expert job. I think he deserves special mention."[8]

"Very well, very well," said English. "I'm sending you right back out there. We need to keep the pressure on and sink some more ships. And I have another job for you, which you might find interesting."

English then launched into a strange and surprising proposal. *Nautilus*, being one of the largest submarines in the US fleet, sported two six-inch deck guns, forward and aft of the superstructure. Weapons of this caliber were normally carried by warships the size of cruisers, hence *Nautilus* and her mates *Narwhal* and *Argonaut* were sometimes called "cruiser subs." Though these guns were meant to sink ships, English had another idea.

"Take a look at this." English spread out several detailed charts of Tokyo Bay and the surrounding waters on the southeast side of the Japanese main island of Honshu. He jabbed his finger at a spot on the north shore of Hayama Bay, just twenty-five miles[9] from the Japanese capital.

"Right here is Emperor Hirohito's summer palace, a place called Hayama," said English. He looked up at Brockman. "I want you to shell it."

"Sir?" Brockman was stunned.

"Shell it. I want you to use those six-inch cannons of yours to flatten the palace. We might catch Hirohito at home. Think of what that would do for morale! You'd be a hero, like Doolittle!"[10]

This was a recklessly dangerous idea. The maximum range of the guns was just thirteen miles. To approach the summer palace close enough for an effective bombardment would call for a perilous transit through shallow water teeming with Japanese patrol ships and dotted with navigation hazards. To use the weapons, the submarine would have to surface, revealing

---

8. Extract from War Patrol Report of USS *Nautilus*.

9. Distances are generally given in nautical miles. One nautical mile is approximately 1/60 of a degree of latitude, about two thousand yards, and is a useful unit of measure at sea. Today, it is defined as 6,076 feet (compared to 5,280 feet for a statute mile). A knot of speed is one nautical mile per hour.

10. Lt. Col. (later General) Jimmy Doolittle who led the famous air raid over Tokyo in April, just two months earlier.

its position and exposing it to larger shore-based artillery. *Nautilus* was ill-suited for the task. She was large, old, slow, and lacked the maneuverability needed for tricky near-shore operations. It was clearly a near suicidal feat that amounted to nothing more than a stunt. Brockman studied the chart carefully, quickly recognizing the dangers he and his crew would face. His thoughts turned from the details of the chart to how to deal with his boss and his crazy idea. He noted that English didn't mention any intelligence to support the speculation that the emperor was in residence.

"Admiral, I will think about this," he said carefully after a few minutes of study. "I would like to discuss it with my officers."

"Of course, of course," English replied. "You do that." He knew he could not order Brockman to take such a risk. "You have your patrol orders. Now, get back out there and create some havoc!'

"Aye, aye, sir!" Brockman saluted, gathered the charts, and headed back to his ship. He never brought up the idea with his officers, and the admiral's ill-conceived caper was never mentioned again.[11]

"Ahead full. Steady on course two-nine-five." The officer of the deck, Lieutenant Frank Hess, had directed the massive 371 foot, 4,000 ton submarine out of the Midway lagoon, headed south to clear the atoll, then turned northwest at full speed toward the setting sun. The date was June 9. Their destination, more than 2,100 nautical miles away, was a patrol area a scant twenty miles from the Japanese coast at the approaches to Tokyo Bay. There they would lurk, seeking enemy warships and merchant vessels to attack.

Nautilus cruised on the surface into calm seas, a warm tropical breeze bathing the men on the bridge. The low rumble of diesel engines and sluicing of seawater past the hull were the only other sounds. The vibration of machinery operating below punctuated the gentle pitch and roll of the vessel as it moved though the waves. Captain Brockman stood

---

11. This extraordinary exchange was noted by Clay Blair in *Silent Victory* (1975) among other sources.

beside Hess and a pair of lookouts, contemplating the dramatic events of the past few days, imagining what might be in store in the following weeks for the ninety men under his command.

"Mr. Hess, is the ship rigged for dive?" Brockman already knew the answer, but he was not one to dispense with formalities. The submarine had already been "rigged for dive" shortly after getting underway. This involved making all weight compensations and setting all hull openings in a position of readiness for diving. That way, the officer of the deck could order a dive at any moment to escape attack or detection. A submarine is always ready to dive.

"Yes, sir. All compartments have reported," replied Hess.

"Very well. Go ahead with the trim dive," Brockman ordered. He then descended the bridge ladder and entered the conning tower, a small compartment that sat atop the main pressure hull that housed the attack center.

Pearl Harbor, circa 1940 looking northwest. Battleship Row is center; the submarine base is lower right. U.S. NAVY.

Midway Atoll, November 1941. Eastern Island is in the foreground. Sand Island with its submarine base beyond. U.S. NAVY.

"Go ahead with trim dive, aye, sir," called Hess as the captain disappeared down the hatch, repeating the order to be sure it was understood. He then announced, "Clear the bridge!" followed by an order to the control room below, "Diving officer, submerge the ship!" Immediately, the chief of the watch signaled two blasts on the diving alarm, *ah-OO-gah, ah-OO-gah.* He announced, "Dive, dive," over the announcing system known as the 1MC. Upon this command, the crew sprang into action throughout the ship. Without further orders, the engine room watch stopped the diesels and answered "All ahead standard" speed, the electric motors that drove the propellers now relying on battery power alone. Engine and ventilation intake and exhaust valves were shut. The bridge party scrambled down the ladder into the conning tower, traditionally the officer of the deck at the rear of the procession. Hess closed the conning tower outer hatch and announced, "Last man down, hatch secured." By then, the chief of the watch had already opened the bow buoyancy and main ballast tanks vents, allowing tons of seawater to flood into the tanks. *Nautilus* was on her way down.

Hess quickly took his place at the periscope stand and peered through the raised number one periscope. Looking fore and aft, he noted water washing over the deck and a double row of geysers created by columns of air escaping from the ballast tanks. "Tanks venting," he called, confirming that the vents had opened properly.

In the control room below, Tom Hogan, the diving officer, watched the control panel in front of him covered with red lighted bars. One by one, the red bars changed to green.

"What's Mr. Hogan looking at, chief?" whispered Wane Campbell. An apprentice seaman, Campbell had reported on board shortly before *Nautilus* left Mare Island, California, and sailed into battle at Midway. He and chief electrician Foy Hester were huddled in a corner of the cramped control room—Campbell the trainee, Hester the veteran mentor. Foy was not an imposing figure at below average height and a slender 136 pounds, and he was known to generally keep to himself. Behind his ruddy complexion, dark hair, and deep-set brown eyes was a serious and thoughtful man, an expert in his trade, well respected by his shipmates. Foy had joined the crew in 1936 and was one of the longest tenured men on board. With fifteen years of naval service already behind him, he was a fount of experience and a great resource for young sailors.

"Mr. Hogan is looking at the 'Christmas tree.' That's what we call it on account of the red and green lights. Red means an open hull valve; green means shut. We need them all green before we submerge."

Just then, Hogan saw the last light change from red to green. "Green board," he called out, followed by "Bleed air."

Hester continued explaining to Campbell, quietly so as not to disturb the proceedings, "Now the chief of the watch will let a little high pressure air into the hull to see if it's sealed tight. You watch that needle there on that pressure gauge and see if it moves." Sure enough, the air pressure in the control room (and inside the rest of the pressure hull) rose slightly. The chief shut the valve and announced, "Pressure in the boat!" He vented additional ballast tanks to accelerate the dive.

"Five degrees down, make your depth six-five feet," said Hogan. "Five down, aye!" "Make my depth six-five feet, aye!" The planesmen repeated the order as they twirled their handwheels to set the bow and stern planes. The deck took a pronounced tilt forward as the bow began to settle.

Soon the submarine reached ordered depth. Vents were shut. "Six-five feet," called Hogan. "Very well, ahead one-third," ordered Hess, slowing the ship so Hogan could check the trim.

"What's that, chief?" wondered Campbell, noting Hester writing numbers in a notebook. "That's my dive log," replied Hester. I write down every dive and keep track of our time underwater."

"Oh! Why?"

"Just something I like to keep track of. I've logged every dive since December 7, when the war started. This is *Nautilus* dive number 1,303 since she was launched back in 1930."

"Well I'll be Goddamned!" marveled the young sailor, impressed. "That's a lotta dives!"

Hester winced in spite of himself. A churchgoing man, Hester didn't use vulgar language, though he'd heard a fair share of it over his years of naval service. "Yes, it sure is," he continued. "That's over 142 hours underwater since April, when we got underway from Mare Island and made our first dive of the war. Almost fifty dives. But pay attention. Mr. Hogan is trimming the ship, moving water from tank to tank so we can cruise underwater slowly on an even keel. After refueling, swapping around torpedoes, and taking on supplies, our trim was out of whack, and the diving officer has to adjust it. Otherwise, we might find ourselves bobbing to the surface at just the wrong time. We're lucky to have Mr. Hogan as a diving officer—he's tops."

While Hogan was at work, Lt. Cdr. Pat Rooney appeared at the conning tower's ladder. "Permission to come up and relieve the watch?"

"Granted. Evening, Pat," said Hess, looking forward to a break after his four-hour stint, which had included the demanding task of getting the ship underway. Rooney climbed the ladder, and he and Hess talked over the situation, the time-honored tradition of watch "turnover."

Rooney had already familiarized himself with the current goings-on about the ship, the conditions of the machinery, the tactical situation, the captain's current Night Orders,[12] and the plan for the watch. Most of what Hess told him, he already knew. "OK, we're submerged on course two-nine-five by gyro, making one-third speed on both main motors conducting a trim dive. Navigator is standing by to sight evening stars as soon as we're back on top." A few details about equipment, tanks, and weapons were verified. Satisfied he was ready, Rooney declared, "I am ready to relieve you," to which Hess replied, "I stand relieved." Rooney then announced to the bridge party and the watch standers in the conning tower, "This is Mr. Rooney. I have the deck and the conn." Hess headed below for some chow, and maybe even some well-deserved sleep.

After a short while, Hogan was satisfied. The submarine was neither heavy nor light, and was in trim fore and aft, starboard and port. He reported this to the officer of the deck. "Very well," replied Hess. "Prepare to surface." Back up they went. Next time, they would be in trim for the dive. Hester added another eighteen minutes to his logged underwater time.

Nautilus made daily dives during their following days of transit. The crew strived to take the ship from surface to a keel depth of sixty-eight feet as quickly as possible. At that depth the submarine hull and conning tower were completely underwater, but a raised periscope would poke a few feet above the waves. A quick dive was essential to evade attack from fast-approaching aircraft, and a standard fleet-type boat could complete a wartime dive in about thirty seconds. However, the best *Nautilus* could do was just under a minute, the log showing an average of fifty-eight seconds over ten dives. That was an improvement over their transit from Pearl Harbor in May, when they generally took sixty to sixty-seven seconds.

---

12. The Night Orders detailed how the overnight watches were to be conducted and under what circumstances the captain should be awoken for a command decision.

But Brockman was not happy. Besides its sheer bulk, old *Nautilus* was hampered by lack of a "negative" tank. In a modern fleet boat this tank had a capacity of nearly eight tons and was normally full while on the surface. It provided negative buoyancy (making the ship heavier) for quick diving. In wartime, every dive was a quick dive, and this tank helped the ship submerge faster. Before reaching the desired depth, the negative tank would be blown dry with pressurized air (with the order, "Blow negative!") to restore the vessel to near neutral trim. Without a negative tank, *Nautilus* could not make such a quick dive.

On the surface making thirteen knots, *Nautilus* continued northwest, the sun already below the clear horizon. Twilight faded and stars began to wink in the moonless night sky.[13]

"Mr. Rooney! Contact, dead ahead!" cried out Holtz, one of the lookouts.

"Aye, Holtz, I see it," replied Rooney, apparently unperturbed. "What do you think it is?"

"I see . . . several lights, sir, one of them is red," continued Holtz, a bit puzzled by Hess's lack of concern. "Could be an aircraft, or a ship!"

"Guess again," Rooney replied with a chuckle. "That red one is Mars; the brighter one just on the horizon is the navigation star Procyon. The other two side by side are Castor and Pollux, Gemini, the Twins. We use all of those stars for navigation."

Just then, Executive Officer Roy Benson, who also served as the ship's navigator, appeared at the hatch. "Permission to come up?" he called to the officer of the deck. "Come on up, XO," said Rooney. I was just giving Holtz here a lesson in astronomy. Time for your evening stars, I gather? Are we lost yet?"

"Not hardly," said Benson as he set to work with his sextant.

---

13. According to logs, the sky was actually mostly overcast at that time. Mars and the noted stars, however, were dead ahead and may have been visible, offering a good opportunity to mention navigation.

Nautilus continued northwest, her patrol area over two thousand nautical miles away. Captain Brockman was eager to cover this distance as quickly as possible. Going full speed on the surface, the ship could cruise at fourteen knots[14] and cover 340 miles a day. At that rate, it could make the voyage in less than a week. But Brockman had other concerns. Running at that speed would consume considerable fuel; a more economical ten knots was better for covering long distances. Also, submarines were easy prey for aircraft while on the surface, and in enemy waters would remain submerged during daylight hours. Underwater, relying on battery power alone, *Nautilus* could make a top speed of eight knots, but not for long. At five knots she could remain submerged for about ten hours before needing to surface and recharge batteries. But in the central Pacific Ocean, summer daylight lasted more than fifteen hours so she would have to go even slower to remain submerged all day. Brockman judged that the risk of enemy aircraft appearing out of nowhere, far from any Japanese base, was low, and he chose to remain on the surface during the transit (except for daily training dives).

Another consideration was zig-zagging. Experience with submarine warfare in World War I led surface vessels to alter their course and speed around a baseline direction to help foil submarine attack. There was debate about this practice and a 1918 Office of Naval Intelligence study did not find much value in course changes, though speed changes were helpful. Regardless, the tactic was regularly used. For submarines, with their low surface profile, it was considered less helpful, and of course it slowed overall progress toward a destination. Captain Brockman chose to zig-zag only during periods around sunrise and sunset when he felt the sub was most vulnerable. Taking all this into account, *Nautilus* was able to practically make a bit more than eight knots on average, and would arrive at the assigned patrol area in about eleven days.

The days passed without incident as the submarine neared enemy waters. By midafternoon on June 20, *Nautilus* was a hundred nautical miles from the Japanese mainland. Forward lookouts squinted into the

---

14. *Nautilus* made a top speed of 17.4 knots in sea trials. At a more sedate 10 knots the ship could travel nearly 9,400 nautical miles with a full load of fuel.

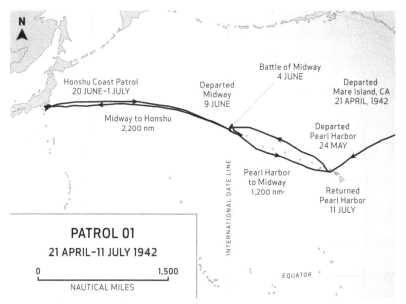

USS *Nautilus* first patrol. The submarine played a key role in the Battle of Midway, then after a brief stop at Midway Atoll resumed her mission, patrolling the entrance to Tokyo Bay off the Honshu coast. ILLUSTRATION BY BETHANY JOURDAN.

late afternoon setting sun as they peered in the direction of the Honshu coast, dead ahead.

"Conn, JK," called Buzz Lee, manning the "JK" sonar listening equipment in the conning tower. He was continuously scanning the surrounding waters, listening for sounds of churning screws of ships. He and his mates were trained to distinguish these distant sounds from other noises in the water, including rain squalls, whales, snapping shrimp, and sounds made by *Nautilus* herself.

"Go ahead, JK," called Ensign Joe Defrees from the bridge above. Defrees, just twenty-one years of age, was the youngest officer on board. Owing to the exigencies of war, his Naval Academy class of 1942 was commissioned early, December 1941. In other circumstances, Joe would have been enjoying college graduation ceremonies instead of sailing into battle. Defrees was a capable and competent officer, steeped in navy traditions, being the son of a rear admiral who was awarded the Navy Cross for distinguished service in World War I.

"Propeller sounds, bearing three-zero-eight true," replied Lee. "Does not sound like a merchant ship, too high pitched." Lee, a radioman by rating, had received extensive training in sonar operations before leaving Mare Island, and had spent the day of June 4 in the conning tower listening to the sounds of the Japanese fleet at Midway. He knew what a warship sounded like.

"Very well," replied Defrees. He did not hesitate. "Clear the bridge!" he called to the lookouts topside. "Diving officer, submerge the ship, make your depth one-five-zero feet!" The men on the bridge scrambled below to man positions in the conning tower, Defrees right behind them. "Last man down, hatch secured!" called Defrees as he closed and dogged the watertight hatch. With the submarine descending, he took his position at the periscope stand and had a last look around before the lens dipped below the surface. "Down scope," he called, snapping up the handles of the instrument so it could slide smoothly down its tube. By that time, Captain Brockman had climbed the ladder to the conning tower and was assessing the situation.

"One-five-zero feet," called the diving officer. "Very well, ahead one-third, both main motors" ordered Defrees. At slow speed, *Nautilus* could remain submerged for most of the day. About that time, Hess appeared to relieve the watch. Defrees explained the situation.

"We have a sound contact at bearing three-zero-eight. We're heading two-seven-five, so it's just off our starboard bow. No visual. We're making one-third speed, at one-five-zero feet." He continued filling Hess in on other details of the ship's condition. Satisfied, Hess announced, "I relieve you." To the room he announced, "This is Mr. Hess, I have the deck and the conn." Defrees moved to the plotting table, just forward of the periscopes, to track the movements of the contact. This was his job as part of the "fire control tracking party," a team that used sonar and periscope observations and a plot of *Nautilus*'s track to figure out a target's motion. The sonar station reported the target passing to starboard and the sound of screws fading, then sonar active pinging was heard. Definitely a warship.

Brockman was thinking, visualizing the geometries, weighing the risks and rewards. He was still fifty miles or so from where he wanted to set up shop and lurk off the approaches to Tokyo where targets should be abundant. Tangling with a Japanese warship now might lead to an untimely end to his patrol. Besides, without a visual sighting, he didn't know what he was dealing with; he thought it might be another submarine. Uncharacteristically, but wisely, he chose caution.

"Mr. Hess, let's see where this target's going. Come to two-two-zero." Hess repeated the order back and had his helmsman turn *Nautilus* to port and head southwest. That change of course would alter the geometry and would help Defrees, at the plotting table, figure out the motions of the target, and a firing solution for a torpedo. After a few minutes Brockman said, "Mr. Hess, bring us up to periscope depth, seventy feet. I have the conn."

"Diving officer, make your depth seven-zero feet. The captain has the conn," announced Hess to the control room and the men in the conning tower. He remained officer of the deck with overall responsibility for ship operations, but Brockman would give steering, speed, and depth orders directly ("conn" the ship). The deck tilted as the submarine nosed up and neared the surface. As the keel depth passed one hundred feet, Brockman called, "Up periscope!" The periscope assistant, Fire Controlman Preston Graham raised the periscope and snapped the handles down as the eyepiece slid out of its barrel in the deck. Graham turned the periscope to the bearing of the target as reported by Lee on the sonar. Brockman stepped forward, grabbed the handles, and peered through the periscope's eyepiece as the lens cleared the surface. He squinted as the sunlit horizon burst into view. Twisting the barrel slightly he scanned for targets. Hess, watching and waiting, saw the captain steady for a moment.

"Surface vessel on the horizon. Bearing?"

Graham checked the bearing ring on the periscope barrel. "Zero-six-seven relative—that's two-eight-seven true," he replied, doing the math[15] quickly in his head.

---

15. Relative bearing is measured from the bow of the vessel, whereas true bearing is given from true north. In this case, the ship was on a true course 220° so an angle of 067° from the bow equates to a target bearing of 287° true. In this narrative, either true or relative bearings are given, depending on what was logged at the time.

"Very well," acknowledged Brockman. "Come right to three-three-zero. Down scope." *Nautilus* turned northeast. After a few minutes he raised the periscope for another glimpse. Leaving the periscope up too long invited detection. "Patrol vessel, looks like a Narvik," he announced, referring to a German destroyer class of vessel. "Come right to zero-eight-zero," he ordered, followed by, "make all forward torpedo tubes ready."

"Shall we go to battle stations, sir?" Hess wondered. "Not yet," replied Brockman. We need to get closer." Another peep though the periscope revealed two ships in company, about six thousand yards distant. This was at the limit of the effective range of the Mark-15 torpedoes carried by *Nautilus*.[16] After another twenty minutes the range closed to 4,700 yards, but as Brockman was about to man battle stations, the ships turned away and quickly passed out of sight over the horizon. Unable to match the speed of a surface ship while submerged, there was nothing to be done. An hour later, Brockman gave the order to surface, and *Nautilus* resumed transit to her patrol area.

June 21 was a quiet day as the submarine crept closer to the enemy coast. Heading northwest, *Nautilus* remained on the surface before dawn cruising at a sedate five knots, keeping her battery fully charged. Only the sighting of a searchlight at 0207 interrupted the midwatch,[17] but did not interfere with progress. At 0346 the ship submerged with the coming dawn and continued on battery power, slowing to just two knots. Tension grew among the crew as the ship neared her patrol area. A sharp look-out was kept using both periscopes, which were manned continuously as *Nautilus* cruised just below the waves. The day passed without sight or sound of any vessel. Finally, at 1934, the submarine surfaced, picked up speed back to five knots, and began to recharge batteries, depleted after close to sixteen hours underwater. Reaching the assigned patrol area Captain Brockman ordered a turn to the southwest, parallel to the coast, heading toward the outer reaches of Tokyo Bay. At 2021, lookouts sighted a flashing light on the horizon, identified as the Katsuura Wan Lighthouse, just twenty-one nautical miles to the west.

---

16. Mark-15 torpedoes were normally carried by destroyers, however the Mark-14 submarine variant was in short supply, so *Nautilus* was armed at that time with the slightly larger surface model.

17. The watch period from midnight to 0400.

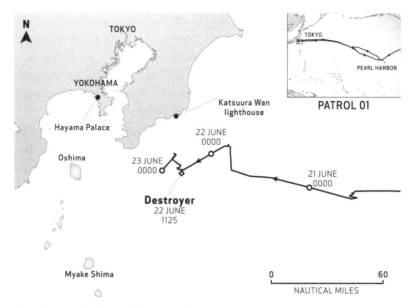

Nautilus attacked an unidentified destroyer on June 22 barely twenty miles from the Japanese mainland. ILLUSTRATION BY BETHANY JOURDAN.

Midnight came and passed. All too soon a faint glow on the overcast horizon signaled approaching daylight and the crew prepared to submerge. Steady white lights to the northwest were noted just before diving, but could not be identified in the deteriorating visibility. Sonar reported nothing. *Nautilus* continued southwest, creeping along at two knots and running just one main motor to conserve the battery charge. The morning passed and watches rotated, lookouts took turns scanning the surface above through the periscopes. Lieutenant Richard "Ozzie" Lynch had the deck for the forenoon watch.[18] He lifted his head from the number two periscope[19] eyepiece and rubbed his weary eyes before resuming his chore, made more difficult owing to growing mist and fog.

18. The watch from 0800 to noon. This was preceded by the morning watch (0400 to 0800) and followed by the afternoon watch (noon to 1600). The watch day ended with the "dog" watch through 2000, and began with the first watch (2000 to midnight).

19. *Nautilus*, like all US submarines, carried two periscopes, allowing the bulk of the vessel to lurk twenty feet or more below the surface while the officer of the deck and a lookout watched the world above the waves. The number one, or "attack" periscope had a slender barrel and was used during

"See anything at all, Ozzie?" inquired Captain Brockman.

"Not much, Captain," replied the lieutenant. "The weather is getting worse. I would say visibility no better than two miles in this soup."

"Not a good day for your camera, then?" said Brockman, a statement more than a question.

"No, sir. I would like to try it if we see something, though." Ozzie had an abiding interest in photography and brought his personal equipment on board, including a still camera and on later patrols, remarkably, a 16-mm movie camera. He enjoyed capturing scenes of life aboard *Nautilus*, and had devised a scheme to attach his camera to the periscope.

Just then, the sonar operator called out, "Conn, JK. Echo ranging[20] ahead."

"Aye, sonar," acknowledged Ozzie, swinging the periscope around to the direction of the sound. "Damn if I can see a thing."

Nautilus motored on, intermittent pinging persisting in the distance. At 1120 the sounds grew stronger.

"Conn, JK. Sound contact bearing zero-three-five. I hear propeller noises. Believe it is the source of the echo ranging!"

"Very well, sonar." This is what Ozzie was waiting for. Without hesitation, he ordered, "Chief of the watch, man battle stations!" Still peering through the periscope, after another five minutes of patient study of the murky horizon, Lynch was rewarded.

"Contact, bearing zero-three-five. Looks like a destroyer. It's close!"

Brockman was immediately on the attack periscope. "The captain has the conn. Get me the recognition guide!" he barked out to no one in particular. The booklet of Japanese ship silhouettes was immediately produced. Brockman took a look at the book, then back to the periscope.

---

approach to a target; the number two periscope, sometimes called the "search" or "night" periscope had a larger head to accommodate a bigger lens and gather more light for nighttime viewing.

20. A warship sonar was capable of making a sharp sound in the water (sometimes known as a ping) that would echo from a submerged target. The time between ping and echo multiplied by the speed of sound yielded distance, or range. Thus, the term "echo ranging." The sound of the ping was generally *not* characteristic of the reverberating "bong" favored by Hollywood, and could exhibit a range of tones depending on the sonar frequency and pulse length. Many sonar frequencies were above the range of human hearing and could be made audible only though electronic manipulation known as "heterodyning." The Japanese attack sonar at the time was described as making a rapping or rattling sound, and when on automatic pinging, resembled the sound of a stick dragging along a picket fence.

He then ordered quickly, "Down scope." Both periscopes were lowered, so nothing appeared above the waves. Nothing for sharp-eyed enemy lookouts to catch sight of. After contemplating the guide and considering the quick glimpse he had of the target, Brockman declared, "It's a *Shinonome*-class destroyer. Set height seven-five feet."

"Seven-five feet, aye," repeated back the periscope assistant. He twirled the dial on the stadimeter[21] to the ordered setting. "Set," he curtly confirmed. Though a respectful "sir" was normally used when addressing a superior, unnecessary verbiage was not used in the attack center during battle stations. Brockman insisted on terse, clear communications.

"Very well. Up periscope, observation," ordered Brockman. Up went the periscope, sliding out of its oily well. Brockman was on the target immediately. Adjusting his handles, he called out, "Bearing . . . mark!"

"Zero-three-five," called out the assistant.

"Range . . . mark! Down scope." The assistant, looking at the stadimeter, called, "One-zero-two-zero," as he lowered the periscope. At 1,020 yards, the destroyer was almost on top of them. Brockman ordered, "Flood tube two, open the outer door!" The command was relayed to the torpedo room where John Sabbe and his team scrambled to make the torpedo tube ready to fire.

By then, the conning tower was fully manned, ten sailors filling the cramped eighteen-foot long cylinder, just eight feet in diameter, that also contained periscopes, a plotting table, sonar gear, steering station, piping, valves, and other equipment. Pat Rooney took over as officer of the deck so that Ozzie could man the TDC[22] with an assistant. Chief radioman Ike Wetmore manned the sonar station. Joe Defrees ran the plot, with an assistant. Executive officer (and navigator) Roy Benson led the team as "attack coordinator," there to make sure the party operated smoothly, and information was shared smartly. Along with the captain, his periscope

---

21. The stadimeter, when engaged, showed the periscope observer a split image of the view, with one image offset vertically based on a dial setting. If the height of a target was known, and that value set in the dial, adjustment of the prism control to merge the split image would yield, by simple triangulation, the range (or distance) to the target.

22. Torpedo Data Computer, an analog computer, technology not far removed from a cash register, that took in sonar bearings, periscope sightings, and speed estimates to solve the geometry problem of firing a torpedo.

assistant, and helmsman at the steering station, the space was crowded, hot, and busy.

"Diving officer, make your depth seven-zero feet," ordered Brockman. With the destroyer so close, he did not want the periscope to poke up too high when raised, more the risk of detection. Unluckily, at that moment the battle stations diving officer, Tom Hogan, was just taking over and other personnel were shuffling around in the control room below. Suddenly, Brockman saw green water through the periscope.

"Diving officer, what's your depth?" he called sternly.

"Uhh . . . seven-five feet sir. Coming up," replied Hogan, realizing that in the transition in worsening seas his team had lost control and gone too deep.

"Get me up, Hogan, I can't see and we're in the middle of an attack!" growled the captain. Without waiting for a reply, he barked to Lynch, "TDC, status?" Without an accurate periscope bearing the TDC had little to work with. "Not yet, captain," said Lynch, peering at the clacking device and worrying the "banjo"[23] slung around his neck. "I need another bearing."

"Damnit," swore Brockman. "I said seven-zero feet!" Moments later, the periscope cleared the surface. "OK, I see him." After a quick look, he lowered the periscope. Bearing, range, and angle on the bow[24] were fed into the TDC. "I've got a solution," reported Lynch after a few moments. "He's opening range." At over two thousand yards and increasing, they had to act fast.

"Very well. Single shot, tube two, middle of target. Final bearing and shoot," ordered the captain in rapid succession. He chose not to test the repair on the balky tube number one that gave them so much trouble at Midway. "Up scope." The shiny cylinder slid up. Brockman crouched to meet the eyepiece as it emerged from the deck. Snapping down the handles, his assistant trained on the target bearing as the captain watched

---

23. Technically, "Submarine Attack Course Finder," essentially a circular slide rule that helped calculate the best course for approach and the torpedo firing solution without resorting to an electro-mechanical machine. In use since World War I, the device was known as a "banjo" because of its shape. Submariners also liked to call it an "Is-Was," for its use in predicting where a target will be based on where it "is" and where it "was."

24. Angle on the bow tells how the target ship is pointing in the periscope view.

the lens break the surface and the scene reappeared. "Standby forward," Brockman called, warning the torpedo room to be ready to fire, and the diving officer to be ready for the nearly two-ton torpedo to leave the ship. "Bearing," he called, "mark!"

"Three-two-two," called the assistant.

"Set!" Lynch reported his TDC had received the information and was ready. "Shoot!" he called as the firing key was triggered. "Fire two!" He waited for a report from the torpedo room.

"Tube two fired electrically!" came Sabbe's report from the torpedo room.

"Very well," replied Brockman. "Sonar?"

"Torpedo running true and normal!" Wetmore could hear the high-speed whine of the Mark-15 torpedo propeller. "Echo ranging from target. He's picking up speed." The destroyer heard the torpedo as well and was frantically seeking the source of the attack.

"Very well. Shut the outer doors. Down scope. Diving officer, make your depth two hundred feet."

"Two-zero-zero feet, aye!" Hogan replied. "Ten degrees down. Make your depth two-zero-zero feet," he ordered to the planesmen.

"Torpedo room, reload tube two," Brockman ordered. To the men in the conning tower, "I lost the target in the fog." Silence fell in the conning tower. There was nothing more to do but wait. A minute passed. The speedy Mark-15 torpedo should have covered the short distance already. Another minute. Finally, a call came from forward, "Conn, torpedo room, we hear rumbling sounds."

"Sonar?" inquired Brockman.

"Nothing, sir," replied Wetmore, puzzled.

A few more minutes. Suddenly, a loud explosion was felt throughout the ship.[25]

"Rig for depth charge!" ordered the captain, somewhat belatedly. "Diving officer, make your depth seven-zero feet!" Confused by the lack of ship sounds on the sonar, Brockman wanted a look. Up they went.

---

25. In his patrol report, Brockman described this sound as "the same as that of a depth charge five hundred yards abeam." He may have been right about the source.

Raising the periscope, he trained it on the bearing of the target. Visibility was a scant three thousand yards. He saw nothing.

"Down scope. Make your depth one-five-zero feet. Come right to course one-five-zero."

The crew acknowledged and set to work, accustomed to Brockman's rapid-fire string of orders. Back down they went, sonar listening for any clues as to what became of the destroyer that had faded as suddenly as it appeared. Just fifteen minutes had elapsed since the first sighting of the enemy warship. Doubling back to the northeast, they checked in case the fast-moving destroyer had slipped behind them. Finally, after nearly half an hour, sonar reported, "I hear screws . . . intermittent." Soon, the propeller noise stopped, for good.

"That's it," said Brockman, "I think we got him!" He believed the single torpedo hit the destroyer, and it finally sank. An improbable shot, but enough evidence for a cheer in the conning tower.[26]

"OK, quiet down," said the captain. "Secure from battle stations. Come right to two-two-five. Mr. Defrees, you have the conn." Brockman turned the duty over to the regular afternoon watch section and went below to record the events of the attack in his official diary.

Lt. Cdr. William Brockman as he received the Navy Cross for heroism at Midway, Pearl Harbor, November 7, 1942. U.S. NAVY.

---

26. This claim of sinking was not recognized in Admiral English's endorsement of Brockman's patrol report, the evidence considered "so meager." Likewise, it was not credited by JANAC, the Joint Army/Navy Assessment Committee formed at war's end to assess Japanese naval and merchant marine shipping losses caused by US and Allied forces during World War II.

Lt. Cdr. Roderick S. (Pat) Rooney, First Lieutenant on *Nautilus*, shown here at the christening of USS *Corvina*, which he commanded. Rooney was killed in action aboard *Corvina* on her first patrol in November 1943. U.S. NAVY.

Lt. Joseph R. Defrees Jr., shown here as a midshipman graduating from the US Naval Academy in December 1941. He served on *Nautilus* at the Battle of Midway and was killed in action aboard USS *Sculpin* in November 1943. U.S. NAVY.

Radioman First Class Harold "Buzz" Lee is decorated by Admiral Chester Nimitz, Commander in Chief US Pacific Fleet, on the occasion of the award of the Presidential Unit Citation to USS *Nautilus*, December 1942. The citation read in part, "For outstanding performance in combat during three aggressive war patrols in enemy-controlled waters." U.S. NAVY COURTESY HAROLD LEE.

First Class Electrician's Mate Foy Hester with wife Lorene at their home on Kaili Street in Honolulu, Territory of Hawaii, circa 1939. COURTESY FOY HESTER JR.

Cdr. Richard Barr "Ozzie" Lynch, executive officer of *Nautilus*. Lynch went on to command the submarines *Seawolf* and later *Skate* on which he won the Navy Cross for valor. U.S. NAVY.

Lt. Cdr. Roy Benson, executive officer of *Nautilus*. Benson went on to command USS *Trigger* on which he received two Navy Cross awards, the second being presented by Admiral Chester Nimitz in this 1942 photo. U.S. NAVY.

Nautilus continued her submerged patrol, creeping along at barely two knots through the water, conserving precious charge in the battery. Though she was pointed southwest, a strong northerly current carried the boat ever closer to the Honshu coast, and by late afternoon she was barely twenty nautical miles from the enemy mainland. Keeping a sharp eye through the periscope, Pat Rooney sighted a ship at 1722, identified as a sampan,[27] just two thousand yards away. Battle stations were manned, interrupting the rest of the men who had just settled in after relief from the previous watch. Brockman turned west and picked up speed in an effort to attain a firing position for his deck guns. However, the speedy little vessel opened the range and a half hour later passed out of sight. Battle stations were secured, and weary men headed back to their bunks. *Nautilus* continued her slow submerged drift for another hour and a half before surfacing in the falling darkness of the evening. Picking up speed while charging batteries, the submarine continued southwest to patrol the outer approaches to Tokyo Bay.

After the excitement of June 22, the next day was quiet. Other than routine operations, the only events deemed worthy of note in the deck log were the sightings of a patrol plane in the morning and the Japanese outer island of Myake Shima[28] in the afternoon. The captain's patrol report, however, noted a trailing oil slick, visible in the periscope. Rather than risk detection by continuing to leave a telltale stain in the ocean behind them, Brockman decided to run south, away from the main shipping lane and try to repair the oil leak, suspected to be from an exhaust valve gasket. Sure enough, the fix took care of the problem, and *Nautilus* turned north to scurry back to the patrol line before dawn. June 24 passed without incident, the submarine patrolling back to the east across expected routes of cargo shipping lanes.

---

27. Sampans are small boats generally used for transportation or fishing in coastal areas. As the war progressed, the Japanese increasingly used them to transport troops, supplies, and equipment. The US Navy authorized attacks on these small civilian vessels as early as March 1942. They were attacked at close range with deck guns, as torpedoes would not have been effective and wasted on such small targets. Captain Brockman tended to refer to any small patrol vessel as a "sampan."
28. A volcanic island south of Tokyo known today as Myakejima.

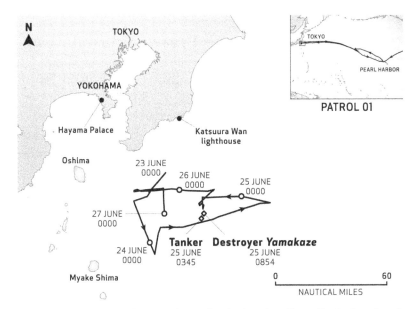

Nautilus attacked a tanker, earning a depth charging, then attacked and sank the destroyer *Yamakaze* on June 25. ILLUSTRATION BY BETHANY JOURDAN.

Excitement resumed with the approach of dawn on June 25. Ens. Joe Defrees had the conn with the sub cruising on the surface and getting ready to submerge for the day. Scanning the horizon, the lookout suddenly called out.

"I see a ship to port, bearing one-eight-five. A large vessel, sir!"

"I see it," said Defrees. "Clear the bridge! Chief of the watch, submerge the ship!"

The men scrambled down the hatch and secured it as the ship began its dive. Brockman, never far from the conning tower, quickly appeared and was on the periscope.

"Man battle stations. Mr. Defrees, I have the conn."

Nautilus had been caught silhouetted against the dawn sky. Fears that they had been detected by sharp-eyed Japanese lookouts were soon realized. Brockman saw a destroyer fast approaching from the south.

"Echo ranging on automatic!" Wetmore heard the destroyer's sonar reaching out to seek the underwater threat. Automatic echo ranging came soon before a depth charge attack. The pings from the Japanese destroyer were clear over the sonar loudspeaker: *pa-ching . . . pa-ching . . . pa-ching, pa-ching pa-ching . . .*

"Rig for depth charge," Brockman ordered. Throughout the ship, men hurried to their stations and prepared the ship to better withstand a depth charge attack. Watertight doors between compartments were shut and dogged; ventilation systems were secured; interior communication phones were manned. One by one, compartments reported they were rigged and ready.

Moments later, the crew felt the first thundering of a volley of undersea explosions as the destroyer passed to the starboard quarter and started a depth charge attack from one thousand yards. The crew of *Nautilus* had been through this before, having weathered forty-two depth charges during the day of the Midway engagement. Though it was tempting to dive deep to try to escape the worst of the barrage, Brockman knew that they were not in serious danger of damage from explosions a thousand yards away, and he preferred to keep tabs on his attacker through the periscope rather than try to run and hide. He was also keen to press an attack on the large vessel first seen, which he judged to be a tanker of ten thousand tons.

"Designate target, large tanker. Make ready tubes three and four." Throughout the ship men scrambled to prepare *Nautilus* to attack from below, all the while under attack from above.

Depth charges rolled off the stern of the Japanese destroyer. Down they sank, triggers slowly squeezed by sea pressure. Suddenly, the men in the submarine heard a sharp, shrill whistle over the sonar loudspeaker, then an enormous deep boom like the beating of a huge drum as the 220 pound explosive charge detonated, followed by a second, longer boom and roaring sound as the exploding bubble of gas collapsed.

. . . FWEET . . . BOOM . . . BOOOOM . . .

In the submarine's hull, the men could feel the steel deck shudder. The deafening blasts repeated and became stronger as the destroyer closed the range to five hundred yards. Brockman kept his cool, determined to get off a shot. His demeanor helped the men manage their own fears as they kept busy working to line up an attack.

"Observation," he called to the tracking party. "Bearing, mark . . . range, mark!" His assistant sang out the numbers, which Lynch fed into the TDC and Defrees plotted on his chart. "He's within three thousand yards! I need a firing solution, now!" called Brockman sternly. He slewed around and took a peek at the attacking destroyer before lowering the periscope. Depth charges continued to explode around them.

BOOM . . . BOOOOM . . .

"One more bearing, captain," called Lynch, almost shouting over the din, but trying for a measure of composure in the face of his commander.

"Very well. Final bearing and shoot!" Up went the periscope. The numbers sang out.

"Set!" called Lynch. "Fire three!" Moments later, "Fire four."

"Tubes three and four fired electrically," reported Sabbe from the torpedo room. "Torpedoes running true and normal!" called Wetmore from the sonar station.

"Make your depth two hundred feet," ordered Brockman. Down they went. Depth charges continued to roar. In between reverberations, Wetmore listened for the torpedoes. "Still running, sir," he announced. "Still tracking to target." After about two minutes he reported, "I hear a rumbling sound and crackling noises. The tanker's screws have stopped."

Nautilus stayed deep, running silently, making barely two knots as she tried to evade the attacking destroyer. The depth charge barrage ended after about an hour, with twenty-one explosions counted. As the echoing of the undersea blasts faded, the men took stock. *Nautilus* crept along—the charges were not close enough to cause much more than pounding hearts and cold sweats among the men in the submarine.

Suddenly, almost an hour after the torpedo attack on the tanker, the men were startled by three loud explosions, which shook the boat more than the depth charges had and reverberated longer in duration.

"What the hell was that?" Benson exclaimed. "Could that have been our tanker?"

"Let's take her up and see," said Brockman. They ascended to periscope depth. Nothing was on the horizon. The nature of the explosions remained a mystery.[29]

Another hour passed. Men relaxed as well as they could while remaining at battle stations positions. Stewards brought coffee to the watch standers, "black and bitter" or "blond and sweet" as to order. Benson, now the officer of the deck of the morning watch, kept his eye to the periscope. At 0522 he had something.

"Captain! Ship on the horizon . . . looks like a warship."

Nautilus, submerged and thus with limited speed, tried to close the contact. Brockman judged it to be a *Shigure*-class destroyer. He increased speed to four knots, drawing heavily on the battery, a risky move so early in the day. Try as they could, the destroyer passed from view to the west at nine miles. Brockman secured battle stations, giving his crew a rest. At 0718 he ordered course back to the southwest to continue to patrol what was becoming a fertile hunting ground. Barely an hour later, the busy morning continued with yet another warship sighting, beginning with a report from the attentive sonar listeners.

"Conn, JK, echo ranging bearing zero-nine-zero!"

Ozzie Lynch, now on watch, spun his periscope around to the aft port quarter and peered intently to the east. The skies had cleared somewhat, and the seas were rough but abating, with visibility improving. In a few minutes his efforts were rewarded with the view of a warship, judged to be an *Amangiri*-class destroyer. *Nautilus* had found *Yamakaze*. One of the most powerful destroyers in the world, she was armed with five 12.7 cm (five-inch) naval guns, antiaircraft guns, torpedoes, and depth charges. Her steam turbines could propel the 1,700 ton ship to a top speed of thirty-four knots, fast enough to run circles around the pokey *Nautilus*. The veteran vessel had participated in the invasion of the Philippines at the time of the Japanese attack on Pearl Harbor, and was credited with assisting in the sinking of a Royal Dutch Navy minesweeper off Tarakan Island. In the Battle of the Java Sea, *Yamakaze* helped sink the

---

29. In spite of this evidence, and a huge oil slick discovered that night, neither Admiral English nor JANAC credited *Nautilus* with sinking the tanker.

American destroyer USS *Pope* as well as the British cruiser HMS *Exeter* and destroyer HMS *Encounter*. She had used her deadly cannons to sink the submarine USS *Shark* in the Makassar Strait, the first US submarine to be lost to enemy antisubmarine warfare.

Enemy ship recognition was not counted among Brockman's many abilities, at least not on his first patrol. He repeatedly identified Japanese destroyers as cruisers, and misidentified the battleship *Kirishima* and carrier *Kaga* during the Midway engagement. In this case, he got the type correct, but he was looking at a *Shiratsuyu*-class vessel. Fortunately, the ships were similar, and the error was inconsequential. He correctly noted that it was not the same warship that they had unsuccessfully chased earlier in the morning.

"Mr. Lynch, man battle stations. Ready tubes two and four. We're in a good position this time and I want to get off a shot before that Jap gets away! We don't have enough battery charge left for another chase."

The battle stations announcement and the attention-grabbing *BONG BONG BONG* on the submarine loudspeakers jolted the crew back to action. Within minutes, *Nautilus* was again ready to attack. With glimpses through the periscope, bearings from sonar, and a glance at the plot, Brockman changed course to the southeast to intercept the enemy ship. The bow swung around as *Nautilus* crept slowly and silently to a firing position. The torpedo tube outer doors hung open, the deadly Mark-15 weapons inside ready to speed to their target.

Brockman let the destroyer close the range, the enemy unwittingly approaching danger with every minute. The men in the conning tower worked together quietly and deliberately as the picture on the plot began to take shape in what was turning out to be an orderly approach. Lynch, now working the TDC, announced, "Captain, I have a good firing solution. He's walking right in to this one!"

"Very well," said Brockman. "Final bearing and shoot. Up periscope!"

Nautilus was at seventy-one feet keel depth, so the attack periscope barely cleared the whitecaps. The lookouts on the Japanese destroyer never saw it, and had no idea a submarine was lurking nearby. That was about to change.

"Ready forward. Bearing . . . mark!" said Brockman, as he centered the periscope crosshairs on the target. His assistant called out the bearing.

"Range . . . mark!" Brockman tweaked the stadimeter dial to match the split image in his view. His assistant read the number off the dial, "One-three-zero-zero yards!"

"Dip the scope!" The captain had the periscope lowered just enough to hide it under the surface but ready to pop up for a quick look. The destroyer was very close.

"Set!" said Lynch as he entered the final bearing, then, "Shoot!" as he triggered the firing key. "Fire two!"

"Two fired electrically!" came the report from Sabbe in the torpedo room.

"Torpedo running true and normal!" called sonar.

Moments later tube four was fired. "Up scope!" Brockman watched the bubbling tracks of the two torpedoes as they headed toward the enemy ship at forty-five knots. Covering 1,500 yards every minute, at such close range they would reach their target in moments. Brockman stared intently at the unsuspecting quarry. There was no evidence that the Japanese lookouts noticed the torpedo tracks all but lost in the rough seas and whitecaps.

Suddenly, Brockman gasped. He then let out a whoop. "Bullseye! First torpedo hit amidships! I see flame coming from the aft stack and it seems like the amidships portion is raised a couple of feet. We might have broken her back. Lynch, get your camera!"

"Aye, sir!" Ozzie, no longer needed at the TDC, grabbed his still camera and the apparatus that connected it to the periscope.

Seconds later, Brockman drew a sharp breath. "My God! Second torpedo hit forward. Damage is terrific . . . she's already down by the bow. Ozzie, raise number two scope and get some shots of this!"

Sonar began to report sounds of minor explosions and turbulence as *Yamakaze* heeled and began to sink. Lynch quickly fixed his camera to the number two periscope and began to frame the image. He snapped several photos. "I see men scrambling into the water!" said Brockman, still watching the tableau through the attack periscope. The ship, broken in two, listed heavily and began to sink fast. The stern disappeared, leaving the bow jutting out of the waves, the forward gun turret just awash, those deadly five-inch cannons silenced for good. A rising sun emblem was clearly visible on top of the structure. In ten minutes, it was over. *Yamakaze* slipped under and disappeared from view.[30]

Once the camera was removed and the periscope lowered, Benson asked, "Ozzie, did you get the shot?" "We'll see what develops, XO" replied Lynch, with a smirk.

Japanese destroyer *Yamakaze* photographed through the periscope of *Nautilus* by Ozzie Lynch, June 25, 1942. U.S. NAVY.

---

30. Neither Admiral English nor JANAC had any argument with this one. *Nautilus* and Brockman were credited with sinking one 1,600-ton DD (destroyer).

Fine 18"x15" enlargement of this painting, suitable for framing, will be sent on request while supply lasts. Write to our New York address for Lithograph C, enclosing 10¢ to cover postage and handling. (Sinking Jap warship from Official U. S. Navy Photo taken through periscope.)

Revenge IN THE PACIFIC

3 Ships . . . 3 Candles!

Submarine cooks take special pride in preparing tempting meals in their compact galleys. And the Navy sees to it that they get the finest food in the fleet! Besides good eats, submariners enjoy many advantages: 50% higher pay; pleasant, informal living, air-conditioned quarters; opportunity for first-hand study of diesel engines and other fascinating technical subjects; and, of course, exciting action and adventure.

BUY WAR BONDS

THREE enemy warships blasted in a single action by one U. S. submarine alone! Four 10,000-ton Jap transports sunk within 2½ hours by another! A convoy of four troopships and their destroyer escort sent to the bottom by a third! That's the kind of vengeance our subs are taking on the treacherous Japs . . . socking them where it hurts most . . . smashing their sorely needed vessels *right in their own back yard.*

More than any others, the men of our Navy's submarine service are carrying the war to the enemy's homeland. The daring officers and crews of our subs maneuver their craft right up to the coast of Japan. There they lie in wait for ships enter-ing or leaving Japanese harbors, and attack them in full view of astounded Japs on shore. Frequently they even slip inside the harbors and blast ships and shore installations with deck guns and torpedoes.

Already U. S. subs . . . the *fastest, safest, most comfortable* and *deadliest* submarines ever known . . . have badly crippled enemy shipping. As this goes to press, the latest Jap ships sunk or smashed since the beginning of the war! And thanks to your purchases of War Bonds, more and still more U. S. submarines are being speeded from the yards of the Electric Boat Company to the naval battle fronts of the world.

Submarine Officers' Insignia

ELECTRIC BOAT COMPANY
33 Pine Street, New York 5, N.Y.

Motor Torpedo Boats	*Submarines*	*Electric Motors*
ELCO NAVAL DIVISION	NEW LONDON SHIP AND ENGINE WORKS	ELECTRO DYNAMIC WORKS
Bayonne, N. J.	Groton, Conn.	Bayonne, N. J.

Copyright 1943, Electric Boat Co.

1943 Electric Boat advertisement featuring color artwork of the sinking of *Yamakaze*. U.S. NAVY PHOTO COURTESY OF TOMMY TRAMPP.

As the sailors secured from battle stations, Campbell fell in with Chief Hester. "Hey chief, I have a question . . ."

"What is it, Wane?" Hester was heading back to the chief's quarters but stopped for his trainee. Foy was a quiet man who didn't much go for conversation, but he felt an obligation to help the younger sailors whenever he could.

"Chief, when we were hit with those depth charges this morning, I was at my station in the control room. Just before they went off, I heard a whistle over the loudspeaker. I remember a couple of weeks ago at Midway hearing clicks sometimes when they were close. What is that?"

Foy had to admit he didn't exactly know. He was an electrician, not a sonar man, and after all, the depth charging at Midway was his first time experiencing the awful ordeal himself. "Why don't you ask Chief Wetmore?" he replied, seeing the sonar chief coming down the narrow passageway. "Hey Ike," he greeted him.

"What'd ya want?" growled Wetmore, unkindly. He'd been at battle stations or on watch all morning, his ears glued to the sonar headphones, and was exhausted, grouchy, and impatient.

"Campbell here wants to know what that shrill whistle is that you hear on the speaker before a depth charge blasts," replied Foy.

"It's heterodyning," said Wetmore, unhelpfully. "Go ask Lee in the sonar shack. I'm hitting the rack." Wetmore disappeared into the chief's quarters. Foy was unruffled. He was used to the grizzled chief's manner. He advised Campbell to go see Lee.

"Hey, Wane!" Buzz Lee greeted the young seaman warmly. Lee was a colorful figure, with a zest for life and the gift of gab, always glad for a conversation. Shipmate Red Porterfield later said, "Buzz likes—and is good at—telling sea stories, and I think he has told some so many times he believes them himself!"[31] Though just short of twenty-five years old, with four years' service and sonar school under his belt, he was a seasoned veteran to Campbell, who had just enlisted in January. Buzz had already gained valuable experience during the Midway battle. Due to illness of the chief radioman Wetmore, he found himself perched on a folding

---

31. Interview with Floyd "Red" Porterfield, August 2006.

camp chair in the conning tower helping to man the JK sonar. Campbell posed his question, which invited Lee to tell him everything he knew about depth charges.

"First of all, forget about "heterodyning." Chief said that just to get rid of you. The ash cans the Nips use are just bombs in a can, set to go off at one hundred or two hundred feet depth. We can dive deeper than that, so that helps, but even if we're at three hundred feet the upper part of our hull, like the conning tower, is pretty close if one is dropped right on top of you. Time to cash in your chips."

"So, what happens is, the bomb goes off—KAPOW!" Buzz clapped his hands to emphasize the point, "and this makes a pressure pulse called a shock wave. Kind of like a sonar sound pulse, except a shock wave goes faster than sound. Don't ask me why.[32] When it hits our hull it makes that metallic click we sometimes heard at Midway. Then the blast of the detonation hits—*BOOM!*" Buzz threw his arms out, knocking a clipboard off its perch in the confined space of the sonar room. "And then it reverbs, like beating on a drum. The blast travels at the speed of sound, so the farther away you are the longer the time between click-BOOM, kinda like the difference between lightning and thunder."

Buzz was enjoying himself and would have kept on, but Campbell was finally able to interrupt him with a question. "So, how close does it have to be to get us?"

"Well, I'm not sure. I know when I was in the conning tower at Midway, a thousand yards was no problem, though it scared the shit out of us. Five hundred yards was close, but nothing serious broke. I tell you, I made sure I took my headphones off when I heard that click! I would not want to be a hundred yards away when one of those things went off! That's all she wrote!"

Research performed after the war showed that a close explosion, within twenty-five feet, could rupture a pressure hull by action of the shock wave or gas bubble. Within fifty feet, the shock wave could deform

---

32. A shock wave is a pulse cause by the sudden displacement of water as the charge detonates. This propagates by actual motion of the water, unlike an acoustic (sound) wave, which propagates though changes in water pressure. A shock wave is not limited by the speed of sound in water and can propagate at a higher speed.

a hull or cause serious damage to machinery. Beyond one hundred feet, only minor damage to fittings would be expected.[33]

"But Buzz, what about heater-dying?" asked Wane.

"Heterodyning, you moron. I told you not to worry about that. But since you asked, here it is. Those clicks I told you about? The actual shock wave is too high pitch for human ears to hear, like a dog whistle," said Buzz. "The click is when it hits the hull, like a bell ringing. But the sonar we listen to can hear the actual shock wave. A lot of the sounds we listen for in the ocean are like that. So that we can hear them in our headphones, the gizmo converts them to a lower pitch. That's heterodyning. To us, it sounds like a whistle."

"Oh, I see . . ." said Campbell, not seeing at all.

"Well, don't worry about it. You want to be a torpedoman, anyway, right? All you need to know is how to run a chain fall and a knucklebuster."

Campbell was familiar with Buzz's schtick and was undeterred. "C'mon, Buzz, I really want to know this shit. It's not just the sonar shack that gets depth charged!"

"You're right. We're all in it together when the Japs start banging on our metal mousetrap."

The physical and psychological effects on the crew during a depth charge attack are hard to appreciate. The pressure pulses and sound waves hitting the hull transmit energy into the air, spiking pressures, creating deafening booms, and shaking one's insides. Lights dim, or blink out as bulbs shatter, the hull creaks and bangs as metal flexes and fittings stress, water spurts from pipe joints, and loose items of any description fly about the spaces. A 1945 Hydrographic Office[34] report on war damage suggested that "luminous gases, visible shock waves or smoke from close underwater detonations may have entered the interiors of the ships concerned, either through packing glands or hatches which opened momentarily." Crew stationed in torpedo rooms reported balls of fire or momentary jets of flame entering though torpedo tubes and air pressures spiking at 130 pounds per square inch, almost nine atmospheres. One

---

33. *War Damage Report No. 58*, January 1, 1949, by the US Hydrographic Office.
34. Ibid.

explanation for these astounding, but consistently reported, phenomena is physiological, relating to the behavior of vision under stress. The report goes on to say that "changes in the pressure, volume or velocity of blood in the retina will cause some people to see momentary grayish or purplish luminous clouds that sweep over the field of vision. Others may see rivers of light or a succession of scintillations that resemble fireworks."

Fortunately for *Nautilus* and her fellow submarines, there was safety in depth. Japanese depth charges could be set for a maximum of two hundred feet, and American subs could evade them by diving to their designed test depth of three hundred feet—or even greater. In April 1942, the ship conducted a test dive to 350 feet off the California coast, and Lee reported similarly deep dives in *Nautilus* during depth charging. USS *Grouper* claimed to have descended to as much as six hundred feet, losing depth control during an attack. This tactic was effective in the early part of the war, allowing American submarines to eventually slink far enough away to escape detection by the attacking destroyer's sonar.

After an eventful morning, the rest of the day was mercifully quiet, allowing the crew to recuperate and revel in their morning's successes. "We took care of that bastard!" "Scratch one tin can!" Details of the sinking of *Yamakaze* filtered through the boat. That evening, just after surfacing and beginning to charge the depleted battery, *Nautilus* ran through a huge oil slick, described as a mile across and several miles wide. Brockman judged it to be from the oil tanker that was attacked just after sunrise.[35]

It was a quiet night as *Nautilus* cruised on the surface, charging batteries and clearing the stench of diesel fumes, cigarette smoke, and sweaty bodies from the spaces with fresh tropical air. Shortly after submerging with the dawn on June 27, the periscope watch reported a contact—an enemy destroyer. Battle stations were manned, and the submarine attempted to close the target, but the speedy warship moved off, unaware of the near encounter. The rest of the day was uneventful. Brockman complained in

---

35. There was not enough evidence to convince English or JANAC that the tanker was sunk.

his patrol report that "weather conditions made navigation difficult," as overcast skies persisted. A two-knot northeasterly current was posing an additional challenge for Benson the navigator as he tried to make educated guesses about their movements. At least the wind and seas were subsiding, and Brockman logged "Fugi Yama in clear sight as well as the coast of Honshu, O'Shima, and Miyaki Shima.[36] Sea glassy calm."

"Mr. Lynch!" called Brockman, peering through the number two periscope. "Come here and bring your camera!" Lynch hurried to the conning tower, eager to know what the captain thought was worth photographing.

"Take a look. It's Mount Fuji, clear as day. You can see the snowcap. Get a shot of this, will you?" Brockman stepped aside so Lynch could attach his equipment. Working quickly, he removed the eyepiece and fastened a homemade adapter to the barrel.

"How far away is it do you reckon, sir?" asked Lynch.

"The plot shows us to be about seventy-five miles." Brockman had moved to the number one periscope. He spun around, looking for contacts. "Hurry up, Ozzie. I'd like a few others to get a look, then I want that periscope down. The seas are too calm."

Mount Fuji taken through the periscope of a US submarine, April 1943. U.S. NAVY.

36. Fujiyama, or Mount Fuji; Oshima, a large island near the entrance to Tokyo Bay, and the aforementioned island Myakejima.

Brockman was worried that they'd be easy to spot without the clutter of waves and whitecaps to disguise the periscope. Lynch finished his work and went below with his precious film.[37]

That evening, while cruising on the surface, Joe Defrees spotted something ahead.

"Captain, bridge, contact off the port bow, bearing one-seven-five." In less than a minute, Brockman was in the conning tower, on the periscope. "What do you make of it, Mr. Defrees?"

"Sir, I believe it's closing. It's definitely a ship, and I believe it changed course."

"He may have seen us—visibility must be at least ten thousand yards. Take her down, Mr. Defrees, we'll conduct a periscope approach."

Reversing course to keep the contact from closing too quickly, Brockman ordered number six (stern) torpedo tube readied, and within fifteen minutes they were in firing position. The vessel, identified as a sampan or small patrol vessel, about 1,500 tons, was not worth more than one valuable "fish." Brockman allowed the unsuspecting enemy ship to close to a mere one thousand yards before firing. Watching through the periscope, he saw the torpedo hit. An eruption lit the night sky.

"Bullseye!" he called excitedly. "I see flames!" Seconds later, sonar reported "Conn, JK, hearing sounds of explosions!"

"Right! And more flames! That Jap's a goner!" Brockman continued to watch as fire on the patrol boat lit the scene. "It's sinking by the stern. Mr. Defrees, surface the ship."

"Surface the ship, aye." Defrees gave the orders and *Nautilus* broke the surface. Men scrambled topside, lookouts scanning the horizon. The patrol boat was gone.

"Scratch another!" It was a perfect scenario—a lone vessel, quick sinking, and no depth charges to weather. And solid evidence.[38] *Nautilus* continued west, drawing ever closer to the enemy coast. Shortly before dawn on June 28, the prowling submarine was a scant seventeen

---

37. Red Porterfield claimed that Lynch photographed Mount Fuji and later submarine photographers certainly did, but Ozzie's reputed image has not been found.

38. Certainly Admiral English was impressed, and credited this sinking in his patrol report endorsement. Amazingly, the ever-conservative JANAC did not.

nautical miles from the Honshu coast, directly astride the main ship-ping channel leading from Japan's largest population and industrial region. Hayama palace was just forty miles to the north, but Brockman was not tempted to nose any closer. Before submerging for the day, he reversed course and headed southeast to open the range from enemy shores while remaining in the shipping lane. Soon, the sonar watch was rewarded with the sound of beating propellers to the east, and ten minutes later, Joe Defrees, the midwatch officer of the deck, sighted a large patrol vessel. Battle stations were manned, the start of what was to be a very long day for the crew of *Nautilus*. After forty tense minutes, unable to catch the enemy vessel, the crew stood down and the subma-rine resumed her submerged patrol.

Nautilus turned southwest, slowly and silently creeping along the coast, making barely two knots through the water. Currents were logged as "various," swirling about the offshore islands and making it difficult to hold a steady course. Throughout the rest of the morning and into early

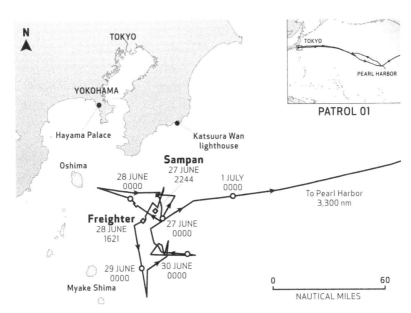

Attack on a freighter on June 28 led to a severe depth charging and heavy damage to the submarine. ILLUSTRATION BY BETHANY JOURDAN.

45

afternoon the crew patiently watched and listened. Finally, at 1604, they were rewarded.

"Multiple contacts, bearing three-two-nine true!" Benson, standing the dog watch, was on the number two periscope. "I see two ships, look like merchants. Man battle stations!"

BONG BONG BONG! The general quarters alarm rang throughout the ship. Men rolled out of their bunks or dropped whatever they were doing and rushed to their stations. The galley was secured, the evening meal in mid-preparation. Turning sideways to squeeze by in the narrow passageways, men tried unsuccessfully to avoid bumping into each other as well as the valves and fittings protruding from every direction. "Up ladder!" "Down ladder!" they called in an attempt at traffic control on the constricted connections between decks. By now, the practiced crew could negotiate the mazes and bottlenecks of the three-hundred-foot pressure hull with ease and barely a minute passed before all stations reported, "Manned and ready!"

Brockman was, of course, already in position. With some further peeks through the attack periscope and a look at the Japanese ship recognition guide, he announced, "Down scope. We have two merchant ships, one resembling the *Kamakura Maru*, 17,500 tons. Designate 'target one.' The other looks like a tanker, *Arimasan Maru*. Make ready tubes two, three, and four, MOT[39] with one degree spread. I have the conn. Diving officer, make your depth seven-one feet."

A chorus of acknowledgments followed the captain's typical barrage of orders. The submarine eased a few feet deeper so the periscope would less likely be seen in the calm seas. Sonar called bearings to the chosen target as the TDC began to reckon a firing solution in its little electro-mechanical brain. Joe Defrees was working the plot, doing the same with pencil and straightedge. Ozzie Lynch was studying his Is-Was,[40] calculating the torpedo settings by hand in case the TDC stopped working at the worst moment. The "Ready" light came on, telling Brockman torpedoes

---

39. Middle of target. Brockman wanted the salvo of three torpedoes to be centered on the target with one degree angle between them. This would improve the changes of at least one weapon hitting the target even if their firing solution was off or if the target maneuvered.
40. Submarine Attack Course Finder, also called "banjo."

were set and could be fired at any time. As usual, John Sabbe and his team were on the ball.

"Firing point procedures. Up scope. Observation," called Brockman. Up slid the shiny metal tube. The head of the periscope poked just a few feet above the waves as the captain put his eye to the lens. "Bearing . . . mark! Range . . . mark!" His assistant called out the numbers. Brockman slewed the barrel slightly. "Third contact, a warship, cruiser, or destroyer. I see three stacks. Down scope."

The stakes had just been raised. This would not be an easy shot at an undefended target like last time. "Range is closing. Mr. Lynch, status of the TDC?"

"Solution looks good captain. Is-Was agrees," replied Lynch, with a glance at the analog computing device while adjusting the circular slide rule hanging around his neck.

"Very well. Final bearing and shoot. Up scope!" The assistant immediately raised the periscope and pointed it to the bearing shown on the plot.

"Ready forward . . . bearing, mark! Dip the scope," called Brockman.

"Set!" Lynch reported his TDC had received the information and was ready. "Shoot!" he called as the firing key was triggered. "Fire two!"

"Two fired electrically!" came Sabbe's report from the torpedo room. "Torpedo running true and normal!" Buzz Lee could hear the high-speed whine of the Mark-15 torpedo propeller.

"Shoot," Lynch repeated, and again hit the firing key. "Fire three!" and in succession "Fire four!" Three undersea missiles were speeding toward the unsuspecting freighter.

"Reload tubes. Up scope," ordered Brockman. "Reload tubes two, three, and four," acknowledged Sabbe. Torpedomen shut the torpedo tube outer doors, depressurized and drained the empty tubes, opened the inner hatches, and winched in fresh warshots. The men sweated and strained to move the two-ton weapons with block, tackle, and muscle. Mattresses and personal gear were shoved aside to make room to move other torpedoes in position for the next reload (when not at battle stations, the forward torpedo room served as berthing for a handful of the crew).

Meanwhile, Brockman was watching the proceedings as the torpedoes sped to the target. "The cruiser may have seen the bubbles from our torpedoes. It's turning toward us. Down scope, make your depth two hundred feet. Rig for depth charge."

"Ten degrees down, make your depth two-zero-zero feet." Hogan gave the orders to the planesmen, who spun their big handwheels to set the bow and stern planes. The deck tilted as *Nautilus* headed down and the crew prepared for the inevitable depth charges. Riveted steel hull plates, internal frames, and bulkheads creaked and popped as sea pressure rose. At two hundred feet, almost ninety pounds per square inch squeezed the boat, causing the pressure hull to measurably shrink. Hogan ordered several thousand pounds of water pumped from auxiliary tanks to sea to compensate for the loss of buoyancy.[41] Lee listened over the sounds of the shrinking, creaking hull and humming trim pump to the high-speed propeller whine of their three torpedoes as they sped toward the Japanese freighter, just three thousand yards away. Then another sound pierced the sea.

"JK, echo ranging on automatic!" The Japanese cruiser was closing in. "Splashes in the water!" The enemy was so close Lee could hear the depth charges hit the surface as they rolled off the stern of the attacking ship. In a few moments they would sink to the trigger depth and detonate.

"Make your depth three hundred feet!"

"Make my depth three-zero-zero, aye. Passing two hundred feet!"

A sound like a severe hammer blow hit the hull, *CLICK* . . . then *BOOM* as the first depth charge exploded. Before the reverberation ceased another *CLICK . . . BOOM* filled the ship with an enormous blast. With clenched jaws and white knuckles, men squeezed their eyes shut, stared without seeing, or just looked at their shoes.

CLICK . . . BOOM . . . CLICK . . . BOOM . . . CLICKBOOM . . . BOOOOM . . .

---

41. Sea pressure caused the hull to shrink, displacing less seawater and reducing buoyancy. To compensate, Hogan had to pump water out. Keeping a submarine in trim (neutrally buoyant) depended on many factors, including depth, water temperature, and salinity. It was a full-time job for the diving officer of the watch.

The assault was thunderous. The last charge was so close there was almost no time between the shock wave and explosion. The hull reverberated and riveted plates snapped as the boat headed deep to escape the onslaught. Frightened men prayed. Some shouted aloud, voices unheard over the din. Lights dimmed and bulbs shattered. Debris from the decks underfoot and bulkheads flew in all directions; grease fittings shot from their sockets like bullets. The conning tower shook as though it might tear free of the pressure hull.

Seaman Galli, standing watch in the windlass room forward, let out a wail as an indicator housing shattered and shards of metal lacerated his stomach. In the control room, electrical cables were forced into the hull and water gushed though the openings.

"Flooding in the control room!" yelled Red Porterfield, the chief of the watch. He spun around to try to locate the source of water as it streamed through the cable seals. "Grab a DC kit and pound those seals back in place! Get a bucket under that leak" he ordered to the damage control team. To the conn, he reported, "Streams of water pouring into the compartment. We are forming a bucket brigade to keep water off the equipment." Men quickly formed a line and handed buckets of seawater down below to the bilge, empty buckets coming back up.

Throughout the ship, water was leaking through seals and patches, high pressure air roared through cracked joints, and hydraulic fluid spewed from ruptured hoses. Men rushed to shut valves and secure equipment to stanch the flows. The pharmacist mate, Joe Hudson, hurried to the windlass room to treat the injured sailor.

"Right full rudder, come to course zero-five-five," ordered Brockman, hoping to evade the Japanese ship that was lining up for another attack.

"Right full rudder, aye, my rudder is right full. Coming to zero-five-five," called the helmsman. Then, from the engine room, "Conn, engine room. The rudder ram is making a loud banging sound and moving in jerks." At the same time, sonar reported, "Conn, JK, the rudder is making an awful noise. I'm sure the Japs can hear it!"

"Very well," replied Brockman. "Rudder amidships. Engine room, report status of damage to rudder ram."

"Aye aye, sir!" But the engine room had nothing to report. Obviously, something was wrong with the rudder, and the ram seemed to have a terrific load on it, but nothing from inside the ship could explain it. It seemed that damage to the rudder mechanism during the depth charging of June 4 had worsened.

Soon enough, the cruiser was back. Three more splashes were heard as depth charges hit the water. This attack was less severe, but hardly less frightening to the men below. Brockman changed course to the north, heading toward the coast and shallower water, hoping to evade his pursuer with an unexpected move. A third attack with three more charges followed, but from farther away. Then, there was blessed silence as the cruiser moved off, the captain's maneuver having thrown off the attack. Silently, *Nautilus* slowly opened the range, creeping along at three hundred feet. The bucket brigade in the control room labored as quietly as possible while other crewman worked to seal the leaks. Damage control reports filtered to the conn as men made inspections and tested equipment. The list was long. Besides the cracked pipes, ruptured hoses, and leaking seals, the trim pump sea valve was knocked loose and the stern torpedo tubes were leaking excessively. Later inspections found the outboard diesel exhaust valves were leaking, putting full sea pressure on the inboard valves, the only line of defense from full-scale flooding of the ship. The rudder appeared to have been knocked loose and continued rattling and banging.

Benson, the executive officer, and the man in charge of damage control, reported all of this to the captain. "Sir, every compartment thought that first barrage was right on top of them. That one must have come within twenty-five yards!"

"Yes," replied Brockman. "But we are still here. That old, riveted hull can really take it!"

Nautilus remained deep and quiet for the next hour until the cruiser's echo ranging became distant and then finally stopped. They slowly made their way up to periscope depth. Sonar reported some cracking sounds off in the distance, but could not identify them. At 1829, Brockman put up the periscope and took a look around, but nothing was in sight. At 1906, battle stations was secured. Minutes later, sonar reported a rumbling sound as if a strong detonation erupted at a great distance. Finally, at 1935 they surfaced in the dark, reversed course, and resumed their patrol to the southwest. The balky rudder protested but responded. The diesel roared to life and the boat filled with fresh air, washing the stink of fumes from the below compartments. The stench of fear would be slower to subside.

Brockman felt they hit the freighter with two of the three torpedoes, and the distant rumbling they heard was evidence of sinking.[42]

During the night a number of small boats, or sampans, were sighted, but nothing worthy of a torpedo. With the approaching dawn, *Nautilus* submerged, just thirteen miles east of Myake Shima (now called Myake-jima). Still nursing the wounds of the prior day's beating, Brockman decided to loiter in the vicinity of that island and the smaller Mikura Shima just to the south and out of the shipping lanes so as to further appraise damage and repair what they could. The crew was shaken and exhausted from the strain of battle and hours of labor stopping leaks and patching up gear. The submariners had been at sea for more than five weeks since leaving Pearl Harbor in May (expect for their brief repair visit to Midway Island), and fatigue was setting in. The submarine itself was wounded and some of her injuries, like the protesting rudder, could not be repaired at sea. To make matters worse, the weather was deteriorating, and seas were rising.

Regardless, Brockman, *Nautilus*, and her intrepid crew resumed their mission. On June 29, after submerging in the morning, masts were sighted on the horizon and the submarine tried to get into a firing position, but was unable to close. Seas continued to rise, making for an increasingly uncomfortable ride on the surface that evening. Any serious attempt to repair equipment was put on hold as the ship pitched and rolled in the heavy swell. The next morning yielded some relief as the boat submerged, but the diving officer found it impossible to hold

---

42. Admiral English and JANAC, characteristically, did not agree.

periscope depth as the seas alternatively pushed the hull down and sucked it back up with each passing swell. Brockman ordered a depth of ninety feet, then one hundred feet to keep from bobbing to the surface. That precluded a periscope watch, and the sonar men could hear little but the sloshing waves above. Captain Brockman commented in his diary, "It is the opinion of the commanding officer that this ship should not be subjected to any more depth charge attacks due to damage."

Even so, *Nautilus* remained submerged on patrol, later in the day passing over the spot of the sunken *Yamakaze*, her wreck some 11,000 feet down on the seafloor below. In the evening they surfaced in heavy swells and resumed bouncing through the waves, off-duty crew trying unsuccessfully to sleep in corkscrewing bunks. After a laborious night they submerged with the dawn, seventy miles south of the Katsuura Wan Lighthouse and fifty miles from the Honshu coast. Periscope patrol was impossible in the raging seas and Brockman judged they were on the edge of a typhoon. They spent the day at one hundred feet, drifting along at less than two knots, unable to see anything nor hear much.

On the evening of June 30, *Nautilus* surfaced, and the corkscrewing resumed. Brockman called Benson to his cabin.

"Roy, what's the condition of the ship?"

"Well, Captain, I don't have a lot of good news. The rudder is a big worry. It's making a heck of a noise, and if it breaks for good, well, we're stuck. Still a lot of leaks, but the pumps are keeping up with it for now. The trim pump is erratic and vibrates . . . it may not last. The bow planes indicator is busted, so we're only guessing at their angle." He went on to describe a lengthy catalogue of serious damage: warped torpedo tubes; cracked buoyancy tank; noisy periscope hoist; gyros out of alignment; cracks in engine manifolds; leaking exhaust vales; flooded antennas . . . the list went on. Just about every major system on the ship from weapons to engineering to communications to navigation was affected.

"If our rudder goes, we're doing circles out here forty miles from the Jap coast," mused Brockman. "Can we even be sure the tubes will fire?"

"No, sir, I can't guarantee it. Sabbe and Chief Porterfield are real good, but they can't unwarp a tube. And if we get a fish out there, we can't be sure it'll run straight with the gyro problem. That and most everything else will require yard work to repair."

"OK," said Brockman after just a moment's further thought. "We're done out here. We can't patrol if we can't see and can't shoot. And I don't think we can take another pasting like that last one." He grabbed his interior communication phone and rang the bridge. "Officer of the deck, set course for Pearl Harbor. We're headed home."

"Aye, sir," replied Rooney, from the bridge. "Changing course to zero-nine-three." Under the circumstances, Rooney was not surprised at the decision and had already plotted a course to take them east. "All main engines ahead full!" *Nautilus* increased speed to thirteen knots and put her stern to the Honshu coast.

The transit back to Pearl Harbor passed without incident, a quiet Independence Day celebration and a sighting of Midway Island as they passed to the south the only events worth noting. An umbrella of US Navy PBY patrol craft comforted the crew as the submarine crossed into the Western Hemisphere and approached Hawaii. Finally, on July 11, *Nautilus* made contact with her escort vessel, USS *Allen* (DD-66), assigned to accompany her into the harbor. The island of Oahu came into view. At 1155, *Nautilus* made fast to the submarine pier, forty-eight eventful days and 10,400 nautical miles after departure from the same pier on May 24. Waiting to meet them were two prominent figures: Admiral English, commander of submarines in the Pacific, and the US Pacific Fleet commander himself, Admiral Chester Nimitz. Captain Brockman rushed topside. With a crisp salute, he greeted his bosses. "Good morning Admiral Nimitz, Admiral English." He had a folder of papers in hand. "Here is my patrol report, sir."

Nimitz returned his salute, then offered his hand. "No need for that now, commander. This is an informal visit. I just wanted to welcome you and your crew home and congratulate you on a successful mission! From your radio reports it sounds like you had quite the time out there."

"Thank you, sir. Yes, we did. I'm afraid we're going to need a stint in the yards to get *Nautilus* ready for sea again. But she brought us home." He turned and appraised the black steel warship behind him, six-inch cannons flanking the looming conning tower. Sailors were busy topside, stealing glances at the admirals as they conversed with their captain.

"Would you like to come aboard for lunch, sir?"

"Yes, I would like that, and a quick tour belowdecks if that would not be an imposition," said Nimitz politely. English nodded his agreement.

"Not at all, Admiral. The crew would be proud to see you and show off their ship," he replied. "I'll have to warn you, though. It doesn't smell so good down there!"

Nimitz chuckled as he and English climbed aboard.

Later that evening, Brockman was in his stateroom when there came a knock.

"Enter." It was Ozzie Lynch. "What is it, Lieutenant?"

"Sir, I thought you might like to see this." From under his arm, he produced a folder and carefully removed the contents. On Brockman's desk he placed a black and white photo enlargement. Brockman gave a low whistle.

"Holy cow, Ozzie, you got it!" Brockman was looking at a photograph taken through the periscope of the Japanese destroyer *Yamakaze* in its death throes. Most of the ship was already down, but the bow stood out of the water, canted crazily to port. The forward gun turret was just awash, rising sun emblem visible on its roof, gun barrels aiming uselessly at the sky. Struggling men were in the water, scrambling to abandon their swiftly sinking ship. A periscope's crosshairs and reticule left no doubt as to the source of the image.

"Well done, well done!" beamed Brockman. "Is this a copy? I want to take it right over to English. This is outstanding!"

"Thank you, sir!" Lynch swelled with pride. "I have some other photos from the patrol that you might like to see later, but I knew you would want to look at this one right away. Please take it to the admiral. I will make more copies."

"Thanks, Ozzie, good work. This should be in a magazine! Unfortunately, it will probably be censored and never see the light of day."

Brockman was wrong. Ozzie Lynch's photograph was published in the August 3, 1942, issue of *Life* magazine, and was lauded as one of the year's outstanding photographs in the December 1942 issue of *U.S. Camera* under the title "Doom of Jap Warship."

On just his first war patrol, Captain Brockman proved to be an outstanding submarine commander. He was technically competent, aggressive, made good decisions, and was a competent leader. He lauded his crew in the conclusion of his patrol report, saying, "The work of all hands has been of the highest order and there was no 'let down' noticed at any time except immediately following depth charge attacks." He singled out several of his officers for praise, including Benson, Hogan, and Lynch. His officers, along with senior petty officers including Red Porterfield and Foy Hester, certainly contributed to the high level of competence and morale of the crew.

Brockman's superiors were effusive with praise in their endorsements of the patrol report. Captain J. M. Harris, the division commander, recommended Brockman be awarded the Distinguished Service Medal, noting that he had already been recommended for the Navy Cross for his performance at Midway. The latter is the highest honor the navy can bestow, topped only by the Medal of Honor (awarded by the president in the name of Congress). Letters of commendation for the officers and crew were recommended. The squadron commander, Captain J. H. Brown, noted, "The action of the commanding officer in coming to periscope depth while, or soon after, being depth charged is noteworthy and deserves commendation. It has great merit as an aid in conducting evasive tactics." All his superiors concurred with the decision to cut the patrol short in the face of damage to the submarine.

The ninety-one[43] young men who left Pearl Harbor in May, having never before sailed into battle, returned in July hardened by the experi-

---

43. Eighty-five enlisted men and seven officers including Brockman (ninety-two total) left Pearl Harbor. One man (Troutman) debarked at Midway.

ence of their first war patrol. They had taken what the enemy and the weather had thrown at them and found themselves worthy. Their submarine, however, was a wreck. Brockman included a three-page detailed listing of "major derangements" arising mainly from the depth charging of June 28, and the vessel would require an extensive month-long overhaul before she was ready to return to sea.

CHAPTER TWO

Makin

NICK BRUCK SAT HUNCHED OVER HIS COFFEE CUP, CRADLING IT AS THE boat rocked gently in a light swell. *Nautilus* had gotten underway from Pearl Harbor that morning and was headed southwest. Bruck sat shoulder to shoulder in the crowded messroom, filled to capacity with Marines from the 2nd Raider Battalion. Across the table, similarly hunched with coffee cradled in hand, was his friend John Sabbe.

Bruck stroked his dark mustache. Hailing from Earling, Iowa, the twenty-six-year-old first class machinist's mate was the second of nine children from a Catholic family. Wiry and angular, he sported a tan from a few weeks in the Hawaiian sun, a feature he would lose in the ensuing weeks underwater. He and his wife, Alma, were married on New Year's Eve of 1940. He reported on board *Nautilus* just six months later. In the navy since 1936, he had earlier served on her sister ship *Narwhal* and was one of the more experienced crewmen on board. Nick and John Sabbe were among the seven men who would sail on all fourteen *Nautilus* war patrols.

"Well, I guess I have to call you Chief Sabbe now," he remarked. "Hope we can still be buddies." The young torpedoman had sufficiently impressed the captain and the navy to warrant promotion, confirmed while in port.

"You can stick to John. Of course we're still pals! Anyway, you're a machinist, so I won't have to boss you around. Hey . . ." he nudged the Marine next to him. "Would ya mind passing the 'side arms' down here?"

"Sure thing, pal," said the marine, as he reached for the canned milk and sugar. "Here ya go."

"Thanks," said Sabbe, who proceeded to "rig" his coffee. He said to Bruck, "Sorry to see Dad go." Bosun's mate Warren McLauren was among the twenty-five crewman leaving *Nautilus* after her first war patrol. One of the oldest members of the crew, traditionally known as "Dad," McLauren had joined the boat in 1933 and was the longest tenured wartime crewman with almost nine and a half years on board. By war's end, Foy Hester would be the second with eight years.

"Yeah, and Chief Hudson," replied Nick. "He did a nice job on Galli." Sabbe agreed. The young seaman had suffered serious lacerations during the previous depth charge attack but was back on the job working in Sabbe's torpedo division. "Whaddaya think of the new pecker checker?"

"He'll be OK, I guess," mused Sabbe. "He sure had a way of getting to know the crew!" Nick chuckled. The new hospital corpsman, Joe Potts, had the unenviable duty of checking the crew for signs of venereal disease after their month in Pearl Harbor. Potts would eventually advance to chief pharmacist's mate and sail the remaining thirteen war patrols on *Nautilus*.

"Any scuttlebutt on the new officers?" asked Bruck. "Is Ensign Ray[1] a ninety day wonder? I hear he didn't go to the trade school[2] like the rest of them."

"No idea," replied Sabbe. He quickly changed the subject, not wanting to be caught gossiping about the officers, especially with all the visiting Marines about. "So what happened to you on liberty in Pearl? Any Jane action I should know about?"

"Naw, nothing like that," replied Nick.

"Oh, yeah, I forgot you're a shack man,"[3] teased Sabbe.

---

1. Ens. Sherry Buford Ray, who hailed from Toronto, Canada, served two patrols on *Nautilus*. Promoted to Lt. (jg), he was transferred to USS *Pickerel* (SS-177), which was lost with all hands off the Honshu coast by depth charging on April 3, 1943. *Pickerel* was the first US submarine to be lost in the Central Pacific area.

2. Naval Academy.

3. Married.

"Yeah, let's leave it at that. Sounds like Red had a time, though!" Chief Porterfield, a colorful figure, and a bit of a carouser, had been nabbed for intoxication, violating curfew, and being out of uniform, warranting a captain's mast and punishment of ten days deprivation of liberty. Nick and John continued gabbing about their month in Pearl Harbor. After their harrowing first patrol, Captain Brockman gave the crew as much R&R[4] as possible, and Hawaii was the place to be, particularly the nearby Waikiki Beach. The most prominent features of the beachfront were the stately Royal Hawaiian and Moana hotels, the former's striking color scheme lending it the nickname "Pink Palace of the Pacific." Normally a haven for high-end tourists, the Royal was closed to visitors during the war and instead served as a place of rest and relaxation for US submariners. Busses would shuttle crews from the navy base, and open barbecues with beer and wine were held on the lawn all day long.

About that time, Porterfield showed up and stuck his head in. There was no room to squeeze in the crowded space. Spotting Sabbe and Bruck, he growled, "If you guys are done beating your gums, there's work to do. Bruck, Chief Donovan is lookin' for you. Something about his precious diesels."

"Sure thing, Chief. How was liberty?" he chided. Red's ten-day suspension expired just about the time they got underway. That got a chuckle out of the Marines, who were already clued in on Porterfield and his reputation.

"What are you, a comedian? Get cracking! T.N.T.!"[5] Then to the Marines, "You mud eaters enjoying yourselves? I'll bet it's not every day you get a luxury cruise like this with gourmet food. Soon enough you'll be back to jawbreakers and battery acid!"[6]

"We love it, Chief! Better than dog food![7] Gung ho!"

"Gung ho . . . what the hell does that mean?" growled Red as he headed to the chief's quarters.

---

4. Rest and Relaxation.

5. T.N.T. = Today, not tomorrow.

6. Army biscuits and artificial lemonade powder included in K-rations. The latter was considered undrinkable and regularly discarded or used as cleaning solution.

7. Corned beef hash. A favorite.

"Gung ho" was the rallying cry of the 2nd Marine Raider Battalion, led by Lt. Col.[8] Evans Carlson, who coined the phrase. Carlson joined the US Army in 1912 at the tender age of sixteen (representing himself as a twenty-one-year-old to meet the minimum age requirement). He served in the Philippines and France, and left the army as a captain.[9] Carlson's leadership qualities were evident from those early years. He wrote, "I will lead a man, if he will be led. But I'll get him to where he's got to go, even if I have to drive him. I will never ask a man to do something I won't do myself." Carlson rejoined the service as an enlisted marine in 1922, and was quickly restored the officer ranks. He served in China, then Nicaragua where he experienced his first combat on jungle patrol, and was awarded the Navy Cross for valor. A subsequent posting with the president's guard led to a friendship with Franklin Roosevelt and his son, James.

Carlson returned to China in 1937 as naval attaché to Chiang Kai-shek and the Nationalist army, who were already fighting the Japanese. Hearing of Mao Tse-tung and the Red Army fighting in the north, he joined them to learn of their tactics. After spending much of 1938 with the Red Army, he became enamored of their military philosophy and lightly armed mobile forces able to live off the land and operate behind enemy lines. The philosophy was codified by the term *gōng hé*, meaning "to work together in harmony," which Carlson anglicized to "gung ho."[10] Returning from China, he lobbied along with army Col. William Donovan to form commando-type units that could land ahead of conventional troops and perform behind-the-lines special operations. Senior officers in the Marine Corps did not support the idea, considering Carlson a renegade and the concept a risk to the Corps identity. However, at the urging of the commander-in-chief, the Marines reluctantly went along with the plan, and in January 1942 two volunteer commando-type units were activated and designated "Raider Battalions." Evans was put in command

8. Lieutenant colonel in the Marines or army is equivalent to a commander in the navy.

9. Equivalent to a naval full lieutenant.

10. The term is an acronym for the Chinese industrial cooperative organization *Gōngyè Hézuòshè*, and the meaning is an Americanism probably invented by Carlson or one of his comrades. Today, it is often taken to mean "overly enthusiastic" and can be derogatory.

of the 2nd Battalion, and he chose his friend, Maj.[11] Jimmy Roosevelt, as his executive officer.

Roosevelt was no one's idea of a marine, much less a commando. A Harvard graduate, his experience was in business and in the movie industry, but his father, the president, Franklin D. Roosevelt, commissioned him as a Marine lieutenant colonel without benefit of military training. He had poor eyesight and flat feet that required him to eschew combat boots in favor of sneakers. Though athletic in college, chronic illness led to hospitalizations and removal of part of his stomach. Uncomfortable with his high rank and public criticism of it, he resigned his commission in 1939, but with war brewing he rejoined the Marines at the lower rank of captain. Among other jobs, he worked on Donovan's staff and helped promote Carlson's ideas. Despite his physical limitations and lack of experience, Roosevelt possessed two qualities that Carlson valued above all others: leadership and bravery. He was absolutely devoted to the cause and was much admired by his men.

Carlson's command philosophy, influenced by his experiences in China, tended to egalitarianism, and reinforced his reputation as a renegade. He abolished ranks and insignias, dividing his team into "leaders" and "fighters," with no special privileges for the leaders. Teamwork and self-criticism were emphasized, and reason, rather than authority, was the basis for decision-making, though in the field a leader's command could not be questioned. He called his approach "collective consensus and ethical conviction." Anyone who volunteered to become a Raider had to agree to this philosophy. Functionally, he expected his Raiders to operate behind enemy lines on any terrain and in any weather, and march up to fifty miles in a day. His troops learned navigation, hand-to-hand combat, proficiency in small arms of all types (including enemy weapons), camouflage, and night operations. Operating mainly around Pacific islands, infiltration of a force was expected to be by rubber boat, most likely from a submarine.

By the spring of 1942, the Raider battalion was ready. All it needed was a mission.

---

11. A Marine or army major is equivalent to the naval rank of lieutenant commander.

Though the turning point in the Pacific war had passed with the decisive American victory at Midway, Japan had not lost an acre of territory and still possessed a most formidable navy, the most powerful in the world at that time. The coming conquest of the Pacific would clearly be a protracted and bloody affair, and the US war cabinet was eager to go to the offensive as soon as possible. As the top generals and admirals discussed strategy, two distinct options were considered. One was a southern route through the large islands of the East Indies (including New Guinea and the Philippines) as favored by the army, particularly General Douglas MacArthur, who had escaped from the falling fortress at Corregidor vowing, "I shall return!" MacArthur was a popular public figure and touted as a hero, but he possessed a tremendous ego and was viewed as a prima donna within the service, particularly by the navy who feared playing a subordinate role if he were in charge. The second option was to "island hop" along the smaller atolls of the central Pacific, presumably less heavily defended, a task more suited to the navy and Marine amphibious forces. However, the Marine Corps was small compared to the burgeoning army units staging in Australia, and there was no large base of operations in midocean west of Hawaii to support a campaign. Stormy interservice negotiations ensued as General George Marshall (chief of staff) and Admiral Ernest King (commander of the US fleet) wrestled with debatable strategic options and formidable personalities. In the end, a compromise was reached. Both strategies would be pursued in parallel, with distinct boundaries between forces and division of command. As early objectives, Guadalcanal in the Solomon Islands was assigned to the navy led by Marines with army troop support, while MacArthur and the army would launch from bases in Australia to New Guinea, with support from naval transport and bombardment units.

This settled, the island-hopping campaign would have to start somewhere, and Carlson's Raiders were looking for a job. With Roosevelt's personal interest in mind, Admiral Nimitz met with Evans Carlson to discuss the matter. The Raiders were a small, mobile force that could support a larger amphibious operation or could conduct a diversionary or disruptive attack, but could not hope to prevail against a heavily garrisoned island on their own. Hit-and-run targets like Wake, Tinian, Attu, and even the Japanese home island of Hokkaido were considered but rejected, being too far away and too heavily garrisoned. A location was sought that was not too far from US bases, not too strongly defended, and one that might divert Japan's attention from the upcoming Guadalcanal landings. Around mid-July, a small Japanese outpost in the Gilbert Islands was selected: Makin Atoll. It was hoped that the raid would deter immediate reinforcement of Guadalcanal, about one thousand miles to the southwest. The date was set for mid-August.

What the US military called Makin Atoll[12] was actually known as Butaritari, and today is part of the island nation of Kiribati.[13] It is a small bit of a 1,500 nautical mile chain of dozens of islands that stretch from the Gilberts in the south (including Tarawa) through the Marshalls (Mili, Jaluit, and Kwajalein) to Wake Island in the north. Many of these islands were former German possessions granted to Japan at the end of World War I, and were garrisoned by the Japanese in early 1940s. Wake was a US possession invaded the day after the Pearl Harbor attack. Butaritari (Makin) was likewise occupied in December 1941. Together, these island fortresses were meant to extend Japan's Pacific sphere of control and isolate Australia from the United States.

Makin, less than two hundred nautical miles north of the equator, consisted of an irregularly shaped coral reef surrounding a lagoon, about ten by fifteen statute miles in extent, with a very narrow border of dry land at most five hundred yards wide running along the south side. Along that area was a thick covering of coconut palms, salt-scrub brush, and scattered breadfruit trees. The lagoon side was lined with mangrove swamps. A smaller eight-mile islet jutted to the north, known as Makin Meang (Little Makin), or today just Makin. A small population of native islanders lived on the main island, mostly in a settlement on the southwest end known as Ukiangong Village. The Japanese established a modest seaplane base and weather station there, and held it with a small

12. Properly pronounced "Muc-kin" but called "Ma-ken" by US forces, who referred to the entire atoll as Makin.
13. Pronounced "Ki-ri-bas." Butaritari is pronounced "Pu-tari-tari."

seventy-three-man contingent of guard and air flotilla personnel led by Warrant Officer Kyuzaburo Kanemitsu.[14] Very little of this was known by the Americans about to attack, who possessed only prewar navigation charts and some aerial photographs collected by navy carrier-based aircraft. Dense vegetation effectively hid installations on the ground from airborne reconnaissance, so the latter was not particularly helpful. A local fisherman was found and interviewed, who thought there were about fifty Japanese marines guarding the island. Naval intelligence estimates held the number to be higher, possibly as great as 350, and Carlson guessed the garrison to number about 250, a bit larger than his attacking force. This cautious assumption would affect Carlson's judgment and actions over the course of the engagement.

But how to get even two hundred men onto the island for a surprise amphibious attack? Nimitz asked Carlson how many submarines he would need to transport his troops, and he is reported to have answered immediately, "Twenty." This was not a practical number. The US Pacific Fleet began the war with just thirty submarines in the theater, and though numbers had grown in the ensuing months with new construction and consolidation of the Asiatic force, Nimitz had to manage operations from Hawaii to Japan to Alaska to Australia, and there were not enough boats to go around. Blockading the Japanese fleet base at Truk alone required seventeen of his boats. Seeking the most effective way to use his limited forces, the admiral settled on his three cruiser subs as candidates to transport the Marines.

The conclusion of the Great War saw the victors (Great Britain, the United States, France, Italy, and Japan) meet in Washington, DC, to discuss limitation on naval armaments. A treaty was signed in 1922 that limited construction of battleships, battlecruisers, and aircraft carriers. Limitations on smaller vessels, particularly submarines, were not addressed. British demands that submarines be abolished altogether were opposed, so that in the end no agreement on undersea vessels was

---

14. A warrant officer is a rank falling between senior enlisted ratings (chief or sergeant) and junior commissioned officers (ensign or second lieutenant). Originating in the British Royal Navy, usage of the position and details of its status vary among countries. In World War II, the Japanese military called this position *heisōchō*.

reached. A subsequent meeting in Geneva, Switzerland, in 1927 aimed to extend the existing limits to smaller vessels, that is, cruisers, destroyers, and submarines. US president Calvin Coolidge called the meeting, but only representatives from Great Britain and Japan attended. Japan, in particular, was concerned with amending the prior treaty, which limited them to three-fifths the size of the US or UK fleets. In the end, no agreement was reached. A third conference was held in London in 1930 with all five parties (the defeated of World War I remained uninvited) where, finally, submarines were limited in displacement and caliber of guns (but not in numbers).

In the meanwhile, the United States was developing new submarine designs, including V-boats. The first three were of modest size, but V-4 (later named *Argonaut*, SS-166) at 4,231 tons was the largest submarine the US Navy ever built until the advent of nuclear powered boats in the 1950s. She was commissioned in 1928 before the London Naval Conference limited future submarines to a much smaller size. *Argonaut* was originally designed as a mine-laying vessel, but was converted to a troop-carrying ship (designated APS-1) early in World War II. Likewise, V-5 and V-6 were commissioned just before the 1930 conference and were slightly smaller at four thousand tons but of similar design to *Argonaut*. V-5 became *Narwhal* (SS-167) and V-6 *Nautilus* (SS-168). The three became known as "cruiser subs" with large guns, large capacity, slow speed, and long range. Subsequent V-boats and the later US designs observed treaty limitations and were much smaller.

V-boats were large by submarine standards, but by any other measure were cramped, confining, and claustrophobic. The huge hulls at more than 370 feet with a thirty-three foot beam were longer than a football field. From keel to the top of the bridge the ships measured forty-five feet, as tall as a four-story building, with periscopes and masts extending as much as thirty feet higher. Two huge six-inch caliber naval cannons, mounted fore and aft of the conning tower, were the size carried on light cruisers, and the upper structure bristled with small-caliber machine guns. But much of this bulk was filled with tanks, external machinery, superstructure, and fairings. The pressure hull, where the crew lived, worked, and fought, was contained inside that shell. A twenty-one foot diameter

Driving first official rivet on ways for submarine V-6 (later renamed *Nautilus*) at Mare Island, California, August 2, 1927. U.S.NAVY COURTESY DARRYL L. BAKER.

Officers and riveting gang participate in keel laying ceremony at Mare Island Navy Yard, California, August 2, 1927. U.S. NAVY.

Miss Jean Keesling, daughter of a prominent San Francisco attorney, was the sponsor of the V-6 at its launching at Mare Island on March 15, 1930. U.S. NAVY.

Miss Keesling, was sixteen years old, wore a red dress and used a quart of cider to christen V-6. U.S. NAVY.

Rear Adm. George William Laws, Commandant of Mare Island
Navy Yard, with sponsor Miss Jean Keesling just before the
launching of the new submarine V-6. U.S. NAVY COURTESY BILL
GONYO.

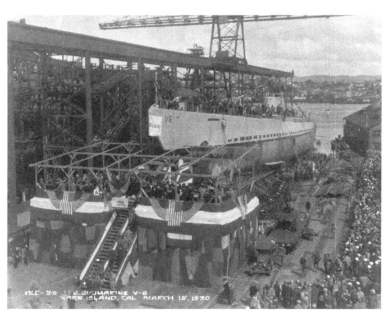

V-6 at her launching at Mare Island on March 15, 1930. U.S. NAVY PHOTO
COURTESY OF THE VALLEJO NAVAL AND HISTORICAL MUSEUM & DARRYL L. BAKER.

cylinder about three hundred feet long, tapered at the ends, the space was crammed with machinery, weapons, supplies, and equipment. Four diesels hammered the heartbeat of the boat in the engine room, by far the largest space in the vessel. These machines spun generators that in turn powered electric motors that drove the propellers in a diesel-electric configuration, common to US submarines. Of course, the diesels could only operate while on the surface, so the electric motors relied on stored battery power while submerged. Two battery rooms and a pump room held other vital gear. Torpedo rooms fore and aft held six tubes and as many as twenty-four torpedoes; along with ammunition magazines, weapons occupied one-fifth of the interior space. The control room, maneuvering room, and conning tower filled another one-tenth. This left just about two thousand square feet of deck space for the crew: berthing, heads, galley, and mess. Ninety or more men lived in a space about the size of a typical four-bedroom home on patrols that could last eight weeks or longer.

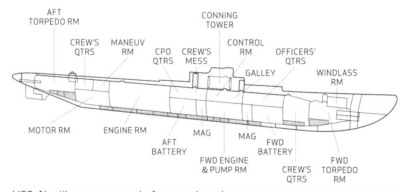

USS *Nautilus* arrangement of compartments. ILLUSTRATION BY BETHANY JOURDAN.

As with all World War II vintage submarines, the sealed chamber called the "conning tower" was contained within the external structure and sat atop the main pressure hull. The periscope stand, steering station, and other equipment were located within that chamber. When submerged, the ship was "conned," or controlled, by a small party including the officer of the deck and a helmsman. The chamber was connected to the main pressure hull below by a hatch on the deck; a ladder from that hatch led down into the control room and provided access into the main hull. Another ladder led up to an overhead hatch that gave access to the external bridge when surfaced. Both hatches were normally closed when submerged, isolating the small conning tower and the men in it both from the sea and from the main pressure hull. During battle stations, ten men would occupy and fight enemy ships from this confined and sweltering space.

The ship, originally designated V-6, was laid down[15] August 2, 1927, at Mare Island Naval Shipyard in Vallejo, California, just two days before the Geneva Convention ended, and was commissioned July 1, 1930. *Nautilus* served as the flagship of Submarine Division 12 in Pearl Harbor and operated in the Pacific for the decade preceding World War II. She entered the shipyard at Mare Island for modernization in 1941, which included new engines and an air conditioning system, much appreciated by crews operating in tropical waters. She departed Mare Island in May 1942 for Pearl Harbor, in early June she went on to patrol the waters west of Midway Island, followed by action off the Honshu coast through early July. She returned to action after repairs in time to support Carlson's raid. *Argonaut* (V-4) spent the interwar period in Newport, Rhode Island and San Diego, California, before moving to Pearl Harbor and becoming the flagship of Submarine Division 4. In 1931, the submarine was featured in *Seas Beneath*, an American action film directed by John Ford. The Pearl Harbor sneak attack found the submarine patrolling the waters near Midway where she tried unsuccessfully to approach Japanese destroyers shelling the island, and later narrowly escaped bombing by friendly aircraft. She returned to Mare Island for a major overhaul that included the conversion to a troop transport, which was hastily completed in time for the August raid on Makin. *Narwahl* (V-5) served in Submarine Division 12 with *Nautilus* before the war, and was in Pearl Harbor during the Japanese attack. She joined *Nautilus* again in defense of Midway, but saw no action. At the time of Carlson's raid, she was patrolling Japanese waters off Hokkaido and was unavailable for the mission, though she and her sister ship would team up in future operations.

---

15. A vessel is "laid down" when the first part of the keel is put in place around which the ship's hull will be built and formal construction begins. Once the hull is completed the ship is launched, that is, floated out of the construction drydock. Construction continues until the vessel is ready for operations, at which point it is commissioned.

V-6 in San Pablo Bay west of Mare Island on October 8, 1930. U.S. NAVY COURTESY
OF THE VALLEJO NAVAL & HISTORIC MUSEUM & DARRYL L. BAKER.

Nautilus (aka N-2) alongside tender USS *Holland* in San Diego Harbor, November
10, 1932. Also visible are *Narwhal* (N-1), *Bass* (SS-164), and another unidentified
submarine. U.S. NAVY.

Nautilus operated out of New London, conducting special submergence tests, until March of 1931. The boat is pictured here in New York City. U.S. NAVY COURTESY OF SAN FRANCISCO EXAMINER & DAVID S. SMITH.

USS *Nautilus* takes a tour around New York Harbor on her way to the Brooklyn Navy Yard on April 8, 1931. U.S. NAVY.

Nautilus (now designated SS-168) near the Mare Island Navy Yard, on April 15, 1942, following her modernization. In just a few weeks she would depart for Pearl Harbor and her first war patrol. U.S. NAVY.

Saturday morning card game on board *Nautilus* circa 1940. U.S. NAVY PHOTO BY BILL AZBELL COURTESY HAROLD LEE.

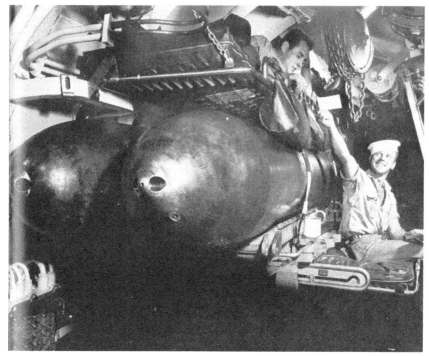

Torpedo room berthing aboard a US submarine, August 1943. U.S. NAVY PHOTO BY LT. CDR. CHARLES FENNO JACOBS, USNR.

Admiral Nimitz told Carlson he could spare two submarines, *Nautilus* and *Argonaut*, and to build his plan around those assets. Carlson set about figuring how he could cram a two-hundred man contingent of his battalion into the two submarines, which by normal standards were already more than full.

The battered *Nautilus* limped back into Pearl Harbor July 11, 1942, after her arduous first patrol. The next two weeks were a chance for the crew to get some well-earned rest while shipyard workers prepared the boat for dry docking. For the most part, the young sailors enjoyed themselves but kept out of trouble, with a few exceptions. The deck log noted several men brought to captain's mast for violation of curfew and being "out of uniform," earning deprivation of liberty as punishment, including the aforementioned Red Porterfield. Second Class Petty Officer Gus McCall was brought aboard by shore patrol "slightly intoxicated" while "carrying concealed a dangerous weapon while on liberty." This incident merited a court-martial, though no punishment was mentioned.

There was some enlisted crew turnover with twenty-four men detached for other duty and twenty-three new men coming aboard. Two members of the wardroom departed, most notably Roy Benson, designated to command USS *Trigger* (SS-237). Known affectionately to his crew as "Pigboat Benny," Benson went on to earn two Navy Crosses for valor, operating in enemy controlled waters in the Sea of Japan. Serving under him as a junior officer was Edward Beach, who went on to a storied career and eventually became the best-selling author of the classic submarine tale *Run Silent, Run Deep* (1955). After the war, Benson married the former Vida Connole, widow of Commander David R. Connole who was the last commanding officer of *Trigger*, lost off Japan in March 1945, just months before the war's end. Benson was described by Buzz Lee as "devoted to the navy . . . the navy was everything to him." He went on to a distinguished career, rising to command the Pacific submarine fleet (COMSUBPAC), and later serving as assistant vice chief of naval operations. He retired as a rear admiral in 1969.

Also departing was Frank Hess, who eventually commanded USS *Angler* (SS-240). These capable officers would be sorely missed, but the lessons they learned during their service under Brockman and first taste of battle would be valuable to the fleet. Pat Rooney took Benson's place as XO, and two new officers, Lt. Cdr. Scott Gibson and Ens. Sherry Ray, came aboard. The wardroom was also complemented by the addition of Clingmon Bowman, former chief electrician who was advanced to warrant officer. Foy Hester took his position as the senior chief electrician on board. Ten other officers came on board temporarily during the time in port to help with repair work and to give the remaining men some time off.

Preparing the ship for dry docking was an undertaking in itself. On July 21, all the ammunition was offloaded, including hundreds of six-inch shells weighing 105 pounds each, and all the torpedoes. Finally, on the morning of July 26, the submarine was nudged into dry dock, along with fellow Midway veteran *Growler*, and the dock was pumped down, exposing the hull for maintenance. Workers swarmed over the two submarines, sitting side by side on keel blocks. A hull inspection found a problem with the rudder, three faulty flood valves, and corrosion of recently welded seams. The propellers were removed for refurbishment, a change of pitch, and reinstalled. Just six days later the dock was flooded, and the two submarines returned to their pier-side berths. *Nautilus* began reloading ammunition and reprovisioning for her next patrol.

Captain Brockman, meeting with Admiral English to receive his next patrol orders, saluted the admiral. English returned Brockman's salute.

"Sit down, Bill. How is the repair work going?"

"Quite well, Admiral. The rudder tiller pins and bushings were removed and repaired, which was my biggest concern. The dock workers have done a fine job, and the temporary officers have served well. Lieutenant Commander Gibson should be a good addition to the wardroom." Brockman added a few details, waiting for English to clue him in on his next assignment.

"Very good," replied English. "Sounds like *Nautilus* is ready for action."

"Yes, sir." Brockman waited. English picked up a folder labeled "TOP SECRET" in red capital letters.

"Your new orders," he said as he passed the folder across the desk. "Ever heard of the Marine Raiders?"

"No, sir," admitted Brockman as he opened the folder and tried to read a few words while keeping his attention on the admiral.

"Well, you'll be meeting them soon enough. Lt. Col. Evans Carlson will be commanding a team of about 220 Marines. You and *Argonaut* will be taking them southeast about two thousand miles to an island called Makin. The Japanese are occupying it. You will deploy them in rubber boats and recover them the next day. Their mission is to destroy the Japanese installations there, gather intelligence, and capture prisoners." He did not mention the concurrent invasion of Guadalcanal and the hope that the raid would divert attention from the bigger mission. He went on, "*Nautilus* will be the senior boat of the task group . . ." he paused and looked down at his copy of the document, "Task Group 7.15. Evans will embark with you. Commander Haines will ride with you as well and be the task group commander." He looked up and added, "By the way, the XO of the outfit is Maj. James Roosevelt, the president's son."

"But how . . ." Brockman started to protest. His first question was where to put the Marines.

"I know, I know," English anticipated his question. "*Nautilus* is a big boat, *Argonaut* even bigger. She was recently outfitted as a troop carrier and can handle about 130 passengers. You will need to carry 85 or 90. You'll leave some crew behind, and some torpedoes. Commander Haines is already working out plans to outfit you with additional berthing."

"Aye, aye, sir," Brockman responded, details of the task ahead already swirling through his thoughts. "I should go see Commander Haines right away, and then brief my officers."

"Right," said English. "But remember this is top secret. We don't want the world to know where you're going and who you're taking. Make that clear to your officers."

"Aye, aye, sir," Brockman repeated. He saluted and took his leave.

Later, in the *Nautilus* wardroom, Brockman gathered his officers and shut the door.

"OK, here's the plan. We are leading a task group consisting of us and *Argonaut* and will ferry a unit of Marines to an island. It will take us about a week to get there. We'll deploy the troops in rubber boats and stand offshore to offer fire support. When they're ready, we'll recover the Marines and head back to Pearl." He let that sink in. Hogan, just promoted to lieutenant commander, was the first to speak.

"How many Marines, sir?" he asked, assuming a dozen or so.

"Figured you'd ask. I've been in touch with their commander, Lieutenant Colonel Carlson. He plans to bring along most of two companies from his battalion. He'll be on *Nautilus* with . . ." he paused for effect, "ninety Marines."

"WHAT!?" several officers cried in unison. "Where are we going to put ninety men?" asked Rooney, the XO. "And their food?" wondered

Defrees, the commissary officer. "And their weapons and equipment?" pointed out Lynch, the gunnery officer, incredulous. Gibson and Ray just sat, stunned.

"OK, pipe down," said the captain. "We've got it easy. *Argonaut* is taking 130. Let's think this through and figure it out. We have work to do!" He went over several details of the operations order and his conversation with Haines. Much discussion ensued. Finally, Hogan made a suggestion.

"Captain, we're just going there . . . wherever 'there' is," making the point that Brockman wouldn't even tell them where they were going, "and back, right? Our mission doesn't include a regular patrol. What are the chances of seeing any Jap ships?"

"Not much," replied Brockman.

"OK, so why don't we leave behind all our torpedoes except for the ones topside, and most of our six-inch ammo. Then we could use the torpedo tubes for storage and the torpedo rooms for berthing."

Lynch immediately objected, "We can't leave our fish behind! We'd be defenseless!!"

Brockman said, "We'll need the six-inch ammo for fire support. But Hogan's right, we won't need many torpedoes. The external tubes will have to do." *Nautilus* carried four torpedo tubes mounted on deck that could be preloaded and fired while underway. Additional topside stowage allowed as many as sixteen additional torpedoes to be carried in this manner, though of course the tubes could not be reloaded while submerged.

Lynch was not happy, but quickly accepted the situation at hand. "Well, sir, if we're not carrying inboard torpedoes, we can pull out the racks. They take up a lot of space." Hogan piped in, "We can add more bunks in their place." Discussion continued as the men set about to imagine how they could accomplish the impossible.

In the end, wooden bunks were installed in the torpedo rooms and the six twenty-one-inch diameter torpedo tubes were crammed with food and other supplies. Tom Hogan later wrote,[16] "We had to have additional air conditioning but none was available. A bright young engineer from

16. From *Memories . . . Thirty-Eight Years Later* by Tom Hogan (1980).

the squadron said not to worry. He would get us some. He went downtown to Honolulu and got two cabinet type commercial machines. This required removal of soft patches[17] to load them aboard. Then the problem of cooling water. . . . Easy! Take salt water from the WRT[18] tanks!"

To further accommodate the Marines, Brockman decided to leave a few crewmen behind. Eighty-three enlisted men and eight officers, plus Commander Haines were to be joined by ninety Raiders, totaling 182 men who would sail in *Nautilus* for Makin Island a few days hence.[19]

Having figured out how to carry the Marines, the crew had to organize debarkation and recovery, at sea, at night. To this challenge was added the need to coordinate with *Argonaut*. The submarines were equipped with rubber boats known in military parlance as LCR(L), or "Landing Craft, Rubber (Large)." They were stored topside and inflated from the submarine high-pressure air supply just before deployment. Measuring sixteen feet long, they were designed to carry ten men each (though twelve or more could be squeezed on), and could be paddled or powered by a small Evinrude outboard motor. Weighing nearly four hundred pounds, the boats were unwieldy to handle, especially at night on a pitching deck. The motors were found to be unreliable and easily contaminated with salt water. There would be only one chance to practice this evolution, a "dress rehearsal" that was scheduled for August 6.

The Raiders came aboard for the first time on the afternoon of August 5. The event was remembered by Tom Hogan:[20]

---

17. A soft patch is a hull plate that can be unbolted to allow removal or installation of equipment too large to fit through a hatch.

18. WRT = water (a)round torpedo. These are variable ballast tanks used for flooding or draining the torpedo tubes.

19. The numbers quoted here come from the official *Nautilus* muster roll compiled at date of sailing, which listed men aboard by name. Smith (2001) excludes five men from his listing. Campbell (2016) lists only eighty-one Raiders on *Nautilus*. Sources (including unit musters and the operations order) disagree about the number of Marines embarked on *Argonaut*. Smith includes a roster of 134, while Rottman (2014) mentions 136. The total strength of the Raider task unit was said to be between 219 and 222 men, which suggests that *Argonaut* carried no more than 132. *Argonaut*'s patrol report states 114 men, and seven officers were on board, totaling only 121, for a task unit tally of 211. As will be seen, the poor mustering of men in the task unit was a recurring problem that contributed to missing Marines at the end of the operation.

20. *Memories . . . Thirty-Eight Years Later* by Tom Hogan (1980).

Well, the day came for a practice embarkation by the Marines and medical contingents. It was scheduled for 1730 on a Wednesday afternoon so as to keep a cover on this Top Secret operation. We were tied up just back of what is now known as Lockwood Hall. Everyone not required topside was kept belowdecks. At 1730 twenty trucks came bearing down alongside, disgorging Marines who disappeared below on the double. Then we noticed that the hedge around the sides and back of SOQ5 [senior officer quarters] were lined with guests at a cocktail party, who nonchalantly viewed the proceedings. There went the cover.

That evening *Nautilus* got underway for the exercise. At 0330 the next morning the Marines deployed and paddled ashore. Admirals Nimitz and Ray Spruance witnessed the proceedings on land and were surprised they could not detect the approaching boats until they were just fifty feet from the beach. Though the Marines had practiced relentlessly, and were proficient in operating the boats in full combat equipment in any condition, this was the first time they had actually deployed from a submarine.

The submarine returned to Pearl Harbor and the Marines debarked, having had a taste of what was in store for them in the cramped quarters they would occupy in the coming weeks. Final preparations were made, and remaining supplies loaded. At 0730 on August 8, the troops returned and quickly came on board, settling into their new temporary homes. At 0900 *Nautilus* got underway in formation with *Argonaut* and a small escort vessel. The raid was on.

Red Porterfield sat in the CPO[21] quarters smoking his pipe as *Nautilus* rocked in calm seas, cruising on the surface. Chief Hester was trying for some privacy in the cramped space while writing a letter home. It was Sunday evening, August 9, and the crew finally had a little time to relax after the hectic departure the day before and a very busy morning.

---

21. Chief Petty Officer.

Captain Brockman called for a quick dive at 0821, then battle surfaced to man the deck guns and fire a few rounds for training. At 0940 the Marines were allowed topside for drills and calisthenics, as well as a little fresh air, all the while the ship cruising at thirteen knots. At 1017 the crew practiced firing the machine guns, and while hurrying topside for the drill Buzz Lee cracked his skull, requiring three stitches courtesy of corpsman Potts. Another practice dive in the afternoon and an evening drill for the Raider detachment rounded out an eventful "day of rest."

Porterfield drew on his pipe and nudged Hester. "Whatcha writing?" he asked.

"Nothing, Red. Just a letter home," replied the chief.

"Writing to your mother again?" he chided. "You know there's no mail buoy[22] out here!" The gregarious Red liked to try to draw out the reserved and quiet Hester.

"That's OK, I like to write things down while they're fresh."

"Hey," said Red, changing the subject, "Did you see Major Roosevelt? I mean, before they got on *Argonaut*?" Having the president's son on the operation was a morale boost for the crew.

"I just saw him with the group. Lee said he talked to him, though. Said his voice sounded just like FDR's."

"Aww, Lee and his chin music," dismissed Red. "He probably dreamed that up on account of his bump on the noggin today."

Foy laughed. "Yeah, Buzz is an ear beater all right. Did he tell you about Private Carson's boots?"

"I heard he was looking for new laces. What happened?"

"Well," said Foy, "he convinced Campbell to let him hot bunk. So he climbs in the rack and takes off his boondocks and ties them onto a pipe over his head. Starts snoring. Next thing he knows we're diving. The klaxon's going off. He wakes up and sees his boots spinning inches in front of his nose!"

Red laughed, guessing the problem. "He tied them to the bow planes drive shaft!"

---

22. A "mail buoy" is a fictitious sea-borne post office. Senior men were known to order new sailors to man the "mail buoy watch" as a prank.

"Right!" grinned Foy. "The planesman's going a little up, a little down, back and forth, trying to hold depth. They'd spin one way, then the other, so fast he couldn't grab them! Kept going until the laces broke! At least," he allowed, "that's the way Buzz told it."[23]

The chiefs had a laugh together, Red pleased that he had drawn out the taciturn Hester just a bit. It was the longest conversation he'd had with him in weeks.

Hey," Foy continued, "Don't let Captain catch you smoking that pipe. You heard what he said to Benny." Brockman forbade pipe smoking on board, a favorite vice of the recently detached XO Benson. This had led to a bit of tension between the two officers.

"Captain don't mind my pipe," replied Red. Curiously, Porterfield claimed Brockman never bothered him about it. Smoking was generally allowed on board, and most of the crew indulged in the habit. Clouds of cigarette smoke added to the fouling of the atmosphere in the ship, especially while submerged, but the practice was so ingrained that only in extreme circumstances did the captain secure the "smoking lamp." But for some reason he considered pipe smoking inappropriate for officers. Beside smoking, cooking, diesel fuel, battery outgassing, and other noxious fumes, carbon dioxide exhaled by the crew was a problem. Carbon dioxide peaked at about 1.5 percent after twelve hours submerged, leading to complaints of drowsiness and the beginnings of headaches, but within acceptable limits for a World War II submarine.

Besides poor air quality, the crew and Marine passengers suffered from excessive heat while operating in tropical waters with air and water temperatures in the mid to high eighties, day and night. The extra air conditioning units installed in Pearl Harbor proved to be completely inadequate as temperatures in the living spaces climbed to ninety-three degrees with 85 percent humidity, being even hotter in the engineering spaces. Severe cases of heat rash and more than a few cases of heat prostration were noted. The physical and mental condition of the Marines deteriorated day by day under the difficult conditions; however, their morale did not suffer. Captain Brockman wrote in his patrol report, "It

---

23. Anecdote from Smith (2001, 101).

was especially noted that the Marines turned to with a will at standing watches and other duties assigned them and soon became proficient in their work. It was a pleasure to have them aboard." He went on to recommend that they be issued submarine orders for their time on board so that they would receive submarine pay.[24]

Many of the men found alternative accommodations to the ones hastily prepared for them. In particular, some of the taller Marines could not easily fit in the confined temporary bunks and sought space to stretch out wherever they could, including on the passageway decks. Of course, this risked being stepped on or kicked as men on watch moved about. Some Marines worked out arrangements with ship's crewmen to use their bunks when they were on watch, a practice common in the submarine navy known as "hot bunking."

The routine for the next few days varied little. Battle surface drills were held each morning, and the Marines were allowed on deck once or twice a day for training and exercise. The ship remained on the surface and cruised at high speed, not particularly worried about Japanese patrols so far from enemy bases. Partway through the transit Brockman increased speed and dispensed with training dives in order to make better time. The crew made do with facilities that were meant to accommodate half their number. The galley was in use around the clock, in spite of serving only two meals a day (with soup and crackers midday). It took three hours or longer to mess all hands for each meal. The galley became one of the warmest and most uncomfortable spaces on board, but the cooks soldiered on. A single head served the entire enlisted crew. The officer's wardroom was prepared to serve as an operating theater in the event of casualties.

On the morning of August 15, *Nautilus* dived as she approached the Japanese-held island at the insistence of the task group commander. Surprise was an essential element of the attack. That evening, immediately upon surfacing, the Raiders held a final drill as the submarine went to full speed to make the appointed rendezvous with *Argonaut* ahead of the raid.

---

24. US Navy submarine ratings received an extra five to twenty dollars per month, depending on seniority, for volunteering for submarine service.

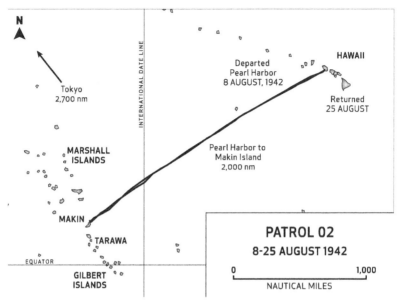

Nautilus was assigned to transport Marines to Makin Island on her second patrol. ILLUSTRATION BY BETHANY JOURDAN.

The cooks prepared a good luck cake for Carlson and his officers, and gung-ho meetings were held aboard both submarines where the troops were encouraged to ask questions. For most of the men, this was the first time they ever heard of Makin Atoll. The target had been kept secret. A motivational speech was read by Carlson and Roosevelt over their respective submarines' announcing systems. Sunday morning, August 16, the ship submerged and cruised on battery power nearing their objective. At 0309 Makin Island was sighted through the periscope and upon daylight *Nautilus* began a reconnaissance of the atoll, Ozzie Lynch taking photos for recording purposes. Over the course of the day Marines pulled their gear from stowage and prepared their equipment for the assault. A hearty supper of ham and mashed potatoes was served.

US Marine Raiders exercise on the deck of *Nautilus* while en route to raid Makin Island on August 11, 1942. U.S. NAVY.

Shoreline of Makin Island, photographed through the periscope of *Nautilus* on August 16, 1942, the day before US Marine raiders were landed. U.S. NAVY.

Lt. Col. Evans Carlson, USMC, cuts "Good Luck" cake in wardroom of *Nautilus*, August 14, 1942, as Captain Brockman looks on. U.S. NAVY.

Two US Marine Raiders below decks on *Nautilus*, ready to go ashore on Makin Island, August 17, 1942. U.S. NAVY.

Corporal Vernon F. Paulstick, a
Marine Raider aboard *Nautilus*
heading topside for raid on Makin
Island, August 17, 1942. U.S. NAVY.

At 1924 *Nautilus* surfaced. At 2116 *Argonaut* was sighted. The ships closed and a barrel was passed between them with final operations orders from Carlson to his XO. Men began hauling equipment topside and were greeted with strong winds, a pitching deck, and passing rain squalls. The crew proceeded to drag out the heavy boats and inflate them, fuel the motors, load gear on board, and strap everything down, all in darkness. It proved impossible to keep seawater out of the fuel, rendering the motors largely useless. The original plan was to load everyone on deck, then submerge the ship under them, but Brockman feared the rubber rafts would be swamped or capsize, so the boats were lowered into the dark water and the Marines had to jump in. Executing this unpracticed maneuver was a challenge, as the men had to time their jumps with the swells or risk a fifteen foot drop, all the while weighed down with equipment. A few were injured and a few missed the rafts altogether and had to be fished out of the sea. A similar exercise took place on nearby *Argonaut*. Finally, twelve boats of Raiders embarked from the larger submarine and paddled over to *Nautilus* to join her eight boats. Everything took much longer than planned, but by 0415 the flotilla was on its way to shore. However, Colonel Carlson and his runner were still on board *Nautilus*, so he called one of the boats to return for him. Lt. Oscar Peatross led one of the few boats with a working motor, so he turned back to fetch the commander and his man even though his boat was already overloaded with thirteen embarked. Carlson was brought aboard with difficulty and transferred to another boat. Peatross returned to the submarine to check for stragglers and became separated from the main body. After getting his bearings, he and his men headed for shore on their own.

At 0513 Captain Brockman established voice communications with the Raiders ashore using their "handie talkie" field radios.[25] At 0543 he received a status message from Carlson: "Everything lousy."

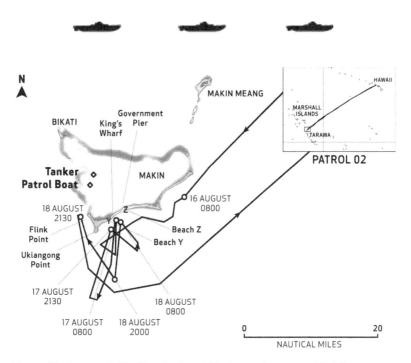

Along with *Argonaut*, *Nautilus* deployed Marines ashore, provided fire support, and recovered troops returning from the raid. The submarine attacked and sank two vessels in the lagoon using her deck guns. ILLUSTRATION BY BETHANY JOURDAN.

---

25. Known to the Marines as a BC-611-A. Also designated SCR-536 and popularly known as a "walkie-talkie."

The official operations order for the Makin raid directed the Marines to land in the early morning at 0400 and sweep through the Japanese held part of the island, killing all enemy troops and destroying installations. They were also to take any documents they could find and capture prisoners for interrogation (though no one had any idea where to put extra men in the already overcrowded submarines). The specifics of going ashore were detailed to the minute and included separate landing points for the two companies. Company A, consisting mainly of men from *Argonaut*, were to land on Beach Y near the southwest point of the island on the ocean side opposite a facility called Chong's wharf. Carlson and his command post would land with Company A. Company B, with a mix of men from *Nautilus* and *Argonaut*, were to land several miles northeast on Beach Z near a small native village opposite Government pier. The land between the two beaches was thought to be the main extent of the Japanese-occupied area and included a seaplane ramp (King's wharf) and a few structures dating back to times of British occupation. A packed coral road ran along the lagoon side of the island's central area. Otherwise, the island was covered with coconut palms, breadfruit trees, and native huts.

The plan was for the two companies to land, hide their boats in the shoreland scrub, and move across the narrow island to the lagoon side, dispatching enemy soldiers and destroying military equipment along the way. There they would turn toward each other and sweep along the lagoon shore in a pincer movement, meeting at a stone pier that marked the approximate center of the occupied area. Priorities included destroying radio stations and any seaplanes found at the wharfs. Operations were to be wrapped up by afternoon, with withdrawal planned for 1830. The Raiders carried light weapons (including a few machine guns, antitank rifles, trench guns,[26] and mortars), ammunition, a canteen of water, and a single four ounce D ration bar. They carried no overnight gear. A medical officer and two corpsmen were to land with each company.

Of course, no plan survives contact with the enemy, and the first enemy was the sea. Winds, waves, and stronger than expected currents slowed debarkation. Noise from gusty winds and heavy surf made it

---

26. A pump-action combat shotgun.

difficult to hear voice commands and added to confusion as the troops tried to gather in the darkness. Two boats and their gear, including machine guns and medical supplies, were swept away from *Nautilus*, but replacements were collected from spares. Carlson decided to scrap the pincher plan and land all the boats together at Beach Z, but two of them became separated and landed to the northeast, one as far as mile away. A third boat, the one commanded by Lieutenant Peatross with thirteen men, had returned to *Nautilus* for stragglers and did not hear of the change in plan. After getting his bearings, Peatross headed for Beach Y as originally ordered. In the event, his raft made it less than halfway as the squad landed about a mile to the southwest of the main group of Raiders, and were now effectively behind enemy lines.

The landing of the main body did not go smoothly, with rafts overturning in the heavy surf and some equipment lost. Drenched with rain and spray, the sodden men made it ashore, and Carlson took stock. Though all the men in the main group reached the beach, some of their weapons were lost. Three of his boats, with more than thirty men, were missing. It was after 0500 and dawn was approaching. An accidental discharge of one of the weapons while being loaded had everyone jumping. Could the noise have alerted the enemy? The situation was indeed "lousy."

By 0600 the Raiders confirmed their location at Beach Z, with Government pier on the opposite (lagoon) side and Butaritari village in between. Men from the two missing boats to the northeast rejoined the group; only Peatross's boat remained unaccounted for. Carlson began to replan the attack on the fly and ordered Company A to advance across the island with Company B deploying on the flanks of the movement. This immediately led to confusion as Beach Z was Company B's landing zone, and in the original plan they would have advanced across the island. Some B Raiders, either not understanding the new orders or acting on initiative, advanced anyway.

The Marines moved quietly across the narrow island, a distance of about four hundred yards, and reached the pier without opposition. Setting up a machine gun post, the company turned and began advancing along the island, approaching the structure known as Government House. All was still. Three troops from 1st Platoon of Company A crept forward cautiously. Then, in a blinding flash, a weapon went off in front of them. Not knowing from where or from whom the shot came, the platoon leader called out the verbal challenge.

"Hi Raider!"

The countersign came back, "Gung ho!"[27] A Company B man had raced across the island to his objective and fired at his own troops with a trench gun. Luckily, no one was hit, and the cool-headed platoon leader chose to confirm the situation rather than firing away at the supposed enemy. The blast and hubbub, however, put an end to the stealthy advance and alerted the Japanese and locals to the presence of the Marines. Natives appeared from their huts. They greeted the soldiers, and some could speak a bit of English. They proved to be friendly and told Carlson where the Japanese were located, near Chong's wharf, which was opposite the original Beach Y landing area. He was unable to get a clear idea of numbers, and continued to overestimate the strength of forces he faced, guessing to be about two hundred soldiers. The Raiders gave the natives some cigarettes and a few of their limited supply of D ration bars. Carlson ordered his troops to deploy on either side of the lagoon road and to advance southwest along the island toward Chong's wharf, about two thousand yards away.

The men moved forward, checking huts and any potential cover for enemy troops. So far, no Japanese had been seen, though occasional shots were taken by Raiders at suspected or imagined targets. A Company's 1st Platoon had the lead and was the first to encounter the enemy as Cpl. Howard Young, on the point, dropped to his knees and waved at the men behind him to hold position. A truck came up the lagoon side road, ground to a halt about three hundred yards in front of the Marines, and disgorged some twenty Japanese troops. More arrived on foot. As the Raiders quietly moved into ambush positions, the Japanese spread into the scattered brush on either side of the road and began to move forward. Advancing in small groups over relatively open ground, they were easy targets for the concealed Marines. As they entered the trap, Sgt. Clyde

---

27. Some sources say the challenge was "Gung" and the reply "Ho," but Rottman (2014) insists this is incorrect.

Thomason opened fire with a trench gun, followed by the entire platoon. The Japanese responded with blistering machine gun fire at close range and deadly sniper fire from men concealed in the palm trees. For the next several minutes a vicious firefight raged, leaving most of the Japanese on the ground dead with nine Raiders lost, most to sniper fire. The melee subsided but the Marines remained pinned down by regular, accurate fire from the trees. Apparently, the attack was expected, and the enemy had taken the time to prepare well-camouflaged positions in the tall palms.

Carlson, from his command post near the landing beach, tried to make sense of the situation. He continued to labor under the false premise that the enemy forces numbered two hundred or more, when in reality a large number of the seventy-three-man garrison has already been killed in the first firefight. Worried that a larger force opposed him, he cautiously ordered reinforcements to the flank. Without clear orders to advance, the Marines continued to lose men to snipers and allowed the remaining Japanese to regroup. Among the casualties was Sargent Thomason, who moved fearlessly up and down the firing line pointing out targets and directing the troops. Lost to a sniper bullet, Thomason became the first enlisted Marine in World War II to receive the Medal of Honor. The Japanese relentlessly targeted officers, medical personnel, and radio operators. Lieutenants and sergeants soon learned to dispense with hand signals, which attracted bullets, and rely on voice commands.

Assuming a concentration of Japanese beyond his lines, Carlson then had Major Roosevelt contact the submarines for help.

On board *Nautilus*, Brockman was having a hard time communicating with the troops ashore. The "everything lousy" message was followed minutes later by a more hopeful, "Situation expected to be well in hand shortly" report, but for an hour after that voice radio was nearly useless. At around 0656 Brockman was able to piece together bits of messages from Major Roosevelt that indicated the Marines wanted artillery fire on Ukiangong Point, where the concentration of Japanese forces was thought the be.

"Man battle station, gun action. Deck gun only!" ordered Brockman. The gun crews scrambled topside to their positions at the fore and aft six-inch cannons and began to prepare the weapons. Plugs and covers were removed and securing brackets were unbolted.

"Target is Ukiangong Point, bearing two-four-four, range six thousand," called the captain.

"Ukiangong Point, aye," replied Ozzie Lynch, the gunnery officer, repeating the bearing and range. Men hauled the 105-pound projectiles and forty-four-pound bags of powder out of the magazines while others loaded the guns. Hand wheels were spun to train the huge twenty-six-foot long barrels. Gunners had the point in their sights.

"Gunnery officer ready!" announced Lynch.

"Very well. Commence firing," ordered Brockman.

"Commence firing, aye," Lynch acknowledged. "Ready one . . . fire one!" Near simultaneous booms erupted as the big guns discharged a salvo. The projectiles screamed through the morning air. Lynch watched with binoculars for the shot to land. A near miss.

"A little short. Increase range one hundred yards. Resume fire!" The second salvo flew with a thundering blast.

"A hit!" Lynch called. The men cheered and continued with their work. Brockman and Pat Rooney, now the executive officer with the departure of Benson, watched the proceedings from the bridge, along with Haines, the task group commander.

"Too bad we weren't able to load out bombardment shells," commented Rooney. The common projectiles *Nautilus* carried were effective against small ships, but were not ideal for land targets. Much of their explosive burst was absorbed by the ground.

"Complain to Commander Haines," quipped Brockman, wagging his thumb at his boss standing behind him.

On the island, Carlson watched as *Nautilus* pummeled the imaginary troops on Ukiangong Point. Then the Raiders, who had reached the lagoon, reported two vessels, one a small patrol gunboat and the other a transport of about 3,500 tons. Concerned that the transport might carry reinforcements, Carlson ordered Roosevelt to redirect fire.

On board *Nautilus*, the radio crackled. Brockman strained to make sense out of the garbled voice, cannons booming around him. After a minute he got the message.

"Check fire! Check fire!" he ordered. "Plot," he called down to the conning tower, "the Marines have a merchant ship eight thousand yards north of Government pier in the lagoon. Give me a range and bearing." Word came back quickly, "Zero-eight-four relative, one-four thousand yards."

"Very well. Helm, steady on course two-six-two. Lynch, new target, merchant ship, bearing three-four-six true, range fourteen thousand." He called for a spotter on the island to watch the fall of shot to no avail. Major Roosevelt could not be raised again on the radio. Finally, at 0716, he decided to fire anyway. The guns erupted, salvo after salvo arcing over the line of coconut palms ashore and disappearing into the lagoon beyond. In the hot morning sun and humid sea air, the men heaved the heavy projectiles and power bags, sweating profusely.

"Mr. Lynch, we can't contact a spotter, so adjust your range and deflection to scatter shot around that part of the lagoon. I want about a thousand yards in all directions.

"Aye, sir," replied Lynch, who set about directing his guns accordingly. Finally, after a few more minutes of firing with another twenty-three salvos expended, Brockman had enough.

"Cease fire! Mr. Lynch, how much ammunition expended?"

"Sixty-five rounds, Captain," replied Lynch.

"Christ!" cursed the captain. "Let's not waste any more. Without a spotter, we're firing blind! Secure the deck guns!"

The troops on the island heard the big guns booming and witnessed the outcome. Sgt. Walter Carroll reported:

> *Got into position on right flank near lagoon side. Saw two ships in lagoon. One seemed to be a tanker or transport, the other a gun boat. Both just at the edge of lagoon. Both at anchor at that time. Guns started firing and they started running in circles in lagoon. Tried to head out towards sea and the tanker was hit near the water line and burst into flames a little later. Gun boat sank after being hit in lagoon.*[28]

Pvt. James Green shared Carlson's concern and later reported regarding the transport, "I gave a silent prayer of thanks for the destruc-

---

28. USS *Nautilus* Report of Second War Patrol.

tion of this ship because without its destruction I am sure we could not have escaped."[29]

Brockman was later gratified to learn that his big guns and imaginative tactic of changing range and deflection to saturate the lagoon were rewarded. Certainly, a large measure of luck was involved, admitted by the captain in his patrol report. *Argonaut*, meanwhile, did not get the word to fire, but observed the *Nautilus* action. Soon, at 0901, the submarines had other concerns.

"Radar contact, four miles," called the radar operator.

"Bearing?" queried Brockman. Just then, the lookout reported, "Aircraft abeam to starboard!" Without hesitating, the captain ordered, "Submerge the ship! Quick dive!" He waited for the men topside to scrambled below before following them down, the submarine beginning its descent.

"Last man down, hatch secured!" called Lynch as he dogged the conning tower hatch. A long minute passed before the diving officer announced, "My depth is six eight feet."

"Damn, I wish we could get down quicker," growled Brockman. Old *Nautilus*, lacking a negative tank, could rarely submerge to periscope depth in much under a minute, about twice as long as a more modern fleet submarine, regardless of the efforts of the crew. Those thirty seconds could be crucial when under attack from a fast-moving aircraft equipped with machine guns and depth bombs. In the event, no attack materialized, and *Nautilus* surfaced at 0958, *Argonaut* fifteen minutes later.

Unaware that they had already sunk the two ships in the lagoon, Brockman contacted *Argonaut*, whose guns had been silent to this point, to direct the submarine to fire on the merchant ship. For his part, Brockman thought to run to the west, around Ukiangong Point, to the lagoon entrance and hoped to bring the enemy ship under direct fire by gun or torpedoes while *Argonaut* was firing indirect. As *Argonaut* was "maneuvering to obtain a firing bearing" the submarines sighted a "two-winged plane," and both immediately dove. Two Type 95 Reconnaissance Seaplanes (US code name "Dave") flew over the island, circled for a while, and dropped two small bombs to no effect.

---

29. Ibid.

Nautilus poked her head up at 1253, but as soon as the radar cleared the surface and could be turned on a new and more serious airborne threat materialized.

The radar watch called out, "Radar contact, multiple targets, at twelve miles and fourteen miles, bearing north! Hogan, the officer of the deck for the afternoon watch, saw them immediately "Captain, I see planes, high altitude, looks like . . . about twelve planes. They could have seen us!"

"Very well," Brockman replied. "Submerge the ship! Let's go to ninety feet." He didn't want to risked being seen at periscope depth in the clear waters and bright morning sunshine. Down they went, quicker this time since they had just barely surfaced. Brockman then turned to Wetmore at the sonar station. "To *Argonaut* on the QC: Do not surface. Air activity. Proceed to Point Baker." Wetmore acknowledged the order and passed it to *Nautilus*'s companion submarine on the underwater telephone.[30] By order of the task group commander, the boats would remain submerged until the scheduled troop withdrawal time of 1830.

The Japanese aircraft swooped over the island. Two Type 2 Emily Flying Boats and six floatplanes were escorted by four Zero fighters.[31] Over the next hour the aircraft made repeated passes over the American positions on the island, strafing and dropping thirty kilogram bombs. A few Marines were wounded to join the growing number hit by snipers, but otherwise escaped much harm. As the planes withdrew, low on fuel and ammunition, one Emily and one Dave landed in the lagoon. The Emily was a four engine transport seaplane that could carry up to forty-one troops. This attempt to reinforce the island was of great concern to Carlson, who already considered himself to be outnumbered. As the Japanese

---

30. The QC (also known as UQC, or Gertrude) was a sonar device that transmitted voice or Morse code signals through the water for communication between submarines. *Nautilus* reported no difficulty communicating while submerged at eleven thousand yards, though the device operated poorly while surfaced.

31. The attack included four Type 94 "Alf" Reconnaissance Seaplanes and two more Dave floatplanes. The four fighters were Type 0 officially designated "Archie," but more commonly referred to as Zeros.

aircraft taxied toward the King's Wharf seaplane ramp, Marines opened fire with three machine guns and two Boys Anti-tank Rifles, the latter firing armor-piercing ammunition. The machine guns had immediate effect as incendiary and tracer rounds set the floatplane ablaze. The Emily flying boat attempted to turn away to escape, and briefly lifted from the lagoon, but riddled with rounds it caught fire and grounded near the seaplane ramp. The Raiders continued to fire on the wreck, hoping to prevent any survivors from making it to land.

Meanwhile, the battle ashore was raging. Carlson had failed to capitalize on his advantage after repelling the initial Japanese attack, and his men continued to be at the mercy of well-hidden snipers. The Marine commander had trouble adapting to the change in plan with both companies intermingled, causing confusion and indecision. The opportunity to outmaneuver the enemy with his superior force of well-trained men was at hand, but Carlson remained overcautious, convinced the Japanese were more numerous.

In fact, the Japanese numbers were dwindling, but they were determined to resist to the last man. A message was intercepted by US naval intelligence that morning from the senior officer on the island, Warrant Officer Kanemitsu, informing his higher command that "all men are dying serenely in battle." At 1130, the waning, but reorganized, force counterattacked the Marines. With shouts and the sound of a bugle, a wave of Japanese emerged from behind two large trees and charged the American positions. This began what came to be called the Battle of the Breadfruit Trees. The Marines fired ferociously and cut down the initial wave, but lost a half dozen men. Surviving enemy troops tried to struggle to their feet but were cut down.

The main body of Carlson's force remained largely in place, having moved barely five hundred yards from their landing spot. The morning was almost gone, little progress had been made, and casualties were mounting. Wounded men were moved back to the beach where they were tended to at a makeshift aid station. The situation started out lousy and had remained so, despite the bravery of the Marines.

One group of Raiders, however, was active and effective. Lieutenant Peatross and his twelve men had landed a mile to the southwest and were isolated from the main body. Their radio did not work and for a while Carlson thought they were lost, though a man was sent to try to contact the commander and did eventually get through. Peatross did not hear back from him, so as he was trained, he took initiative. He sent scouts to the southwest who encountered no enemy, so he rightly concluded the entire Japanese force was between him and the main body of the Raiders. He viewed the enemy as being trapped between his little squad and the main body. He began to advance.

The men came upon barracks and fired on Japanese soldiers moving about the buildings. They cleared out the Japanese headquarters and searched other buildings. A Japanese soldier ran out and was gunned down; he proved to be Warrant Officer Kanemitsu, the Japanese commander. The men continue to advance, wreaking havoc on the Japanese rear, taking out a machine gun emplacement, wrecking a vehicle, and destroying a radio station. Lieutenant Peatross, in fact, accomplished much of what the entire raid had set out to do. Over the next several hours his squad roamed the area killing enemy troops and destroying anything of value. The sounds of battle reached them from the main body, just four hundred yards away, but no word came from Carlson.

The main body saw another ten Japanese gather for a final banzai charge supported by the ever present snipers, but they were quickly dispatched ending the Battle of the Breadfruit Trees. Afterward, resistance all but evaporated, with only about a dozen able-bodied enemy soldiers left on the island. Still, Carlson failed to advance. He had won the island, but refused to believe it. The Raiders continued to stalk individual Japanese, taking potshots from concealed locations, but little else was accomplished the rest of the afternoon.

Late in the afternoon Carlson began to withdraw his troops. Still expecting Japanese attacks, he left some elements in place. At 1630 another wave of planes attacked prompting Roosevelt to recommend withdrawing to the beach. Carlson later reported that he thought a strong force of the enemy still faced him, though by then there could not have been more than a handful of Japanese soldiers left.

Lieutenant Peatross, having done all he could with three of his squad dead and two wounded, proceeded to withdraw as planned. He fetched his raft from its place of concealment and was delighted when the outboard motor immediately started. His troops motored to the rendezvous point and after an hour found *Nautilus*. They were the first Raiders to return.

The other Raiders did not fare as well. Carlson collected his remaining men on the beach, including more than a dozen wounded, and gathered their rubber boats from concealment. He held a farewell meeting with the natives who had helped them and asked them to give his dead Marines Christian burials. Carlson left a dozen troops as a rear guard against the imaginary force of Japanese that he thought still occupied the island. He had the men form into groups of ten to a boat and prepare to brave the heavy surf. Finally, at 1930, Carlson ordered the boats launched. As the waves pounded the beach, the Marines waded into the breakers, pushing the boats until the men were chest deep in water. They furiously paddled, most of the motors failing to start. One after another, boats were swamped, and wounded men were washed overboard. Weapons and equipment were lost to the sea. The Raiders fished their incapacitated mates out of the water and dragged their overturned rafts back to the beach. Many men lost most of their gear, including shoes and clothing. James Roosevelt was said to have rescued three men from drowning.

They regrouped and gathered their strength to try again, with much the same result. Four or five times the troops fought the pounding surf and were mostly washed back to shore. Finally, exhausted, some 120 Raiders, including most of the wounded, fell back on the beach. With no food or water, few weapons, no shelter, and an unknown force of Japanese behind them, the situation had deteriorated from "lousy" to dire.

A few boats managed to push through the surf and paddle out to sea. The men searched the waves for a submarine and safety.

"Surface, surface, surface!" The chief of the watch announced the command on the 1MC, followed by three blasts of the diving alarm. *Ah-OO-gah, ah-OO-gah, ah-OO-gah!* The huge dark hull emerged from the sea in the gathering twilight. Ozzie Lynch scrambled to the bridge and scanned the shore looking for boats.

"I see *Argonaut*," called the lookout, pointing aft.

"Very well," replied Lynch. "Control, energize the green flashing light." *Nautilus* was to be identified by a green flashing light, *Argonaut* by red. It was 1843, and the Raiders were expected to be leaving the beach in about forty-five minutes. Additional crewman made their way topside lugging the bridge machine gun.

"Ahead one-third. Come left to course zero-four-five," ordered Lynch, maneuvering the submarine toward the rendezvous point. "Keep alert for rubber boats," he called, unnecessarily. Everyone topside was staring intently toward the beach, hoping for a glimpse of the Marines. The periscope watch spied them first.

"Sir, I see them. Still on the beach, lining up their rafts."

"Good news," replied Lynch. "Looks like they're on schedule."

The minutes slipped by as twilight faded to darkness; 1930 came and passed. An hour later, still no sign of the Marines.

Finally, at 2050, a boat was sighted. "Hey, Raider," called Lynch. "Gung ho!" was the reply. It was the intrepid Lieutenant Peatross and the surviving men of his squad. They clambered aboard and quickly went below. Brockman and Haines greeted Peatross in the wardroom.

"What can you tell us, Lieutenant? How many other boats are with you?"

"Sorry, sir, I can't tell you much about Colonel Carlson and the main group. We landed about a mile to the west on the other side of the Japanese." He went on to briefly describe his eventful day. Just then Lynch called down from the bridge. "Captain! Two more boats are alongside!" Two dozen exhausted and bedraggled men filed belowdecks. They were without equipment and nearly naked, wet, and hungry. Lieutenant Peatross later wrote, "They all looked like pale shadows of the men I had last seen early that morning . . . the later arrivals looked like nothing less than zombies."[32]

---

32. Peatross was awarded the Navy Cross for his actions on Makin and would later publish a history of the Raiders, *Bless 'em All* (2006). He retired as a major general.

After nearly an hour and a half a fourth boat showed up. That was it for the night. Only fifty-three men made it back to *Nautilus* that evening, and just three boats with twenty-seven soldiers found *Argonaut*. The balance of the force, some 140 men, were either dead, captured, wounded, or stranded on the beach. With no communication from shore since 1030, Brockman and Haines had no way of knowing. The two commanders discussed options.

"Bill, let's go over what we know. What have we learned from the returning troops?" asked Haines.

"Well, sir, what we know isn't good. They have lost a few men, but the rest are gathered on the beach with some pretty badly wounded. They tried many times to ride the surf out, but the breakers were too strong especially for the boats carrying men who could not paddle. Most equipment, including weapons and medical supplies, was lost when the rafts were swamped or overturned. I'm guessing they lost all their radios. Also, there may be more Japanese out there."

"Right, not good at all. They weren't planning on an overnight stay. And it's not going to be any easier tomorrow."

"No, sir. And there's another matter. Major Roosevelt is still ashore." Haines nodded. The missing president's son was of major concern. The risk that he could be lost—or even worse, captured and paraded around Tokyo as a propaganda coup—weighed heavily on the commanders.

Brockman continued, "Lieutenant Peatross has offered to lead volunteers back to the beach with weapons and a radio. That way we'd at least know what's happening." Haines looked downward and considered this for a moment.

"No, let's wait until dawn. Tell the lieutenant to get some rest for now." He looked up at the captain. "Bill, I want to get every living Raider off that island, and we'll stay here as long as it takes!"

"Yes, sir, wouldn't have it another way," replied Brockman immediately. "But we have to get word to Carlson. We'll stay near the beach tonight and look for any signals. In the morning, we can send a rescue party."

Throughout the night, the two submarines cruised slowly back and forth parallel to the reef about three thousand yards from the beach, lookouts searching in vain for any lights or other signs of life ashore.

On shore, an exhausted and discouraged Evans Carlson took stock of his situation. At 2300 a group of eight Japanese had quietly approached but were detected by the rear guard. A brief firefight ensued, and the enemy was beaten back, at the cost of another wounded Raider. This encounter reinforced Carlson's conviction that a Japanese force was still present on the island. He accounted for fourteen dead Marines and twenty wounded, plus several missing.[33] He had no idea how they would get off the beach, and was not even sure the submarines would wait for them. More air attacks would surely come in the morning, and eventually enemy reinforcements. Over the course of a sleepless night, the commander held a gung-ho meeting with his officers and sergeants. Several options were discussed, including fighting on, attempting to reach the submarines, and even surrender.

The latter topic has been a subject of much debate. Many accounts say that at 0330 Carlson had Capt. Ralph Coyte compose a surrender note and attempt to deliver it to the Japanese remaining on the island. Unarmed and accompanied by Pvt. William McCall, Coyte found a lone Japanese sailor and gave him the message. As the sailor departed, he was shot and killed by other Raiders. Supposedly, the note was found days later by Japanese reinforcements and sent to Tokyo, but there is no evidence it was ever used. Others insist that surrender was never discussed. Certainly, there was no mention of this in any official reports, and it is only through testimony years later that the events could be recalled.

Regardless, any thought of surrender was behind them by morning. At dawn on August 18, Carlson told his troops they had two options: either break through the surf to the subs or cross the lagoon. Those that were able to get through the waves were to tell the task group commander that the remaining Riders would cross to the lagoon side dragging any serviceable rubber boats and make their way across to the entrance near Flink Point. There they would hope to meet the submarines that evening.

The breakers seemed to have subsided a bit, and several groups of men decided to make their way through the surf to the submarines, which

---

33. According to later accounts, eighteen Raiders were killed in the first day's fighting, many by sniper bullets.

were by then backing into shore as close as possible. These included most of the men of the rearguard, who had not yet tried the waves. They turned over their weapons and remaining ammunition to the other Raiders and prepared to brave the swells. Among them was James Roosevelt, who Carlson wanted off the island as soon as possible. With fresh paddlers, less rough surf, without the burden of wounded men, and with a measure of desperation, all four boats made it through the waves and out to sea. Paddling mightily, some using palm fronds or rifle butts, the men struggled to safety. Two boats each made it to *Nautilus* and *Argonaut*, totaling around forty men, Roosevelt among them.

Platoon sergeant Frank Lawson came aboard *Nautilus* and reported immediately to Lieutenant Peatross.

"Lieutenant, everybody's been having a helluva time getting off the beach, and when we left, the colonel was getting ready to surrender!"[34] Peatross couldn't believe it. He pressed for more details. Lawson explained the grim situation, including the burden of wounded men and Carlson's plan to try to make it to the lagoon entrance.

"Okay, I'll tell the commander." Peatross quickly found Haines and Brockman and passed on what he knew.

Haines refused to believe Carlson would surrender, but he knew he needed help. "Peat," he said to the Marine lieutenant, "Here's what I want you to do. Find five volunteers and form a party to get a message to the beach. Chief Porterfield will outfit them with a line throwing gun so they can shoot a line across the surf and send a swimmer to shore without taking the raft in. I don't want more Marines on the beach to have to rescue!"

"Aye, aye, sir," replied Peatross. "I'll find the best swimmers."

"You do that. Here's the message: We will wait here for any more boats this morning, and we'll be stationed outside the lagoon entrance by 1930. The submarines will stay until every living Raider is off the island!"

"Yes, sir!" said Peatross, encouraged. He went off to find volunteers. Five excellent swimmers, all good athletes, were selected: Sergeants Robert Allard and Dallas Cook, and Privates Richard Olbert, Donald Robertson, and John Kerns. A raft with a working outboard was found.

---

34. Smith (2001, 162).

At 0750, in full daylight, the boat with the five brave men motored off. Brockman and Haines watched anxiously as they made their way to the reef, lookouts scanning the skies for the aircraft they knew would come.

"I see them at the surf line," reported Lynch, watching with binoculars. "The line is over the reef, and a swimmer is heading to shore!"

The line was anchored ashore, and one of the men used it to swim to the beach with as many supplies as he could carry and the message from Haines.

"He made it!" cried Lynch. "I see him coming back to the raft!"

Just then, the call came, "Radar contact, eleven miles. Aircraft approaching!"

"Lookout, what do you see?" called Lynch.

"Nothing, sir. I can't see anything in the clouds."

"Very well. Keep looking. Radar?" queried Lynch.

"Contact closing at eight miles," came the reply.

"Very well," said Lynch, unsure of what to do. They had to dive, but the men in the raft were still out there. He peered at the surf line.

"Captain, the men in the raft are still there. They must be trying to deliver supplies." From the radar station came the call, "Five miles and closing!"

"OK, we have to dive," said Brockman. "We'll come back for them."

"Clear the bridge!" called Lynch as men scrambled below. "Submerge the ship!" Geysers of spray shot from the ballast tank vents as air was released, allowing the tanks to flood.

"Last man down, hatch secured," called Lynch, as he made his way down the ladder and to his position in the conning tower. "Make your depth eight-zero feet," he ordered. Brockman was already on the periscope watching the shoreline. He grimaced as a Zero fighter swooped down over the beach, guns blazing.

"He's going after the damn boat!" growled Brockman. He watched in despair as the fighter riddled the rubber boat with gunfire, strafing the men in the water. The boat was shredded, and there was no sign of survivors.[35]

---

35. It is not certain that Brockman personally witnessed these details through the periscope, but he noted the event in his patrol report referencing later testimony by Carlson.

Lynch, on the other periscope, was scanning the skies. "Sir, there are other aircraft out there." Just then two explosions were heard as dive bombers attacked *Argonaut*.

"Right. Down scope. Go to one-five zero feet," ordered Brockman. "Those poor Marines are goners."[36]

"Nothing more we can do for them," said Haines. "The planes will be back. Carlson is on his own until nightfall." The submarines remained submerged for the rest of the day. They dove deep below the surface swell so corpsmen in makeshift surgeries could operate undisturbed on wounded soldiers.

Carlson and his remaining men scrambled for cover and watched in horror as the men in the water were strafed and bombs fell about the submerging submarines. *Argonaut*, in particular, suffered some near misses that seemed like hits to the Marines ashore. Huge geysers of spray shot to the sky as dozens of bombs hit the water directly over her position. Fortunately for the submarines, the Japanese bombs were fused to detonate on impact and did not harm the submerged boats; depth charges would have been a different matter. Still, the Raiders had to wonder if their transport home was lost.

Carlson counted seventy-two men still with him on the beach, many of them wounded.[37] The fate of the submarines was unknown, but the arrival of more air attacks and Japanese reinforcements was a near certainty. The men were exhausted, hungry, poorly armed, and ill-clothed. At this point, Carlson took firm command and rallied his troops. He put them to work digging foxholes to establish a defensive position for the day and sent out patrols to scout for remaining enemy presence. With the help of natives, they found food and water. A cache of blue and pink silk underwear found at the pier side trading station was turned into makeshift clothing, an unusual fashion statement for the normally camouflaged

---

36. Unknown to Brockman or Carlson, the five men did survive the air attack and make it ashore, only to meet their fate later.

37. Again, sources vary as to exact numbers.

Marines. Over the course of the morning a few surviving Japanese soldiers made sporadic attacks and were shot. Bodies were counted, and remaining installations and equipment were destroyed. Some of the men even collected souvenirs. During the day, several more air attacks peppered the island with bombs, but the Raiders sheltered in their foxholes and were unharmed.

By nightfall, Carlson was ready to move. He assigned 2nd Lt. Charles Lamb to fashion a raft from available resources. His men dragged three of the remaining rubber boats across the island to the lagoon and lashed them together with a pair of native outrigger canoes. Two working motors were salvaged. Wounded men were laid across the center of the makeshift craft, dubbed *Lamb's Ark*. The bodies of eighteen Raiders were collected and covered by blankets. Carlson said a prayer, and again enjoined the natives to give them proper Christian burials.

It was time to move, but would the submarines be waiting for them? Carlson had no working radio. Signalman Sgt. Kenneth McCullough shinnied up a palm tree with a flashlight and shone his beam toward the dark sea.

A short while earlier, at 1810, the submarines returned.

"Surface, surface, surface!" The black hull of *Nautilus* emerged from the waves. Water sluiced off the dark metal as the conning tower hatch opened and Ozzie Lynch climbed onto the bridge. Lookouts followed.

"Look there, at the beach, where we left them. Do you see anything?"

"Nothing yet, sir," replied one man. Another pointed and called, "I see *Argonaut*, there to the south."

"OK, let's move in closer." Together the boats motored toward the reef, men searching through periscopes and binoculars, straining to see any sign of life on the island. After about an hour, their efforts were rewarded.

"There, sir, I see a flashing light!" The lookout pointed toward shore. By then, Brockman and Haines were topside, along with a signalman.

"We need to be sure it's Carlson and not a Japanese trap," said Haines. He turned to the signalman. "Send the following: 'Who followed my father as A and I?'" The signalman flashed the message in Morse code to the man ashore.

"What's that all about?" asked Brockman.

Haines chuckled. "Carlson and I had an argument on our way here about who relieved my father as adjutant and inspector [A and I] of the Marine Corps. He'll know the answer. No Japs would know that!"

There was a long pause as Carlson got the signal and dictated the answer. Then the light on the island started to flash:

"S Q U E E G I E."

"That's it!" said Haines, slapping his thigh. "Squeegie Long was the guy! It's Carlson, all right. Tell him to send his message." More flashing from ashore told *Nautilus* that the Raiders would meet the boats at the lagoon entrance off Flink Point at 2130. Brockman passed the word to *Argonaut* and the submarines moved off to the new rendezvous point.

On the beach, Carlson was encouraged that the submarines were still there and would be waiting for them. He gathered his men, had the wounded loaded onto the *Ark*, and saw the remaining men aboard. The motors started. Carlson stepped on board and the Marines shoved off into the dark waters.

The little motors coughed and sputtered, and were not powerful enough to push the ungainly craft on their own. Paddlers helped push the raft along. As they approached the open sea, growing waves threatened to tear the boats apart. One of the motors conked out when the fuel ran dry. McCullough kept signaling with his flashlight, which was growing dimmer as its battery weakened. Lashings broke and had to be retied. The appointed hour came and passed as the boats struggled to make headway. The men in one boat asked to cast off and row ahead, fearful that they would miss the rendezvous and the submarines would leave. Carlson unwisely granted permission.

Several shots were heard from the island. A bit later, from the other side of the lagoon, a flare shot into the sky to starboard. Could it be a Japanese patrol boat?

Finally, when the craft made the lagoon entrance, submarine running lights were spotted. The men let out a cheer, but to reach safety they still had two miles to cover in open water. The Marines dug their paddles into the water and put all they had into the job. After an exhausting hour, *Lamb's Ark* came alongside *Nautilus*.

"Turn on the searchlight!" ordered Brockman, heedless of the danger of being spotted by nearby enemy craft. "Haul those men aboard!"

Hauling was required, as the Marines were too exhausted to help themselves. Their condition was shocking, and Carlson appeared to have aged ten years. Their makeshift pink and blue silk garments served to strangely highlight their bedraggled appearance.

"Get everyone below on the double! Slash those boats and deep-six them, and anything else. We don't have time to load luggage!" yelled Brockman. The boats were cast overboard, along with the outrigger canoes and the Raiders' remaining gear, including souvenirs. Finally, at 2353 all men were on board. Haines asked, "Colonel Carlson, is that everyone?" "Yes, sir," Carlson replied, confident that he had brought every living Marine off the island. "Then let's get out of here. Clear the area!"

"Aye, aye, sir, with pleasure," said Brockman. "Lynch, take us home," he ordered the officer of the deck.

"Aye, sir," replied Lynch. "Helm, left standard rudder, Steady on one-eight-zero. Ahead full!"

Nautilus turned south away from the lagoon entrance and left Makin Island behind her.

Battle weary Evans Carlson on board *Nautilus* just after returning from Makin Island, August 18, 1942. U.S. NAVY.

Among these returning Raiders from Makin Island on August 18, 1942, is this Marine who hefts a Japanese rifle captured during the raid. U.S. NAVY.

Crew member paints a Japanese flag on one of the six-inch guns of *Nautilus*, representing an enemy vessel she sank during the Makin Raid. U.S. NAVY.

Captain Brockman (left) with Cdr. John M. Haines, Commander, Submarine Division 42, and Lt. Col. Carlson at Pearl Harbor after Makin raid. U.S. NAVY.

By some measure, the Makin Island raid was a success. The objectives of the operation—to wipe out the enemy garrison, destroy installations, and capture intelligence—were largely realized. The Raiders aboard *Nautilus* returned to Pearl Harbor on the morning of August 25 to a heroes' welcome. Every ship's crew in the harbor mustered at attention in dress uniform as bands played the Marine Corps hymn and "Anchors Aweigh." Flags flew at half-mast to honor the fallen. Carlson and his men, dressed in a mix of green and black-dyed utilities, khakis, and borrowed navy dungarees looked out of place among the pageantry.

When *Argonaut* arrived the next day to the same reception, an accurate head count could finally be made. The results were sobering. Carlson had counted eighteen American dead on the island before he left, but thirty men failed to return to Pearl Harbor. No one recorded at the time the names of the five men sent toward shore in the messenger boat that was strafed by the Japanese, and no one knew who and how many men cast off from the *Ark* as the group escaped through the lagoon entrance. No effort was made to discover who was on *Argonaut* and *Nautilus* before the boats departed the island. As was later learned, nine men were left alive on Makin, including the five volunteers on the messenger boat.

The Japanese returned to the island with a force of a thousand men in the days following the Raider's departure. They quickly rebuilt and expanded facilities and fortifications. They found twenty-seven survivors of the original seventy-three-man garrison, most of them wounded, and uncharacteristically did not punish the natives for any help they gave the Americans. Twenty-one Marine dead were found, along with working weapons, ammunition, and grenades. The following year, when the island was assaulted by US Army troops, the Americans faced a reinforced garrison and suffered more than two thousand casualties.

The fate of the nine living Marines left on the island became known after the war ended. It seems that they were able to link up with each other, and with the help of natives, escaped from the main island to Little Makin, just to the north. There they were assisted by natives who provided them with an outrigger canoe so they could try to sail to Hawaii, two thousand miles away. They departed Little Makin on August 24 and were seen by a resident French priest as they paddled out to sea. Shortly thereafter, they were picked up by a Japanese ship. The captives were shipped to Kwajalein Atoll where sometime in September they were beheaded and buried in a pit. No remains have been found.

Many historians, in hindsight, have largely judged the Makin raid to be a tactical and strategic disaster. Carlson was guilty of a number of errors, including changing the landing plan in the middle of deployment, allowing units to intermingle with confusing assignments, and lack of aggressiveness when it might have counted. There is little doubt that the Marines fought bravely, but the strategic goals of the mission were questionable. In debriefings with Admiral Nimitz, the attempted surrender business was revealed. Brockman's patrol report stated, "Loss of armament and equipment of Marines and orders of the task group commander caused ending of this patrol," a less than enthusiastic summary of achievements. Regardless, the operation was declared a success, and public release of news of the landings on Guadalcanal and the Makin raid were great boosts to American morale. Medals were generously awarded, including the Medal of Honor to Sgt. Clyde Thomason and Navy Crosses to Haines, Carlson, Roosevelt, Peatross, and nineteen other officers and men. The submariners presented the Raiders with the Submarine Combat Patrol pin, along with a few dollars of submarine pay arranged by Brockman. And the submarine division commander recommended that the captain's patrol report be changed to read, "Successful accomplishment of the mission terminated the patrol."

Certainly, valuable lessons were learned from what was a pioneering operation. Captain Brockman documented a list of recommendations for future such missions, and Colonel Carlson put his experience to practice in his subsequent deployment on Guadalcanal, known as the "Long Patrol." The bravery and dedication of the Marine troopers on Makin Island has never been questioned.

USS *Nautilus* rested in her moorings in Pearl Harbor, preparing for new assignments. Captain Brockman stood on the bridge with Ozzie Lynch, Pat Rooney, Tom Hogan, and Red Porterfield surveying the harbor. USS *Trigger* (SS-237) was getting underway with her new captain, Roy Benson, and they all wanted to see him off.

"There he is!" called Hogan, the first to see the boat approaching. They watched as *Trigger* slowly motored through the harbor. As the submarine neared, they saw Benson standing proudly on the bridge of his first command. "It's Pigboat Benny on the bridge!" Hogan said, then shouted across the water, "Hey Captain Benson!" Benson had a pipe clenched firmly between his grinning teeth, puffing away as he rendered a salute to his former captain. Brockman and the other officers returned the salute to their old shipmate, Brockman growling to no one in particular, "Hate that damn pipe!"[38]

---

38. Interview with Floyd "Red" Porterfield, February 2000.

CHAPTER THREE

Hokkaido

BUZZ LEE WAS HOLDING COURT. A SMALL CROWD OF NEWLY REPORTED men was listening, rapt, as the sonarman described events from the Battle of Midway and *Nautilus*'s role in the engagement. Of course, Buzz tended to portray himself being at the center of the action, which was not entirely untrue as he spent the day of battle in the conning tower. Perched just a few feet from the captain, Buzz monitored the sonar equipment and heard everything going on in the attack center and in the sea around them.

Buzz was technically a radioman (the sonarman rating was not established until later in the war), and he also handled communications. He told his audience that on the morning of June 3, around 0330, *Nautilus* received a coded message,[1]

I get a message in my earphones, addressed to the Nautilus *and I typed it out. It was a code in groups of five letters in plain language telling the captain immediately that this was important. I told the Filipino cook to get the captain down here—and he was there in fifteen seconds. I put the message to decoding, and I saw the captain change before my eyes. He said not a word, grabbed that sheet with my message, and left.*

That message was a part of US history, and Buzz regretted not saving it. He continued on, saying that later that morning Captain Brockman made an announcement to the crew on the ship's loudspeakers,

---

1. This and subsequent Buzz Lee quotes are from interviews that took place in 2006 and 2007.

I have something very important to tell you—first of all, why we're here and why I haven't told you what's up. Admiral Nimitz and his decoding groups have broken the Japanese War Code[2] and we now know they have the largest armada of any place in the world, and they're heading our way. You can expect action at any time.

Nautilus and her untested crew left Mare Island, California, on April 21, 1942, and arrived in Pearl Harbor on the twenty-eighth in the midst of a dire situation in the western Pacific. Since the Pearl Harbor attack in December, the Imperial Japanese forces had been on the move. To the southwest of Tokyo, Hong Kong fell before year's end, and land troops expelled the British from Burma by April. To the south, the battle for the Philippines was in hand, with Manila captured in January. American and Philippine forces, bottled up on the Bataan Peninsula, would eventually surrender at Corregidor in May. Malaya was captured with the fall of Singapore in February and the Dutch East Indies shortly thereafter. The Japanese navy trounced the combined American, British, Dutch, and Australian naval forces in the Battle of the Java Sea, thus controlling access to vast resources of Borneo, Java, and Sumatra, as well as threatening Australia's northern coast. This was driven home with a large carrier-based airstrike of the strategic Australian port of Darwin in February, killing more than two hundred military personnel and civilians. Farther south, Japanese forces occupied strategic bases on New Britain and New Guinea. To the southeast, the island groups of the Marianas, Marshalls, and Gilberts were under Japanese control, and even the American outposts of Guam and Wake had been taken.

Japan had gone to war to seize resource centers in their Pacific sphere and wrest control from colonial powers. By the spring of 1942, these goals had been largely achieved, and Japanese naval and ground forces seemed invincible. After much deliberation and intense interservice contention, Combined Fleet commander Adm. Yamamoto Isoroku convinced leadership that the American carrier forces must be destroyed,

---

2. Brockman certainly did not say this, as the cryptological breakthrough that gave the Americans an advantage at Midway, and the Allies throughout the war, was a well-kept secret. Lee embellished his tale in later recounting.

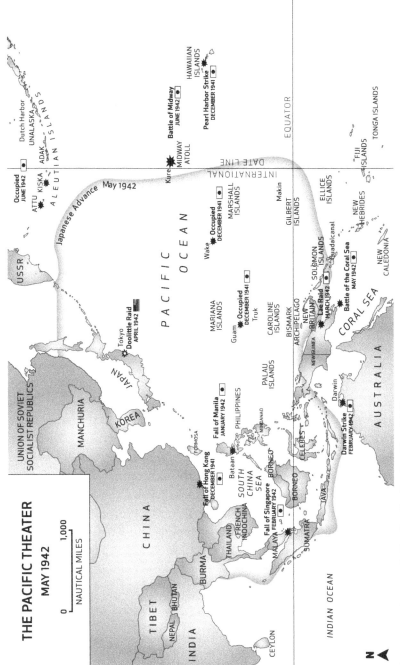

THE PACIFIC THEATER
MAY 1942

0 ——— 1,000
NAUTICAL MILES

Japanese advances in the Pacific theater, May 1942. ILLUSTRATION BY BETHANY JOURDAN.

and the US island base in the mid-Pacific must be eliminated. The date for the invasion of Midway was set for June 6, 1942.[3]

Unknown to the Japanese, American cryptanalysts had broken the Imperial Navy's operational code and were deciphering many of their signals, comprehending enough to anticipate Japanese intentions and guide deployments. Through these means, Admiral Nimitz learned of the impending attack and approximate date. He did not, however, know from what direction the Japanese would approach. He decided to place his three aircraft carriers, USS *Yorktown*, USS *Hornet*, and USS *Enterprise*, to the north of Midway Atoll in a position of ambush, and place most of his submarines in an arc about two hundred miles to the west and northwest of the island. The submarines' mission was to detect the incoming Japanese fleet to give Nimitz a chance to spring his carrier trap, and to strike at the invaders and try to blunt their attack.

Nautilus got underway from Pearl Harbor on May 24 and arrived in her patrol area on the twenty-eighth. She was joined by ten other submarines, each with an assigned arc of coverage. Approaching from the west was a massive Japanese fleet of carriers, battleships, submarines, and other vessels as part of a 192-ship armada aiming to capture Midway, destroy the American carrier fleet, and occupy the US Aleutian Islands of Attu and Kiska to the north. At the spearhead of this juggernaut was *Kidō Butai*, the First Carrier Striking Force, consisting of the aircraft carriers *Akagi*, *Kaga*, *Hiryū*, and *Sōryū*, all veterans of the Pearl Harbor attack. This mighty force, boasting 264 aircraft and escorted by battleships, cruisers, and destroyers numbering twenty-six warships in all, was heading for Midway, and bearing down on the lurking and unseen *Nautilus*.

Brockman had the foresight to look beyond the intelligence provided by his orders and gather his own information through clever use of communications[4]—he knew of the approach of Kidō Butai before any

---

3. Tokyo time. Note that dates cited for Pacific battles and events are confused by the presence of the International Date Line. The Battle of Midway, in particular, took place on both sides of the line. The air attack on Midway took place just after midnight on June 5 (India Standard Time, Tokyo's time zone), which was the morning of June 4 at Midway. Troop landings were planned to take place the next day.

4. Brockman monitored a clear-voice aviation communications channel in addition to reading coded messages directed to his submarine. Thus, he was able to get a sense of the unfolding battle from the

of his fellow submarine commanders. He took advantage of his position and knowledge to place his ship in the middle of the fray. On June 4 at 0824, Brockman raised the periscope to find *Nautilus* at the center of the attacking fleet, Japanese ships swarming around his position, aircraft swooping overhead. Lee continued his dramatic depiction,

> *The captain couldn't believe he saw the entire Japanese fleet in the periscope. Then they were shooting at our periscope. I could hear the gunfire, everyone could. We dove to fifty-five feet and the captain asked me for a sound bearing on that battleship. They didn't hit us, but our orders were to get out of there. We went down deep, to 750 feet[5] and they never got close to us. But it was terrifying.*

Brockman fired torpedoes at the battleship (later identified as *Kirishima*) and observed the carrier *Kaga* and other ships steaming by at high speed, evading attacking American aircraft from Midway. The destroyer *Arashi* was detached to attack and destroy the submarine and dropped depth charges. Brockman struck back with torpedoes, beginning a running duel between the ships that lasted two hours, and saw *Nautilus* dive deep as the fleet disappeared over the horizon. Lee described the terror of being depth charged, trapped and helpless, hoping the hull would withstand the blasts,

> *The enemy ran right down our periscope wake and went to automatic ping, meaning they were dead on us, ka-ching. It was like a mountain exploding. We thought our sub would crack, but we are a riveted hull. Today the subs are welded and can rupture, but the rivets on ours would give between the plates. The Japanese dropped twenty-four depth charges, made a U-turn, and then dropped another twenty, so there was a total of forty-four[6] depth charges dropped over us. Everyone*

---

first dawn reports of enemy planes approaching Midway.

5. *Nautilus*' hull was rated for three hundred feet and they went as deep as 350 feet during the Battle of Midway, but Buzz was prone to exaggeration.

6. Forty-two was the official count, including afternoon attacks.

was so frightened—we knew we were going to die. But then the last one ran over us, and we had made it through.

Brockman came to periscope depth only to find empty seas all around. *Arashi* had been called back to rejoin the Japanese force as US air attacks intensified. As the destroyer made a beeline for her fleet's position, she made a prominent wake that was seen by a flight of thirty-three American dive bombers from *Enterprise*, to that point unsuccessful in their search for the enemy. That provided flight leader Lt. Cdr. Wade McClusky with the clue he needed. He had his aircraft turn and line up with that wake. Five minutes later he radioed, "This is McClusky. Have sighted the enemy." At 1022 the bombers attacked, descending on *Kaga* and *Akagi*. With lucky timing, another thirteen planes from *Yorktown*, led by Lt. Cdr. Max Leslie, dove on *Sōryū* from the opposite direction. Within minutes, the three carriers were in flames and the heart of Kidō Butai destroyed. It is likely that McClusky's bombers would have never found the enemy but for *Arashi's* wake, the ship detained by her duel with *Nautilus.* Thanks in part to *Nautilus* and her crucial role in the battle, the tide of the Pacific War had turned.

Unaware of these dramatic developments, Brockman continue to pursue the enemy. Sighting smoke on the horizon, he closed and came upon the burning *Kaga*, attended by several destroyers, one of which was attempting to take the stricken vessel under tow. *Nautilus* approached and fired three torpedoes, at least one of which hit the carrier but failed to explode. The submarine was rewarded by further depth charging and another harrowing hour of battle, but again managed to evade. From a safe distance, Brockman raised the periscope and saw heavy black smoke as the doomed carrier continued to burn. At 1840, forty minutes later, heavy explosions were detected by sonar and flames were seen through the periscope. Finally, in the waning twilight, *Nautilus* surfaced with a drained battery and equally exhausted crew. No smoke or flame of any sort was seen. *Kaga* was gone.

"We congratulated each other that we were still alive," Lee remembered.

Seaman Bob Burrell, who had come on board just a week before *Nautilus* got underway for her third patrol, took it all in. The story was already legend among submariners, but to hear it from one who was there made a great impression. There was a moment of quiet in the room as Lee halted his narrative, the humming of machinery and the muffled rattling of cookware in the nearby galley the only sounds. The men wanted more. "What happened next, Buzz?" asked Bob, egging him on for more details.

"Well, not much after that," he admitted. *Nautilus* spent the next few days patrolling the approaches to Midway as the toll of the battle became apparent and the threat of invasion subsided. The drama had ended for the submarine, but the action was far from over. The sinking of the three carriers was followed the next day by air attacks leading to the destruction of *Hiryū* and the sinking of USS *Yorktown* and destroyer USS *Hammann* by Japanese aircraft and submarine torpedo attack. The cruiser *Mogami* was also sunk by American dive bombers as the Imperial forces retired in defeat.

Buzz still had an audience, so he continued. "After a few days we were called back to port at Midway for repairs." He went on to describe the scene of destruction on the island and the solemn sight of PT boats carrying dead Marines out to sea for burial. At a point during their short stay at the island, Buzz claimed he spied a figure sitting on the pier,

> *I can still see that guy way down at the end of the dock, sitting there. It was Ensign Gay, the only survivor of that torpedo plane. Nobody knew who he was. He came aboard and told the captain he was floating out there and saw us fire torpedoes at that carrier. He verified everything, saying "I was there! I saw it happen!"*

Chief Porterfield had slipped in a few minutes earlier and was listening to the tale, bemused. Finally, he'd had enough.

"Aw, Lee, that's bullshit!" he growled. "We never met George Gay . . . you made that up!"[7]

---

7. Lee's mention, from a 2005 interview, of encountering George Gay could not have happened, as Gay had been rescued by a PBY flying boat, brought to Midway, and immediately whisked to the hospital at Pearl Harbor with leg and arm wounds before *Nautilus* returned to Midway. Furthermore,

Lee protested weakly, but the spell was broken. Men started to talk and a few chuckled, wondering how much of what they heard was true. Porterfield then turned on them.

"You rookies better believe it," he said seriously. "Buzz may exaggerate, but don't be surprised if you piss your pants the first time you hear a depth charge go off. And you should be proud to be on this boat with this crew and captain!"

Porterfield was justifiably proud of his boat and the crew's actions and achievements on their first patrol. But the eighty-four enlisted men and eight officers sailing west to the Japanese coast on the submarine's third patrol were a markedly different lot from those who fought in the Battle of Midway and sank Japanese ships off the Honshu coast. Bob Burrell was joined by twenty-eight other enlisted sailors who came aboard after the first patrol while thirty men departed, a turnover of more than one-third. Seventeen of these new men were junior seamen, many fresh out of submarine school as the navy strove to quickly expand its ranks. Among those departing were seven experienced chiefs and a half dozen first class petty officers, a core of leadership that could not be easily replaced.

Hardest hit was the twelve-man torpedo division. Experienced chief torpedoman Spurgeon Grove and First Class John Sabbe fortunately remained on board. However, six men from the first patrol had been detached including five petty officers and a seaman "striker."[8] In replacement, the boat received five new men, all junior petty officers and seamen. With six positions changed and one net loss, the division turned over by more than half. Two experienced men were gone, and three of the new men had enlisted just the year before. *Nautilus* did not fire a torpedo on her second patrol, so the men who sailed to Makin on that mission gained no practical experience. The division had a new torpedo and gunnery officer as well, Lt. Phil Eckert. The performance of the division

the location where Gay attacked the fleet was many miles from where *Nautilus* attacked *Kaga*. In Gay's personal account, he remembers being rescued at sea and waking up in Hawaii.

8. A seaman (or fireman in the engineering department) is the lowest enlisted rank in the navy. An enlistee begins his service as a seaman recruit, and can advance to seaman apprentice then seaman, at which point he can select and train for a specialty (torpedoman, machinist, radioman, etc.), a process known as "striking." With experience and qualifications, a seaman can be advanced to petty officer, and eventually to chief (a noncommissioned officer). A few enlisted sailors, through outstanding service and ability, could advance to commissioned officer ranks.

in the coming weeks would reflect this level of leadership and technical inexperience. The torpedomen would have to learn their craft under fire. The crew turnover was balanced to some degree by the experience of the wardroom, featuring four lieutenant commanders among the eight officers. Only Eckert and Ens. Hugh Davis were new, joining Captain Brockman and first patrol veterans Rooney, Hogan, and Lynch. Gibson and Ray remained on board after the second patrol, but Ens. Joe Defrees, battle stations plot coordinator, detached.[9]

Inexperience was not the only challenge facing *Nautilus* as she cruised west to her patrol area off the coast of Hokkaido. She had arrived in Pearl Harbor on August 25, 1942, and completed refit in a scant two weeks. On September 10, the submarine departed Pearl Harbor and conducted gunnery training, having some difficulty with the aft six-inch gun. According to Porterfield, Brockman took a keen interest in any maintenance and repair work on the ship and was leaning over the railing, very close to the gun, when it was test fired. The blast blew off his hat and tore his jacket from his shoulders! The submarine stopped briefly at Midway to refuel and troubleshoot problems with the radar, and was further directed to take on additional torpedoes. Unfortunately, handling gear was not available to load the weapons, and base technicians could not locate the trouble with the radar, so Brockman chose to get underway the next morning regardless. The next few days were uneventful except for problems with the diesel engines that would plague the engineers throughout the patrol. Cracked cylinder liners and broken head studs caused Nick Bruck and other machinists to work day and night with little rest. As *Nautilus* neared the Japanese coast on September 24, the materiel condition of the ship was poor with a malfunctioning air-search radar, balky ammunition hoists, and failing diesel engines. The ship was showing her age, and needed a serious overhaul.

---

9. Defrees was promoted to lieutenant and sailed on USS *Sculpin*, the submarine christened by his mother. In November 1943, *Sculpin* attacked a convoy but was counterattacked by depth charges and forced to surface. Defrees, just twenty-three years old, was killed while on deck attempting to return fire. *Sculpin* sank, taking down most of her crew including wolf pack commander John Cromwell, who was in possession of top secret information and chose to go down with the ship rather than risk capture. For this act of heroism, he was posthumously awarded the Medal of Honor. Twenty-one men survived the sinking and subsequent imprisonment for the remainder of the war.

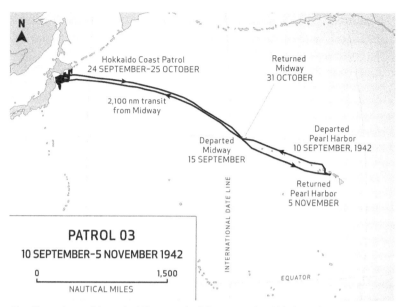

PATROL 03

10 SEPTEMBER–5 NOVEMBER 1942

0   1,500

NAUTICAL MILES

Nautilus returned to patrol the coast of Japan on her third sortie. ILLUSTRATION BY BETHANY JOURDAN.

"Mr. Davis . . . I see a ship ahead, to starboard, zero-six-zero relative!" called the lookout.

Ensign Hugh Davis was the newest and most junior officer on board. Standing one of his first watches as officer of the deck, his immediate reaction was to dive for safety.

"Dive! Dive! Clear the bridge!" he called as men scrambled below. The boat was on its way down as Davis dropped into the conning tower.

"Last man down, hatch secured," he called. "Diving officer, make your depth six-eight feet."

Captain Brockman arrived in the conning tower, along with Phil Eckert, the on-coming officer of the deck.

"Where away?" inquired Brockman as he stepped up to the periscope.

"Bearing three-four-zero, Captain. A surface vessel."

"I don't see it," said Brockman, switching the periscope to full magnification and peering left and right around the bearing. "What kind of vessel?"

The lookout spoke up, "It looked small, maybe a fishing boat. I think it was heading south, sir."

After a few minutes Brockman spied an image of a small vessel in the distance. "Got it. Looks like a trawler, pretty far off. Too small to waste a torpedo. Mr. Davis, battle surface. Go to full speed."

"Aye, sir!" responded Davis. On the 1MC he announced, "Battle surface!" The deck tilted up as *Nautilus* rose from the deep. The moment the conning tower emerged, and the main air induction opened, all four diesel engines roared to life and the ship sped up to fourteen knots. The chase was on.

Men scrambled topside to man the six-inch guns as the submarine plowed ahead in heavy seas. As *Nautilus* closed the range to about five thousand yards, the vessel suddenly turned and headed for the submarine.

"That's no trawler," exclaimed Eckert with excitement. This was his first encounter with the enemy, and he faced it with equal measure of anticipation and anxiety. "Looks like some kind of patrol vessel."

"Right, and armed, no doubt" replied Brockman. "Commence firing!"

The huge guns roared to life as the men struggled to aim at the small target from the submarine's pitching decks. The seas washed over the superstructure, drenching the men as they handled the heavy ammunition. A man by the aft gun was nearly washed overboard. Still, the gunners managed to fire at the oncoming enemy ship, one salvo after another. One solid hit with such a large caliber round would do the trick. After eight salvos the Japanese seemed to realize what they were up against.

"I think that last one was close," called Eckert. "She's turning away!"

The patrol vessel turned and started zig-zagging violently. Splashes and flying debris could be seen around the target as the gunners bombarded it with hits.

Eckert pointed. "She's sinking by the stern!" Just then, a lookout, distracted by the surface action, glance skyward, and yelled, "Aircraft ahead, coming for us!"

"Cease fire! Cease fire! Secure the guns! Clear the bridge!" Brockman yelled over the din. Men scrambled to return the massive guns to diving position, get below, and secure the hatch.

"Aircraft at three-and-a-half miles!" called the radar operator, the unit working for the time being thanks to jury-rig repairs.

"Submerge the ship!" The gunners had made their way below in record time and *Nautilus* headed for the safety of the deep. "Make your depth one hundred feet!"

"Sir, the bow planes are not responding!" called the planesman. The bow planes were used to control depth. Normally folded against the hull while on the surface, they were deployed like small wings while submerged and could be angled up or down. Eckert replied, "Very well, check they are rigged out."

"Aye, sir, they are. But they're not working."

"Very well. Diving officer, control depth with angle." The diving officer would direct the stern planesman to use the planes at the aft end of the ship to adjust the angle on the ship and control depth. A crude method, but good enough to keep the ship at one hundred feet.

"Mr. Eckert," said Brockman, "we'll stay at one hundred feet while working this problem. We'll need those bow planes to hold periscope depth, especially in these seas!"

Investigation revealed that the housing of the huge worm gear that operated the bow planes had come loose. The mounting studs had sheared. The next eight hours saw *Nautilus* keeping depth with stern planes alone as machinists labored to fabricate and weld on new studs. At one point, they descended to two hundred feet when sonar picked up what sounded like a destroyer. One more thing was added to their growing list of problems, this time self-inflicted.

Myles Banbury, gunner's mate, approached the gunnery officer as he ended his four-hour watch. "Mr. Eckert," he said, "can I talk with you?"

"Sure, Petty Officer Banbury," replied Eckert. "What's up? That was good shooting today, especially with the heavy seas. I'm pretty sure we sunk that Jap!"

"Thanks, sir, but we have a problem. We didn't get the guns completely secured before diving," Banbury admitted, looking downcast. "We were in a hurry on account of the plane and left a round in number two. Also, something is wrong with the ammo hoists."

"Oh no, not again! Which one?"

"Both of them, sir. We're working on them. But I have to tell you the guns are out of commission for the moment."

"Damn! Those ammo hoists are stinkaroo! We've had nothing but trouble with them!"

"Right, sir, but we'll get them working again," replied Banbury, optimistically.

Banbury's confidence was ill-founded. The gunners worked around the clock but were unable to make much progress. Upon surfacing that evening, a small sampan was sighted, but avoided as the guns were in no condition to fire. At 2200, on the twenty-fourth, *Nautilus* entered her patrol area, just thirty miles from the north coast of Honshu. She turned south and headed parallel to the shore, seeking Japanese shipping. Lights of small craft were sighted, and again bypassed. Frustrated, Brockman decided to submerge and give his engineers a chance to continue work on the diesel engines while the gunners struggled to repair the ammo hoists, dealing with broken lift chains and grounded electrical circuits. Hours later, with engines back in operation, the boat surfaced on the evening of September 25 in heavy seas and rain squalls. Just before midnight, a sampan was sighted, and *Nautilus* gave chase.

"Mr. Eckert," called Brockman, "Mount the fifty-cal and attack with the machine gun."

"Aye, sir," replied the gunnery officer. Men rushed to the bridge lugging the heavy .50-caliber machine gun and belts of ammunition. Approaching to two thousand yards, Eckert gave the order, "Open fire!" The heavy machine gun burst to life as the submarine neared the two-hundred ton vessel. Rounds appeared to hit it, but had no effect.

"We're scoring hits, sir, but no apparent damage," said Eckert, peering at the target through binoculars. A hundred and fifty rounds had been expended with no obvious consequence. The periscope watch confirmed the puzzling result. Gunner's Mate Banbury said, "Sir, those amour piercing rounds are going right through the wooden superstructure. We should switch ammunition." "Very well," replied Eckert. A special belt that included tracer and incendiary rounds was loaded, and the submarine closed to two hundred yards. The target was staffed across its entire length, and just after midnight burst into flames. It sank at 0055.

Nautilus continued on patrol, reversing course and retracing her earlier path along the busy coast. Many small vessels were seen, none worth attacking. They were looking for bigger game and something worth a torpedo. Finally, at 2340, a large sampan, about five hundred tons, was sighted. Brockman decided not to let this one go. Phil Eckert was again on watch as the .50-caliber machine gun was hauled up, mounted, and manned, this time with incendiary ammunition. At five minutes before midnight, the gunners opened fire and immediately scored hits. Fires started on deck, but the Japanese crew managed to extinguish them as the small ship frantically maneuvered to avoid the onslaught. Over the next half hour, the *Nautilus* crew peppered the vessel with machine gun rounds but were unable to finish her off.

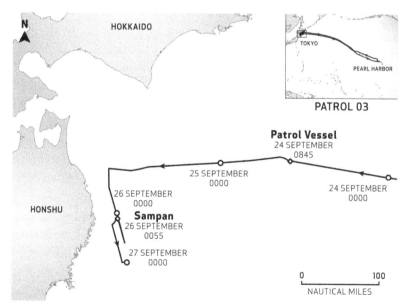

The submarine attacked small vessels with gunfire while approaching the coast of Japan. ILLUSTRATION BY BETHANY JOURDAN.

"Mr. Eckert, man the six-inch guns. We need to end this before they send out reinforcements!"

The gunners had managed to get the forward hoist working, and the aft gun had been left with one projectile loaded. They fired that gun scoring a glancing hit and secured it, then moved to the forward gun. Three more rounds yielded two hits to the superstructure. The Japanese ship was in a shambles and no sign of life was seen on deck, but it refused to sink.

"Secure the guns," ordered Brockman. "This time, do it properly," he added, unnecessarily. Banbury would not make that mistake again. "Mr. Eckert, have some men bring up some oil-soaked rags."

"Aye, sir," replied Eckert, giving the order. He waited for Brockman to tell him what for, afraid to ask.

"Have you ever heard of a Molotov cocktail?" said Brockman finally with a wry grin.

"No, sir," replied Eckert.

"They used them in the Spanish Civil War. We're going to have to make do with oil-soaked rags. We'll set that ship on fire, one way or another!"[10]

The buckets of rags came topside, and *Nautilus* came alongside the now derelict ship. Several men were sent on deck and set the rags afire, dropping them and quickly returning aboard. The submarine backed away and the men watched as the vessel burned. Finally, at 0217, the ship exploded and sank. It was an unconventional, but successful, attack.

Nautilus resumed her patrol up the coast of Honshu, approaching to within ten miles of shore. Many small sampans were sighted close to the beach during the day and not worthy of attack. Finally, at 2231 on September 27, the light of the nearly full moon revealed an escorted convoy

---

10. Brockman referred to the Molotov cocktail by name in his patrol report, and recommended that submarines be furnished with such devices in future patrols. The improvised petrol bombs were first used in Spain against Soviet forces in 1936, and later in Mongolia and Finland. The British perfected the device and trained the Home Guard in their use, producing more than six million of the cheap bombs by 1941 for homeland defense.

of six ships heading south along the coast. One of the vessels, dropping astern of the group, seemed to be having engine trouble as evidenced by billowing smoke. Consulting the recognition guide, Brockman guessed they were looking at a passenger ship of about nine-thousand tons, similar to the *Shoei Maru*. A very worthy target!

Again, Phil Eckert was officer of the deck standing the 2000 to midnight watch. Brockman joined him on the bridge.

Informed by the plotters below, Eckert called out, "Sir, estimated range six miles." Looking toward the east, he noted, "We have the full moon behind us." The moon was very bright in the clear night sky, about halfway to the zenith. The submarine would be silhouetted in the moonlight as seen from the Japanese ship, but there was no alternative. Surface speed was needed to approach this target.

"Understood. Remain on the surface. Man battle stations. Make ready tubes three and four."

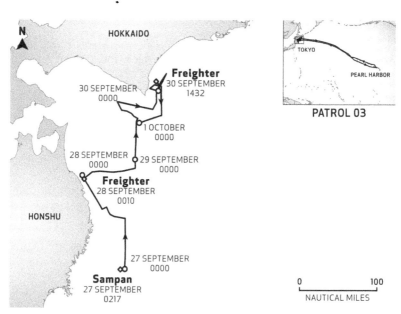

Nautilus attacked and sank a freighter on September 28 in a dramatic night engagement. ILLUSTRATION BY BETHANY JOURDAN.

"Aye, sir," replied Eckert as Brockman went below to the attack center in the conning tower. The torpedomen set to work preparing to fire. In the conning tower, the TDC computed the gyro angle for the weapons. It was a perfect setup with a slow moving target. At nine hundred yards, Brockman gave the order.

"Match final bearing and shoot! Set!" he called as he centered the crosshairs of the periscope on the enemy ship. "Fire three!" called Lynch, operating the TDC, follow shortly by the command, "Fire four!"

"Torpedoes running," called Lee, manning the sonar. "Tracking . . . sir, they are not turning. Torpedoes tracking straight!" he called after a minute. The fish had been set to make a twelve-degree turn after firing but for some reason did not take the ordered gyro angle.

Brockman cursed. Another equipment failure. But there was no time to troubleshoot. "Make ready tube one. We'll maneuver to fire on zero gyro angle." If the gyro setting wasn't working, they would try a straight shot. In a few minutes they were in position. "Fire one!"

From the torpedo room came the report, "Misfire! Misfire tube one!" It seemed that a pressure regulator on the air supply used to launch the weapon had failed. The torpedo remained lodged in the tube. More problems in what was becoming a fraught attack.

"Misfire, aye . . . what next?" replied Brockman, becoming exasperated. Forcing himself to remain focused, he considered the situation for a moment and then ordered, "We'll maneuver for a stern shot. Aft torpedo room, ready tube five!" *Nautilus* changed course to bring the stern tubes to bear. By now the Japanese ship was alerted to the submarine's presence and was turning away. "Fire five!" The torpedo left the tube. "Torpedo running," reported sonar, "Straight and normal!"

"Thank God," breathed Brockman with a sigh of relief. He reported, "I can clearly see the torpedo wake in the moonlight." After a minute his demeanor changed. "Target maneuvered! The wake just passed along the port side!" The torpedo continued past the target and hit the beach, exploding. If there was any doubt that the convoy was under attack, this settled the question. *Nautilus* had lost the element of surprise. Still, Brockman was keen to press the attack.

At that point, Sabbe, in the forward torpedo room, reported, "Conn, we have fixed the gyro problem and the high pressure air regulator and are ready to fire forward tubes." He didn't mention until later that the problem was due to operator error. The inexperienced men in the torpedo room had inadvertently retracted the spindles connecting the torpedo with the TDC information, so the torpedoes went out with zero gyro angle. Only one of the torpedomen in the room had been in battle before.

"Very well. Ready tube three!" Minutes passed as the submarine again reversed course and steadied as the TDC worked a new solution. By 2335, just an hour after initial sighting of the convoy, they were ready to fire their fifth torpedo. Brockman, in frustration, watched through the periscope as the wake passed by the target, missing "by inches." Certainly close enough for the magnetic exploder to trigger. What else could go wrong?

"Battle stations gun one," Brockman ordered. If he couldn't sink this ship with torpedoes, his functioning gun would have to do. Gunners rushed to the deck, and working in the moonlight prepared the forward gun. "Commence firing!" ordered Brockman. The gun roared to life. At point blank range, every round hit, and damage was noted. After ten rounds the gun fell silent. Smoke poured out of the ammunition hoist.

"Fire in the magazine!" a sailor yelled. "The ammo hoist quit running!"

The smoke turned out to be from an overheated clutch, slipping as it tried unsuccessfully to move the broken hoist mechanism. No fire, but the hoist was again out of commission. Sailors struggled to heft the heavy rounds to the deck by hand so the gunners could reload. More rounds were fired by this slow and cumbersome method. The target was on fire, but showed no signs of sinking.

"Continue firing!" ordered Brockman. "We'll maneuver away and try again with torpedoes. Ready tubes two and four!" It was now midnight, and the sea was lit with the full moon, high in the sky. "Fire four!" Again, air pressure was too low, and the tube misfired. "Fire two!" Same result. The burning vessel, still under power, turned toward *Nautilus*.

"Captain! She's trying to ram!" yelled Eckert. "Back emergency!" ordered Brockman. "Right full rudder!" The diesels belched smoke as they ran up to full power, propellers biting into the sea trying to slow the submarine and dodge the ramming ship. The black hull slid by as *Nautilus* backed away. The range opened.

"Rudder amidships! Status of torpedo tubes?" called Brockman. "Tubes two and four ready," replied Sabbe. Air pressure to the tubes had been quickly restored. At a range of barely two hundred yards, with the six-inch deck gun still booming rounds into the enemy vessel, tube two was fired.

"Torpedo fired electrically!" called the torpedo room. The speeding torpedo covered the distance in seconds. An enormous blast erupted from the port side of the enemy ship. "A hit!" yelled Brockman. "Finally!" Within minutes, the ship was seen to be going down by the stern, streaming oil and on fire amidships and aft. Just fifty yards away, two lifeboats were seen in the water.

As the submarine maneuvered away from the scene, two huge waterspouts erupted as a shore battery fired a salvo. The shells landed port and starboard of *Nautilus*, spraying seawater on the ship for a full minute. At the same time, the surroundings lit up as an enemy escort ship, barely a half mile away, turned its searchlight on the scene. From their lifeboats, Japanese survivors cheered as their tormentor came under attack.

"Gun crew below immediately! Forget about securing the gun!" shouted Brockman. "Clear the bridge! What's the water depth?"

"Just thirty-nine fathoms,[11] sir," came the reply from sonar as the destroyer opened up with machine gun fire on *Nautilus*. "Submerge the ship!" called the captain, men rushing below and securing the hatches. "Make your depth one-six-zero feet." The submarine maneuvered toward deeper water. "Rig ship for depth charge!" The words were barely spoken when sonar reported hearing pinging from an antisubmarine vessel. "That destroyer is after us," said Lynch, to no one in particular. The ship became quiet as the crew waited. One-third of the ship's company had never experienced a depth charge attack; the others knew what to expect but were not comforted by the knowledge. Soon enough, at 0021, the onslaught began with an enormous blast.

FWEET! ... BOOM ... BOOOOM ...

---

11. A fathom is six feet. The water depth at that time was just over 230 feet.

Another destroyer joined the attack, and Brockman believed some depth charges were dropped by aircraft. Time and again sonar reported, "Pinging on automatic . . . here it comes!" and another pair of undersea bombs would come tumbling down. Men grabbed whatever was at hand, clenched their teeth, squeezed their eyes shut, and hunched down as though those measures offered any protection. When the blasts came, everything shook, dust flew, lights shattered, and streams of water sprayed from leaking fittings. Men rushed to stanch leaks, glad to take action to distract themselves from anticipation of the next detonation.

Nautilus was in trouble. The Japanese Type 95 depth charge used a simple fuse that could be set to trigger at one hundred or two hundred feet. With the sea bottom at just over two hundred feet, the submarine could not dive below the lethal range of the charges. Knowing this, Brockman chose an intermediate keel depth of 160 feet, trying to thread his way between the worst of the destructive blasts. Still, an accurate drop could be close enough to rupture the submarine's riveted hull, which would spell doom for *Nautilus* and her crew. Buzz Lee described the depth charge attacks as "a moment of hell—nothing in peacetime can prepare you for a confrontation with an enemy bent on your destruction."

"Captain, we have to get to deeper water!" said Pat Rooney, executive officer and navigator. "Recommend heading east, zero-seven-five."

"Very well, Pat. Officer of the deck, turn right to zero-seven-five. Secure from battle stations. We'll continue silent running and head for deeper water. Stay at one-six-zero feet for now."

"Aye, sir," replied Ozzie Lynch, the midwatch officer of the deck, repeating the orders for clarity. Deeper waters were not close. The one-hundred-fathom depth curve on their charts was eighteen miles away.

Some crewmen comforted themselves with the theory that the riveted hull of *Nautilus* could withstand depth charging better than those of the newer welded boats. Buzz Lee in particular believed that there was more "give" in the riveted plates, and he described hearing them "snap" as the hull flexed in response to an exploding charge. He thought that a welded hull would just crack. True or not, Lee shared that opinion freely and certainly the men were glad to hear it.

At 0100 during a lull in the attacks, sonar reported several new sounds. "Sir, I hear crackling sounds on the bearing of the merchant ship we shot." These sounds were thought to be characteristic of a sinking ship, and continued for fifteen or twenty minutes. Brockman considered this evidence they had scored a sinking.[12]

Hour after hour the attacks continued, with some charges coming quite close. None close enough, however, to inflict serious damage, and by 0540 echo ranging ceased and the attacks ended. A total of thirty-two depth charges were tallied. *Nautilus* continued to slink away to the east, assessing damage for the rest of the day. At 1907, the submarine surfaced and the diesels started so that the generators could charge the exhausted battery. Fresh evening air blew into the ship, clearing the spaces of stale fumes and the reek of combat. The previous night's attack alerted the Japanese to the presence of a submarine, so Brockman decided to clear the area and head north to the coast of Hokkaido.

The next day *Nautilus* submerged and patrolled the area just ten miles from shore. The beach was visible under overcast skies. In the early afternoon a lone freighter was seen, estimated to be 6,500 tons, and Brockman called for battle stations. A deliberate periscope approach over the next hour yielded a solid tracking solution and *Nautilus* fired two torpedoes from a mere 1,500 yards, just a one-minute run for the forty-five-knot steam-powered undersea missiles. Frustratingly, a third misfired. Even more vexing, no explosions were heard even though the torpedoes seemed to be headed straight for their target, and sonar did not hear them running after a minute and a half. For its part, the freighter suddenly turned and headed directly toward shore. Brockman tracked it all the way to the beach, and later speculated that one or both torpedoes hit the ship but failed to explode. He wondered if the impact of the inert weapons holed the ship's hull and caused her to run to shallow water.[13]

---

12. Admiral English noted, "It is probable that the ship attacked on the night of 27–28 September sank. However, in the absence of more positive information, the *Nautilus* is credited with having damaged the ship." Intelligence subsequently received confirmed the ship was *Ramon Maru*, 5,200 tons, and that it sank as a result of the attack. JANAC gave *Nautilus* credit for this sinking.

13. By this time of the war, submarine commanders were complaining of regular failures of torpedoes to explode, among other problems. Admiral English brushed off these claims, chalking them up to poor shooting. It was not until Admiral Charles Lockwood took over submarine command

Brockman blamed yet another tube misfire on jammed gyro spindles and inexperienced operators. The spindles were small rods that protruded into the tubes engaging sockets in the torpedoes. They allowed the depth and gyro angle to be set when the torpedo was in the tube and ready to be fired. The gyro setting, in particular, needed to be adjusted at the last moment and the spindle retracted before firing. The inexperienced men operating this complicated equipment had either retracted them prematurely (in the first attack when the torpedoes did not take the course setting) or improperly (causing a jam and a misfire). Brockman was angry and frustrated. John Sabbe and Chief Grove redoubled their efforts to train the new men and improve their performance. They would have another opportunity to redeem themselves the next day.

In an effort to throw off any pursuit, Brockman headed west to the north point of Honshu. At 0635 on October 1, smoke was sighted through the periscope and *Nautilus* headed for it. After an hour's run, a freighter of about 6,500 tons proved to be the source. The seas being glassy calm, Brockman decided to lower the periscope, dive one hundred feet at standard speed to try to approach the target and track it using sonar. By 0815, he had closed to under a mile and soon thereafter successfully fired three torpedoes at the freighter. Two were seen to hit the ship, the vessel covered with sea spray and smoke across its length from the explosion. Soon, a lifeboat with men aboard was seen in the water as the ship began to settle. Further rubbernecking was curtailed by a sudden depth charge attack; apparently an unseen aircraft was overhead and spied the periscope and possibly the hull in the calm seas. Another periscope glimpse a short while later showed no sign of the stricken Japanese ship, but more depth charges discouraged collecting further evidence as *Nautilus* went deep.[14]

Over the next several days, the submarine lurked in a busy area off the Honshu coast, but circumstances deterred any opportunity to press an attack. A bright half-moon rose in the late evening and climbed the

---

in 1943 that a serious investigation into torpedo problems was launched that led to new and more effective designs.

14. Both Admiral English and JANAC found this evidence convincing and credited *Nautilus* with the sinking of a 3,200 ton freighter.

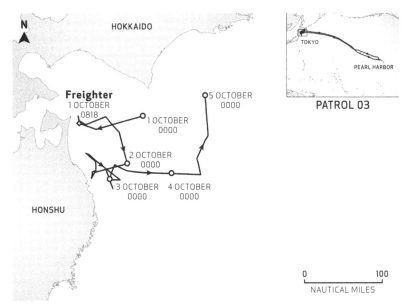

Another freighter was sunk by *Nautilus* on October 1, but worsening weather began to impact the mission. ILLUSTRATION BY BETHANY JOURDAN.

eastern sky until sunrise, making it difficult to creep in on targets hugging the coast to the west. Try as he might, Brockman was unable to maneuver on the surface around enemy ships without being seen by sharp-eyed Japanese lookouts. The reflection of the moon on the water, which Brockman called "moonstreak," made it easier to see the submarine. During the day while patrolling at periscope depth, she was spotted by a destroyer and suffered more depth charges. By October 3, worsening weather became an adversary as challenging as the enemy. Seas became so bad that it was impossible to maintain periscope depth. Brockman noted in his patrol report at 1903, "Surfaced in a very rough sea and high wind. Taking seas over bridge. Made decision to clear coast of Honshu for a few days because at present it is so well patrolled that it is impossible to get in unobserved. Also, it is practically essential we put the seas astern."

Nautilus headed east for a day, then turned north to try patrolling the Hokkaido coast as a period of calm ensued with glassy seas and brilliant sunsets. The sinking barometer, however, warned of the big storm to come. For two days the submarine encountered numerous small sampans, counting at least fifteen in sight at one point, but nothing worthy of a torpedo. On October 8, a typhoon hit. Seas rose, rolling the ship fifteen-degrees side to side while the diving officer tried to hold depth at seventy feet. The suction of the trough of each wave tried to pull the hull to the surface while the crest tried to push the four thousand ton vessel deeper. The planesman struggled mightily to keep the submarine stable as the diving officer tried to find a combination of ballast and angle to keep the ship from broaching. The effort proved impossible as the submarine broke the surface and the diving officer flooded tanks to get her back down. Finally, Brockman had enough. Young Ensign Ray had the watch.

"Mr. Ray, let's go to one hundred feet. There's nothing to see through the periscope in this weather anyway."

"Aye, sir!" replied Ray, relieved. The diving officer was grateful as he ordered the planesmen to ease the ship down. Still, *Nautilus* rolled

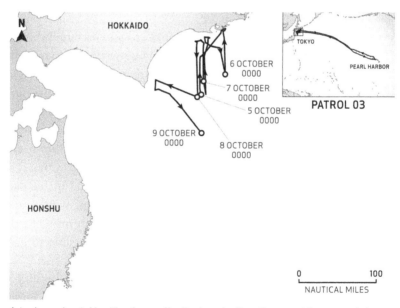

A typhoon kept *Nautilus* from effectively patrolling the coast for several days.
ILLUSTRATION BY BETHANY JOURDAN.

heavily, and even a hundred feet proved a struggle. Brockman ordered 135 feet.

"One-three-five feet," called the diving officer as the ship cruised on battery power at three knots. Speed helped as the diving planes used to control depth[15] were more effective with water rushing more quickly over their surfaces, but *Nautilus* didn't have battery capacity to run at that speed all day.

Suddenly, the diving officer spoke sharply, "Watch your depth!" The depth gage jumped . . . 150 feet, 160 feet, and dropping.

"Ten degrees rise on the stern planes!" ordered the diving office. "Pump auxiliaries to sea!" He was trying to lighten the ship, but it wasn't helping. The sub descended to 170 feet. "Sir, I could use some speed!" he called to Ray.

"Very well, ahead full!" ordered Ray. The propellers spun and the ship picked up speed. Finally, depth steadied at 180 feet before *Nautilus* began to rise. The waves on the surface had pushed the submarine down forty-five feet from the ordered depth of 135 in a matter of twenty seconds. Brockman was back in the control room.

"Mr. Ray, slow to one-third speed and take her to 150 feet. We'll drain the battery at this rate."

"Aye, sir," replied Ray, visibly shaken. He relayed the orders. *Nautilus* held at 150 feet for the rest of the day, still rolling ten-degrees side to side as the typhoon raged overhead. That evening, in need of a battery charge and some fresh air, the submarine surfaced in the middle of the storm. Enormous seas with sixty-foot waves washed over the conning tower. Watch standers and lookouts climbed to the drenching bridge wearing heavy winter clothing to fend off the cold winds. The men quickly became sodden as immense waves and torrential rains buffeted the ship. It would get even worse in the days ahead as the storm roared through the area.

---

15. All submarines are equipped with diving planes, essentially small wings that can be angled to change the forces on the ship as it moves through the water. Stern planes at the aft end of the vessel are normally used to adjust the angle of the hull, and bow planes are normally used to make small adjustments in depth. Modern submarines have dispensed with bow planes and have control surfaces mounted on the conning tower called fairwater planes.

Over the coming days, the ever aggressive Brockman made several attempts to close the coast and carry out his mission to interdict Japanese shipping lanes, but each time was beaten back by the elements. In his patrol report, he continued to describe the seas as "mountainous," on October 10 he commented that they were "the largest any of us have ever seen." Periscope operations were ineffective with the ship rolling fifteen degrees side to side and the sub's depth impossible to control with repeated broaching. At night, while on the surface, Brockman set course to ride out the seas, heading away from the coast. For the crew, life on board the submarine was dreadful. They were crammed into sweltering spaces with ever pitching decks and little to do but wait it out. Repair work was nearly impossible, and even dangerous, as loose bits of equipment easily became flying missiles as the ship lurched and reeled. Sleep was difficult, and even the most effective efforts to wedge in to ones bunk was no guarantee against being tossed out. Minor injuries kept the corpsman busy attending to bruises and twists, though amazingly no fractures were noted in the records. Meals more elaborate than sandwiches were not an option. Any recreation was a challenge as men struggled to keep playing cards on the table or focus on a swaying page of print.

Finally, by the end of the day on October 11, the barometer began to rise and the storm seemed to have passed. Seas remained heavy, but abated to the point that over the course of the next day patrol operations could resume, with difficulty. Having weathered the worst of the hostile storm, *Nautilus* would resume her battles with the enemy and her own aging equipment, with the most harrowing action yet to come.

"Conn, screws bearing zero-four-four relative," called sonar. "Very well," acknowledged Ensign Ray, just coming on the dog watch at 1607. "Captain to the conning tower," he announced. Brockman, eager to go back on the offensive, climbed the ladder into the cramped space and assessed the situation. "What've you got, Mr. Ray?"

"Sir, we have ship screws on sonar off the starboard bow, at zero-one-five. We're headed three-three-zero."

"Very well. Let's take a look. Come to periscope depth."

In spite of the still heavy seas, *Nautilus* came close to the surface, periscope up as high as possible. Even with ten feet of periscope above sea level, waves blocked Brockman's vision 90 percent of the time. A few glimpses to the north were unrewarded. Back down to ninety feet, sonar again heard screws. This time it was the high-speed whine of a warship. Another trip to periscope depth revealed nothing. Sonar reported that the sounds passed by to starboard. Another forty minutes passed, then sonar reported echo ranging, again off the starboard bow. Definitely a warship! The captain ordered the ship back up to periscope depth and changed course to approach. As always, Brockman was eager to take his ship into harm's way.

With difficulty, his crew fighting turbulent waves and uncertain depth control, Brockman sighted what appeared to be two freighters about five miles distant. The source of the high-speed screws and echo ranging was not identified, though the disturbing sounds persisted.

"Mr. Ray, man battle stations. We'll attack those freighters, but we need to be on the lookout for an escort. He's somewhere close!"

BONG! BONG! BONG! Men raced to their positions, eager to get back to work after days of wallowing in the heavy seas with nothing to do. Brockman struggled to get a good range through the periscope, but between his efforts and sonar bearings the TDC became satisfied, and Lynch reported a firing solution. At 1716, two torpedoes left the tubes and sped toward the poorly seen target, 2,250 yards distant. A third weapon failed to fire, the gyro spindle again failing to retract, this time owing to a hydraulic leak. Brockman followed events on the surface with difficulty.

"Two torpedoes hot, straight, and normal," called sonar. Brockman let out an exasperated growl. "Target zigged! Damn, damn, damn!" he snarled. We must have fired on the knuckle of a zig. Or could he have seen the torpedo wakes in these seas?" he wondered out loud. The torpedoes sped by harmlessly. Suddenly, his attention was drawn away from the scene as predator became prey. "Destroyer, heading for us off the port quarter with zero angle on the bow. She's close! Make your depth one-five-zero feet and rig for depth charge!"

The situation called for a quick shot at the oncoming warship to throw off its attack, but with the Japanese ship approaching from behind, the angle was too steep and stern tubes were not ready. Down went the submarine, seeking the relative safety of the deep. The attacking ship had a bead on their position, having seen the torpedo wakes and maybe even the periscope in spite of the rough seas. Echo ranging with sonar helped the destroyer to home in. Three depth charges came down directly above the diving submarine.

BOOM! . . . BOOM! . . . BOOM! Reverberations echoed.

"Those were right overhead," said Brockman looking up at the steel and piping as though he could see through the hull to the enemy above. "But not too close. He probably set them at fifty feet. Go to two hundred feet," ordered the diving officer.

The Japanese destroyer reversed course and passed directly overhead. Men throughout the ship could clearly hear the churning screws as the warship screamed by at high speed. Another pair of charges splashed in the water, which erupted overhead, once again too shallow, but closer, shaking the four thousand ton submarine considerably. The destroyer made two additional passes and dropped another half dozen depth charges, continuing the barrage, each time exploding above the submarine, each adding damage to equipment and terror to the crew. The sound of a second set of screws and echo ranging revealed another destroyer above. *Nautilus* now had a pair of enemy destroyers to deal with. A coordinated attack could make it more difficult for her to evade. Fifteen harrowing minutes had passed since the first charges were dropped.

The two destroyers worked together to keep *Nautilus* pinned between their echo-ranging sonars and the shallow water off the Honshu coast. The men on the submarine could sense that the enemy was in near continuous contact as the sharp acoustic pings seemed to penetrate the hull. From time to time one of the destroyers would shift echo ranging to rapid automatic pinging and make a high-speed run, passing directly overhead and dropping depth charges practically on top of the submarine. *Nautilus* attempted to evade to no avail, and descended to 250 feet to try to put a little more protective water between her thin skin and the detonations just overhead. The bottom was too shallow to go any deeper, and any attempts to evade to the east and deeper water were thwarted by the pressing attacks.

By 1810, the situation had become dire. Damage to the ship from the effects of the blasts was becoming serious, not to mention the physical and psychological harm it had on the crew. The conning tower was a wreck, with lighting receptacles hanging askew, indicator dials broken, engine order telegraphs knocked loose, and even a broken clock. Major valves, fittings, and even the torpedo tubes were shaken violently, leading to binding and leaks. Two of the tubes were leaking seawater into the torpedo room. Most pressure gauges throughout the ship were severely shocked, and either not working or unreliable. The rudder was groaning and seizing, adding to sounds the Japanese were listening for with sonar. Electrical systems tripped out or sometimes energized unexpectedly

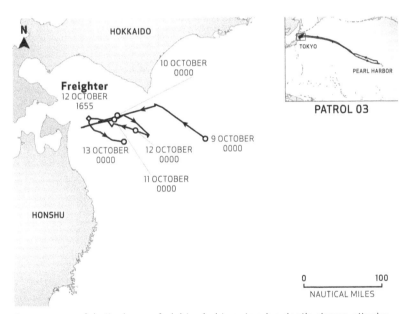

An unsuccessful attack on a freighter led to extensive depth charge attacks by Japanese escort vessels with *Nautilus* pinned near the coast in shallow water. ILLUSTRATION BY BETHANY JOURDAN.

when a depth charge erupted. *Nautilus* and her crew could not take much more punishment.

Throughout the ordeal, Brockman remained calm and patient, looking for an opportunity to slip between the attackers into deeper water. Sonar kept track of the destroyers overheard and warned of fresh attacks. A last minute change of course as a depth charge descended could mean all the difference.

"He's making another run," reported sonar. "Echo ranging on automatic. High-speed screws!"

"Very well," replied Brockman. He had nothing to add. Platitudes such as, "Hold on, men!" had become meaningless. The men knew there was nothing they could do but hope the next detonation would not be too close.

Through it all, the Japanese seemed to have trouble determining the depth of the submarine and continued to set the charges too shallow. Five more underwater bombs descended as the destroyer passed directly overhead. The first two, set at one hundred feet, went off with a roar but did not cause much harm. The next three were set deeper and just about finished the job.

CLICK BOOM! CLICK BOOM! CLICK BOOM! BOOOOM!

Reverberations thundered through the ship as dust flew, pipes shook, glass shattered, and water sprayed from leaks. A high-pressure air line ruptured with a deafening roar as men scrambled to find the valve to secure the air supply.

As the reverberations faded and ringing in the ears subsided, the men looked at each other, a little surprised to be alive. Pat Rooney, the executive officer, huddled with Brockman as they and discussed their next move.

"Those last few were set deeper," Brockman noted, the worry and fatigue in his voice. "A few more like that . . ." He didn't need to finish his sentence as everyone understood the implication. After a further pause he came to a decision.

"Pat, prepare to come to periscope depth. Make ready tubes one and two. We'll try to fight our way out!"

Just then, sonar reported, "Conn, echo ranging. I think he's got us again!"

"Belay making tubes ready," ordered Brockman, having second thoughts, and realizing that trying to attack two destroyers at once was unlikely to succeed. "Change course to one-eight-zero. Sounding?"

Sonar called out the depth of water. Barely fifty fathoms.

"Make your depth three hundred feet. We may scrape the bottom, but it will get us a little farther from those depth charges!" He turned to Rooney, "They know we're trying to head east into deeper water, and they keep cutting us off. Let's try heading south along the coast for a bit and see if we can shake them. They may not expect us to stay so near shore."

Nautilus crept along, heading south. The tactic seemed to confuse the Japanese, who stopped and listened, then started pinging again. No fresh attacks were forthcoming as the enemy seemed uncertain. An hour passed, all was quiet on the submarine, propellers turning slowly. One mile, two miles, they made their way down the coast, just skimming the bottom at three hundred feet. Water from leaks was accumulating, making the ship heavier, but the diving officer was reluctant to use the pumps for fear of making noise that the Japanese would hear. Another hour. At 2026, Brockman decided to make a move.

"Make your depth two hundred feet. Sonar, report!"

As the ship came shallow, the sonarmen listened carefully for activity on the surface.

"Not hearing screws, they must be running slow and listening."

"Very well," replied Brockman. Come up to one-seven-zero feet."

"Conn, sonar. Pinging has resumed, getting louder. They seem to be running parallel to our course but have drawn ahead. Three-zero-five, relative!"

The Japanese ship was still between them and deep water, but seemed to have overshot the slowly moving submarine and was a bit forward of the beam.

"Pat, we may have an opening. Come left and head straight at him. We'll present as small an angle as possible to his sonar and see if we can creep by." *Nautilus* turned directly toward the enemy ship. The whereabouts of the second ship was unknown. Had it left the area, or was it waiting quietly to pounce?

"Captain, the battery is getting low," reported Rooney. "We can't stay down here all day!"

Another interminable hour elapsed as the boat crept southeast, keeping careful tabs on the enemy nearby. Many times it seemed as though the undersea echoes had again revealed their position, but the destroyer continued to draw slowly to the right. By 2220, the Japanese ship had crossed the submarine's bow, leaving an opening to the east. Brockman did not hesitate.

"Come to periscope depth!" Up *Nautilus* rose from the depths, hull creaking and popping as the immense pressure eased. "Up periscope!" Brockman peered into the dark surroundings under a moonless sky. "I see him," called the captain excitedly, "he's now between us and the coast!" The destroyer was still close, but off the submarine's starboard quarter.

"Surface the ship! All ahead full, all main engines!" *Nautilus* leapt from the sea. The four diesel engines belched smoke into the night sky as the engine room came to life. The screws churned the dark water as the submarine picked up speed, heading southeast. Thankfully, the rugged engines had suffered little damage from the depth charging, though one had to be throttled manually. Sonar reported frantic pinging from the destroyer as the Japanese realized they had let their quarry slip away. After about a half an hour, the sounds of echo ranging were lost in the distance astern. *Nautilus* had escaped![16]

"Secure from battle stations, secure from silent running," ordered Brockman. "Pat, let's clear the area and head east for a few days. We need to check damage and see what we can repair."

"Aye, aye, sir!" replied Rooney. "We can sure use a vacation!"

---

16. Brockman described the attacks by the Japanese destroyers as a "work of art," as the enemy ship was able to maintain sonar contact in waters that were purported by scientists to be "bad for sound work." Their depth charge drops were extremely accurate. The only thing that saved *Nautilus* was the Japanese commander's estimate of the submarine's depth as he consistently set his charges too shallow.

The battering *Nautilus* and her crew suffered on October 12 came very close to sinking her. Though the ship slipped away, the vessel was far from fighting trim. Every system on board had suffered some kind of damage and required field repairs if it could be made to work at all. The main engines continued to require attention from the machinists, and even the electric motors were leaking oil from stressed bearings. Diving and steering systems were compromised, from the groaning, seizing rudder to stuck bow planes to failed indicators. Even the diving alarm in the engine room had ruptured. Weapons systems were out of commission including ammunition hoists and deck torpedo tubes. The inboard tubes leaked, and the delicate mechanisms required to set and launch weapons had bent and jammed as the tube nests were shaken violently. The deck guns could be trained only with great difficulty as gaskets had crushed under extreme sea pressure, among other problems. Periscopes were knocked out of alignment and difficult to train. Deck grates on the superstructure had been carried away or buckled from depth charge blasts. Valves everywhere were not seating properly or were operating with great difficulty. Even preservative coatings from inside tanks had shaken loose leaving deposits of shredded plastic in lines, strainers, valves, and pumps. A disturbing oil slick was observed in the ship's wake, a telltale indicator for enemy warships that a vessel was nearby and to follow.

Brockman had ample reason to abort his patrol. The submarine was barely able to fight and was making too much noise to approach a target stealthily or slip away unobtrusively. To make matters worse, on October 13 the weather again deteriorated making depth control difficult. Still, the captain remained in his patrol area, hoping to "increase tonnage" of sunken enemy ships before the end of his assigned mission.

After a day of loitering a hundred miles from the coast away from shipping lanes, *Nautilus* limped back to the waters off the northeast shores of Honshu looking for targets. The crew had repaired what they could, but many work-arounds were needed to accommodate broken equipment. The submarine banged and rattled with unidentified noises, as well as a groaning rudder. The next several days were spent running north and south along the coast, about twenty miles from shore, fighting heavy seas, and dodging destroyers. Brockman was aggressive, but not foolish. He knew

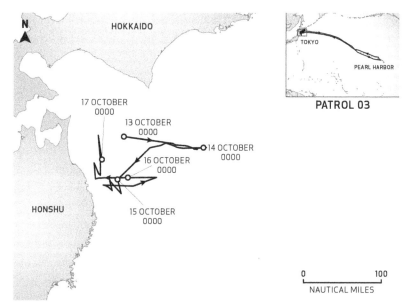

Nautilus escaped after depth charge attacks of October 12, but suffered severe damage. ILLUSTRATION BY BETHANY JOURDAN.

they were in no condition to tangle with a warship and resisted attacking them while carefully avoiding detection. Even though operating in shallow waters, Brockman didn't allow use of the fathometer for fear its pings would be heard. Besides regular sightings of destroyers, echo ranging was heard all around. The Japanese knew a submarine was nearby, and they were keen to avenge their losses from the undersea attacks.

Besides destroyers, sampans were seen in abundance. The small craft were not worth a torpedo, and the guns could not be manned in such heavy weather, especially with jammed ammunition hoists. On October 18 while running on the surface on an extremely dark night, sharp-eyed lookouts spotted what appeared to be wakes of two torpedoes crossing their path. No sign of a nearby ship was seen. Could a lurking submarine have taken a potshot at *Nautilus?* Attack of one submarine on another was very rare, but not impossible.[17] The incident remained a mystery.

---

17. USS *Corvina* (SS-226), commanded by *Nautilus* veteran Pat Rooney would be the only US submarine confirmed to be sunk by a Japanese submarine (I-176) in World War II.

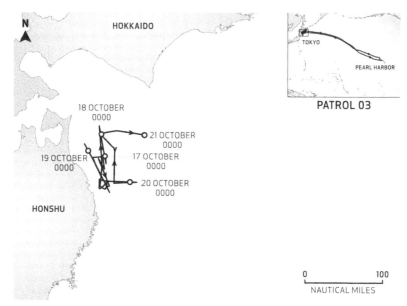

Nautilus continued her mission despite severe damage and heavy weather.
ILLUSTRATION BY BETHANY JOURDAN.

Nautilus continued to battle heavy seas, poor sound conditions, swarming destroyers, and a dearth of worthy targets. On October 19, smoke was sighted in the distance that led them to see a freighter escorted by a destroyer. Approaching to within 5,500 yards while bobbing up and down in crashing waves, Brockman could not get a good periscope observation and sonar could not get a range. Reluctantly, he broke off the attack. Shortly after, a close-by detonation was felt, and water could be heard rushing along the hull. Brockman speculated that an enemy aircraft had seen their oil slick and dropped a depth bomb near their position. Air patrols could now be added to the growing list of enemy efforts to destroy the undersea threat they knew was lurking.

The weather eased that evening. When they surfaced, a heavy oil sludge was present. Oil was emerging from the starboard ballast tanks and a number of air leaks were making telltale bubbles that could give away their presence. The calm waters were welcome, but made it easier for the enemy to see the oil slick and bubbles, especially from patrolling aircraft. Still, Brockman persisted in continuing his mission. He made a run east to the south shores of Hokkaido, hoping for a fresh venue. Frustratingly, other than one freighter that they could not catch, nothing but sampans were seen for the next few days.

Finally, on October 24, the last day of the assigned patrol, fortunes changed. Seas remained calm, but the weather turned dreary with a cold rain and poor visibility. Brockman decided to use the Shiriya Saki[18] Lighthouse on the northern tip of Honshu as a navigation point to allow him to safely approach the coast in spite of the fog and mist. At 1314, after two weeks of patience while enduring weather, balky equipment, and the incessant risk of attack, they were finally rewarded. Phil Eckert had the watch, peering through the periscope into the haze.

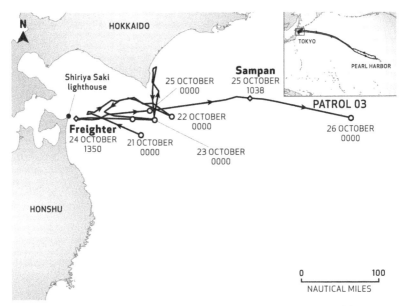

With improving weather, *Nautilus* managed to attack and sink a freighter before ending her third patrol. ILLUSTRATION BY BETHANY JOURDAN.

18. In modern maps this is called the Shiriyazaki Lighthouse.

"Contact bearing three-one-three true. Looks like a merchant." Captain Brockman was finishing lunch in the wardroom. He threw down his fork and bounded up the conning tower ladder.

"What do you see, Mr. Eckert?"

"Sir, I have a merchant vessel about three miles range."

"Very well. Man battle stations submerged. Let's look at the recognition guide."

BONG! BONG! BONG! The battle stations alarm rang out once again. Eckert and Brockman peered at the target through their periscopes and concluded they were looking at *London Maru*, a freighter of 7,200 tons. A worthy target indeed.

"Any sign of an escort?" asked Brockman as he danced around the periscope doing a 360-degree sweep.

"Nothing visual or on sonar, Captain."

"Very well," Brockman replied. "We need to close the range. Down scope. I have the conn. Stay on course two-seven-zero, ahead full." A chorus of acknowledgments followed the captain's string of orders. By then the conning tower was fully manned.

"Listen up!" Brockman said to the other nine men in the confined space. "We have a single merchant vessel with no escort, range about three miles, heading north. I want to run in quickly and sink her before she goes around the point and gets away. We will go at full speed for fifteen minutes, then we'll slow and continue a periscope approach. Make ready tubes one, two, and three."

Nautilus could make eight knots submerged at full speed, but not for long without draining the battery. Surfacing and recharging was not an option until after sunset. Also, the periscopes could not be raised at such a high underwater speed and sonar performance would be degraded, so Brockman was essentially blind for those fifteen minutes. But in that time, they could close the range by two miles. At 1330 he slowed.

"Ahead one-third. Tell me when speed has dropped to five knots."

Moments later the speed was slow enough to raise the periscope.

"Observation. Up periscope!" The target came into view. Brockman called out the bearing and range.

"Down scope. Let's get a little closer and get some good bearings. Angle on the bow starboard zero-nine-zero. We are close to broadside." A few minutes later and a few more peeks through the periscope, range had closed to 2,200 yards and the TDC was ready.

"I have a solution," called Lynch excitedly. "Speed six-point-seven knots, course three-five-six."

"Very well," acknowledge Brockman. "Final bearing and shoot!"

Moments later, at 1342, three torpedoes fired at twelve-second intervals were speeding toward the unsuspecting vessel. At forty-five knots they would arrive in ninety seconds. Brockman called "up periscope" as the time of impact neared. He saw it before sonar heard the explosions.

"Bullseye! A hit amidships!" Moments later sonar reported hearing a muffled explosion. Then another hit slightly forward, followed by a second louder blast on sonar.

"She's broken in two. . . . I see a single screw sticking up in the air aft and the bow tilted up forward. She's sinking fast!" Sonar reported hearing crackling sounds and another loud explosion.

With no escort vessels to be seen, Brockman risked staying in the area and raised the periscope again to give others a chance to see a sinking ship. However, by 1435 there was nothing on the surface to be seen. Crackling noises persisted on sonar for some time.[19]

The captain was elated with one more sinking to add to their tally, a significant one at that. *Nautilus* and her crew had battled weather, failing equipment, inexperience, and the enemy for a month of operations and were ready to go home. Dawn on October 26 found the ship heading east toward Midway. Brockman decided to stay on the surface in daylight hoping to encounter Japanese ships along the northern route to Alaska, lookouts keeping a sharp eye on the sky for enemy aircraft. Late morning a large sampan was sighted, and *Nautilus* opened fire with machine guns, riddling the target and sending the crew sheltering below. Two hundred rounds of armor-piercing .50-caliber made no apparent damage, and no other type of ammunition was left.

19. Admiral English credited *Nautilus* with the sinking of a freighter of 5,863 tons. JANAC agreed on the sinking, but downgraded it to 3,200 tons.

"Mr. Eckert," Brockman called to his gunnery officer. "Status of guns?"

"Sir, both ammunition hoists are out of commission. Bearings are crushed on the guns, but they can be trained with enough muscle. We last fired them when we attacked that freighter back in September and we didn't have time to secure them when we dove. There is still a shell loaded in number one . . . been in there ever since."

"Very well." He turned to Ensign Davis, the officer of the deck. "Go to battle stations surface, gun one!"

Gunner's Mate Banbury spoke up.

"Captain, Mr. Eckert, I recommend a reduced powder charge in that gun. The range is very short, and that projectile has been in there for a month, under sea pressure."

"Right, sir," Eckert added. We don't know what will happen. I doubt that shell will explode."

"OK," agreed Brockman. "And have the crew stand aside when we fire it. Just in case."

The men readied the gun and trained it with great difficulty. *Nautilus* closed to three hundred yards and Eckert gave the order to fire. The gun sounded, and immediately the shell hit the base of the superstructure and exploded with a deafening blast. Debris flew, and the small vessel began to burn furiously.

The men on the bridge looked at each other in amazement. They waited for the Japanese crew to emerge, but no sign of them appeared. Soon the ship was engulfed in flames. They secured the gun and watched the burning pyre for a half hour before resuming their transit east. As they motored away, explosions could be seen on the horizon as the sampan sank.

Nautilus put the perilous Japanese coast astern, but the adventurous third patrol was not over. A rough passage to Midway caused all hands considerable discomfort, and problems with the battery were added to the list of damage suffered during depth charging. The boat arrived at the Midway submarine base early afternoon on Halloween, and the crew was joined by yard engineers as they furiously made makeshift repairs to the diesels and other equipment. Departing the next morning, Brockman received a report that an enemy submarine had been sighted along the route to Pearl Harbor. Early afternoon of November 3, an object in the water was sighted. Brockman climbed the ladder to the bridge.

"What do you see, Mr. Ray?"

"Appears to be fishing gear," Ens. Sherry Ray replied as the submarine slowed to a stop. "I see a large glass float and some netting." He gestured into the water arounds them. "Looks like an oil slick. And more glass floats in the distance. Some poor fishermen bought it here!"

"Conn, sonar!" an excited voice sounded in the loudspeaker on the bridge. "Torpedo in the water bearing one-four-zero relative!" All eyes turned aft to the starboard quarter. Lynch, officer of the deck in the conning tower, did not hesitate. "Ahead full!" he ordered. The diesels belched black smoke as the screws bit into the water. Slowly, the ship moved ahead.

"Torpedo sighted!" called Lynch peering through the periscope. The sea was glassy calm, making it easy to see the yellowish weapon approaching close astern.

"Ahead emergency!" called Lynch. He hoped the jury-rigged engines could take it. "Right full rudder!" The ship lurched as the diesels roared and the boat picked up speed. The sonar man called, "It's close!" and threw off his headphones, grabbing a stanchion expecting impact any moment.

"Torpedoes passing astern," called Lynch with relief, watching the weapons slide by harmlessly, by some reports within a hundred feet. "Ahead full." He slowed the engines but continued to clear the area. After a half hour they stopped and listened with sonar. Nothing was heard, and no periscope was sighted. Old *Nautilus* barely escaped once again.

The balance of the transit to Pearl Harbor was uneventful, though the crew remained alert. No further evidence of an enemy submarine was seen for the remainder of the journey. *Nautilus* moored at the submarine base at 1223 on November 5 after a grueling and harrowing fifty-six days at sea. Brockman submitted a detailed patrol report that included a list of seventy ship and aircraft contacts, nine attacks, and five pages of "major defects," with a specific tally of damage absorbed during the depth charge attack on October 12. Besides the listed contacts, he noted the sightings of more than 250 small sampans. Admiral English gave *Nautilus* credit for sinking three sampans and three cargo ships for a total of 15,163 tons, as well as damage to a one thousand ton patrol trawler, a significant blow to the Japanese war effort.[20] The submarine would spend a considerable time in Pearl Harbor effecting repairs and equipment upgrades, as well as recuperation for the crew.

A few days after arrival, the entire crew assembled wearing their finest dress uniforms as Admiral Nimitz, on behalf of the president of the United States, presented the Navy Cross to Captain Brockman "for extraordinary heroism and distinguished service in the line of his profession as Commanding Officer of the USS *Nautilus* (SS-168), in the Battle of Midway." The citation concluded, "His skill, determination, courage and fortitude were in keeping with the highest traditions of the Naval Service." A second award was given for the balance of the first patrol, citing "extreme courage and expert seamanship [that] enabled him to bring his ship and crew home safely without loss or injury." The Navy Cross is the highest honor the navy can bestow, topped only by the Medal of Honor (awarded by the president in the name of Congress). Brockman would eventually also receive a Silver Star for his performance on the third patrol.

Phil Eckart relaxed on the lawn of the Royal Hawaiian hotel sipping a beer, enjoying a well-deserved day off from duty leading working parties and managing repairs. Ozzie Lynch joined him. As usual, the Waikiki weather was perfect—warm and sunny with a gentle breeze to take the edge off the heat. Men frolicked in the waves off the famous beach, some even trying their luck at surfboards.

"How's the work going on those ammo hoists?" asked Ozzie. He took a sip of beer and waited patiently for the answer, knowing it was a loaded question. The finicky machines had provided Eckert and the gunnery division no end of trouble. The devices would eventually be removed; the

---

20. The ever conservative JANAC lowered the official tally to just the three larger vessels for a total of 12,000 tons.

work of lifting the 105-pound shells and powder bags from the magazine by hand being favored over dealing with a hoist that could not be made to reliably operate.

Finally, Eckart replied, "You know, Ozzie, after I leave *Nautilus* and the war is over, I'm going to requisition the navy to let me take one of those ammo hoists home with me."

"What for?" Lynch was surprised. Was he serious? What could he possibly want with an old ammunition hoist?

"Well," Eckert said ruefully, "I'm going to set it up in my backyard so whenever I want, I can piss on it!"[21]

---

21. Anecdote from a February 2000 interview with Floyd "Red" Porterfield.

CHAPTER FOUR

Bougainville

BROCKMAN STUDIED THE MESSAGE. HIS BROW FURROWED AS HE CON-sidered the content. "Well, I'll be damned," he mused.

"What is it, sir?" queried Lynch, just coming off the midwatch. He had made his way to the wardroom looking for a snack before hitting the rack for some well-deserved shuteye and was surprised to see the captain up and about at four in the morning.

"Seems like we have some new orders. We'll be having guests on board," replied Brockman, somewhat cryptically.

"What? Guests? What guests?" asked Lynch, puzzled. Just then there was a knock at the open wardroom door. Red Porterfield looked in. "Excuse me, skipper," he said.

"What is it, Red?"

"I'm volunteering, sir. Chief Killgore too. We'll need a motorman."[1]

"Volunteering for what?" said Lynch, more puzzled than ever.

Brockman shook his head. "Word sure gets around here fast," he said ruefully. "I'm going to have to have a word with Petty Officer Lee about communications security!" he said, just slightly in jest. Lee had received and decoded the message, and the basic contents were already scuttlebutt around the ship.

Lynch was still in the dark. "What's going on?" he demanded.

"Tell him, Red, since you seem to know everything already," said the captain.

---

1. According to Porterfield in a February 2000 interview, Brockman told him he was "volunteering."

Porterfield proceeded to outline what he knew, and Brockman filled in details. *Nautilus* was being directed to Teop Harbor on the northeast coast of the island of Bougainville to effect the evacuation of civilians fleeing Japanese occupation of the island. The operation would involve using the submarine's small boat and inflatable raft to steal ashore in the middle of the night and pick up the refugees. Lt. Jack Reed of the Australian Royal Navy, among the Allied troops still resisting the Japanese there, would coordinate activities from shore, signaling the embarkation point with a beach fire. Details of where to take the rescuees would be forthcoming.

"There are nuns, sir," concluded Porterfield.

"Nuns?" asked Lynch, taken aback by this news, and looking a bit dazed.

"Catholic nuns," explained Brockman, looking at the message. "Says here there are 'seventeen white women' in danger of capture. Among them four Sisters of St. Joseph."

"You'll need an officer in charge," said Lynch, regaining his composure. "I'll volunteer!"

"Good," said Brockman. "I was going to volunteer you anyway. Now you and the chief here start making plans. The Japanese are on their tails, and we don't want to let them down! We'll try to go in tonight if we see a signal. Oh, and figure out where we're going to berth seventeen women on this ship."

"Yes, sir!" said Lynch, knowing he would get no sleep tonight. "Let's go, Chief!"

As they left, Brockman rung up the bridge. "Mr. Winner, set a course for Teop Harbor on the north coast of Bougainville. Go to full speed." The submarine turned to the northwest and accelerated to fourteen knots. There was no time to lose.

The battle for Guadalcanal was raging. US Marines had stormed ashore on August 7, 1942, the opening salvo of the Solomon Islands campaign, the first steps in the retaking of the Pacific from the Japanese Empire.

The Japanese fought fiercely to hold the island and aggressively reinforced and resupplied the front with ships operating from their huge naval base at Rabaul on the island of New Britain[2] to the northwest. These heavily escorted convoys sailed routes along the island of Bougainville and between the islands of Santa Isabel, New Georgia, and others forming a stretch of water called "The Slot." These shipments, known to Americans as the Tokyo Express, ran a gauntlet of air and submarine attacks before reaching Savo Sound just north of Guadalcanal. Several major naval engagements were fought there over the course of the campaign leading to the sinking of thirty-three Allied warships (including seven cruisers) and seventeen Japanese (including two battleships). So many hulls litter the seafloor there that this body of water was renamed Ironbottom Sound from a nickname given by Allied sailors. Fighting on and around Guadalcanal would involve more than sixty thousand Allied troops facing more than thirty-six thousand defenders and would last until the Japanese evacuated some eleven thousand men in early February.

At the north end of The Slot rested the island of Bougainville, the largest bit of land in the Solomon Islands. About as long, but a bit narrower, than Puerto Rico, the island is covered with dense tropical rainforest and features a central spine of volcanoes, the northernmost conspicuously active. At the beginning of the war, the territory was occupied by Australia and was a focus of Catholic missionary activity, to the extent that much of the native population had converted to Christianity. The Japanese arrived in 1942 and garrisoned the island, but a few Australian troops, among them the famous Coastwatchers, took advantage of forest hideouts and their connections with the native and expat civilian population to remain and collect intelligence.

The Coastwatchers were a formal Allied organization of military intelligence operatives who were stationed on remote Pacific islands during the war to observe enemy movements and aid Allied personnel caught behind lines as the Japanese occupation swept over the region. The group was formed in 1922 by the Australian navy. Over the course of

2. Today part of Papua New Guinea, a nation on the island of New Guinea formed after World War II.

World War II, about four hundred men served as Coastwatchers, among them Australian and New Zealand military personnel, Pacific Islanders, and escaped prisoners of war. One notable exploit of these intrepid volunteers was the rescue of Lt. (jg) John F. Kennedy, future US president, after the sinking of *PT-109*. These men generally operated alone, lived off the land, and if captured, were savagely tortured. One of the more famous Coastwatchers, Sgt. Maj. Jacob Vouza, was captured and brutalized by the Japanese, managed to escape, and yet continued to volunteer as a scout after recovering from his wounds.

Among the missionary groups on the island was a party of the Sisters of Saint Joseph, four of whom had recently arrived from their convent in Orange, California, for duty. Sister Hedda Jaeger kept a detailed journal of their experiences, beginning with the three-month journey from California through Hawaii, Samoa, Fiji, New Zealand, and Australia, finally arriving on Bougainville in December 1940. There they joined a small group of nuns on Buka, a smaller island on the north end of Bougainville, where they served as nurses, teachers, and spiritual leaders for the native population. Just a year later, the Japanese bombed Pearl Harbor and began moving through the South Pacific, and the sisters were encouraged to leave Bougainville. However, they all agreed to stay, expecting that their mission and neutrality would be respected by the Japanese. When the invading army arrived in 1942 their expectations went largely unrewarded. With rare exception, the occupiers treated the native population as a source of labor and raided their food supplies. The missionaries were treated with suspicion at best, and sometimes imprisoned or even killed when suspected of aiding the Allies. The sisters found themselves on the run, fleeing air attacks and Japanese patrols, moving to the main island, and retreating to hideouts deep in the forest when threatened. The rest of the nonnative population, including plantation owners and farmers harvesting coffee or copra, were likewise threatened.

At great risk of capture and ill treatment, or worse, the local bishop and priests tried repeatedly to negotiate with the Japanese for the safety of the missions. In particular, in March 1942 Rev. James Hennessey was taken prisoner, court-martialed, condemned, and sent to a prison camp. It was later learned he was eventually shipped to Japan, but on the way his vessel was torpedoed by an Allied submarine, and he was lost along with some 1,100 other civilians and military prisoners. At the same time as Hennessey's capture, plantation owner Percy Good was executed. In August, Father Joseph Lamarre, who tried to continue Hennessey's work, was captured, and spent the rest of the war in a prison camp. Finally, by December, the situation was dire, with eleven American and French sisters and two priests sheltering in a northern coastal retreat called Tsipatavi, awaiting instructions, having been ordered (not just recommended this time) to evacuate. The party was eager to comply after a nearby plantation was raided and burned to the ground, the owners barely escaping with their lives and families. Father Albert Lebel, leading the evacuees, kept in communication with the missionary network through notes carried by natives and by trekking along secret jungle trails to secure meeting places. Through these means, he learned that the Japanese were looking for them and was directed to lead his group to a new hiding place where they could connect with Australian soldiers.

At 1:30 a.m. Christmas morning, the group set out with what they could carry with the help of native porters. The nuns, as always, were wearing their white habits, Sister Hedda clutching her precious diary. They were warned that they would be cold, wet, and hungry. Guided by a bight moon hanging in clear skies, they were able to make their way through steep gorges, across streams, and into forests where heavy foliage cause the moonlight to be "fitful and uncertain," making it very hard to follow the trail. Two of the French sisters were ill or injured and had to be carried on stretchers, which were hauled up and down steep ravines by natives. A brief stop in a local village offered a short rest and a chance to eat a biscuit before trudging on. By morning of Christmas Day, after crossing a particularly daunting gorge, Father Lebel called a halt to make camp. A small area was quickly cleared, and banana and taro leaves were gathered to provide shelter and a place to rest. The sisters prepared tea, fried eggs over a smoky fire, and even produced a small bottle of rum to lace the father's drink. In a short time, the sisters now numbering fourteen, and the rest, were sound asleep, curled up on giant mat of six-footlong banana leaves.

That afternoon Lebel made contact with the Australian soldiers, and the next morning he dispatched a message through Coastwatcher Lt. Reed to appeal to the Americans at Tulagi for help, stating, "Seventeen white women were in danger of capture by the Japanese or death from fever or starvation in the mountains." They were told it was now safe to return to Tsipatavi and await further instructions. The day found them retracing their trek back to the coastal retreat, this time aided by daylight and a good night's rest. Upon arrival, Father Lebel made his way back to investigate the situation at Tinputz, a once flourishing mission that had been ransacked by the Japanese. What was not stolen was destroyed, and the locals reported the invaders were asking where the missionaries had gone. Thankfully, the natives refused to tell them, and a few of them kept watch while Lebel snuck into the compound and collected several valuable items he had buried for safety.

The refugees had been hoping they would be airlifted to Australia by the army, but on New Year's Eve they were told to be at the beach at Teop Harbor that evening, bringing as little baggage as possible. They gathered their bags and meager supplies while Lebel organized carriers to transport the two nuns who could not walk. By then their footwear was in tatters, so Lebel gave his two last pairs of tennis shoes to the women while he pulled on a pair of army boots given to him by the Australians. The soldiers had also been generous with their food supplies whenever they could. In the early afternoon they set out in a heavy rain, crossing rivers and mountains, as they made their way to the coast. Three hours later they reached the beach and found Lieutenant Reed working his radio. He immediately sent them to a nearby coffee plantation, about an hour's walk away, to await further word. By dusk they arrived and set about drying their sodden clothing by the kitchen stove.

Before they had a chance to rest, one of the fathers arrived breathlessly and told them to gather their possessions and head back to the beach where they would meet other evacuees at the shoreside home of Mrs. Chris Faulkner. As they descended the steps of the plantation house to leave, the father said, "A submarine is going to pick you up!" Sister Hedda wrote, "Our hearts must have stopped beating for a moment. We hadn't anticipated this means of deliverance!" Following Lieutenant Reed by lantern light, the party, occasionally balancing on log bridges, followed a boggy path. A sister called, "Wait—I've lost my glasses!" to be met with the stern reply, "Move along faster!" They reached Mrs. Faulkner's house around 11:00 p.m., to be greeted by a proper English lady wearing a black lace gown. Initially, she declared she would not be joining the evacuation to the great anger and frustration of Lieutenant Reed who had gone through Herculean efforts to arrange the proceedings. He argued, demanded, and threatened, to no avail. Finally, Faulkner was persuaded by Father Lebel to change her courageous (but foolish) attitude. Meanwhile, the nuns set about cleaning up and swapping their sodden and filthy habits for fresh clothing, including discarding their navy-blue veils, their only concession to camouflage in the bush. With fresh white habits and veils, the sisters were ready to meet their rescuers.

At midnight two Australian soldiers appeared. They wished the gathering a Happy New Year and asked if the nuns would send messages to their families back home. An hour later a native boy came running in, saying excitedly, "Boat he come! Boat he come!" Everyone grabbed their remaining possessions, Sister Hedda with diary in hand, and headed to the beach.

Nautilus had gotten underway from Pearl Harbor on the morning of December 13 after more than a month of extensive repairs. Among modifications made to the ship was the installation of four 20-mm antiaircraft guns to the ample bridge. The crew was disappointed not to be upgrading the air conditioning system; as they headed south, the captain noted in his patrol report, "It now appears that this trip is going to be excessively hot." After their harrowing experience on the previous patrol Admiral English decided that *Nautilus* and her sisters *Narwhal* and *Argonaut* were too big, slow, and clumsy for Japanese Empire waters, so Brockman was being sent south to the Solomon Islands theater. With the Guadalcanal battle in full force and Japanese ships and aircraft swarming the area, the days ahead would prove to be hot in more ways that the weather.

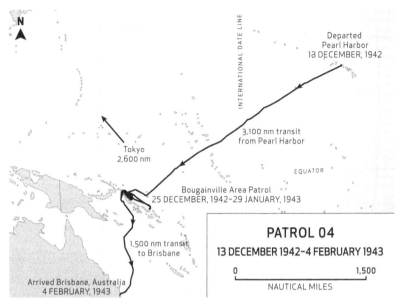

For her fourth patrol, *Nautilus* was assigned to interdict Japanese shipping off the coast of Bougainville in the Solomon Islands. ILLUSTRATION BY BETHANY JOURDAN.

Twenty-one crew members detached, including Ike Wetmore the experienced sonar chief, recently promoted to ensign. Twenty-three replacements came aboard, including veteran torpedomen Pat O'Brien and Ed Navratil, who had sailed with *Nautilus* on her first patrol. The wardroom welcomed three new officers including Lt. Milton Foster, Ens. George Davis, and Ens. Hal Winner, and bid farewell to Pat Rooney and Sherry Ray. Rooney would be lost commanding *Corvina* in November 1943 and Ray, promoted to Lieutenant (jg), would go down on *Pickerel* (SS-177) in April of the same year. They were among the nearly 3,500 US submariners who perished during the war.

Another departing officer who would be sorely missed was Tom Hogan, who went on to command the submarine USS *Bonefish* (SS-223) and would win the Navy Cross for valor on his first patrol operating in enemy controlled waters in the South China Sea. In the tradition of his former commander Brockman, Hogan pressed home persistent attacks despite vigorous antisubmarine measures, and was successful in sinking five hostile merchant vessels and damaging two additional ships. Hogan would win two more Navy Crosses for heroism on subsequent *Bonefish* patrols.

On the twenty-third the submarine crossed the equator. The crew commemorated the event by erecting a sign on the bridge that read, "Dear Santa Claus, please bring us a fat old Jap cruiser for Christmas." Christmas Day was spent reconnoitering Ontong Java, an atoll due north of Guadalcanal. Seeing nothing of interest, Brockman declined to spend another day in the area as planned and proceeded to his assigned patrol area off the northwest coast of Bougainville. The ship spent the next few days lurking around the south end of the island, seeing nothing but a distant destroyer patrolling the far end of Bougainville Strait. On December 29 they received the urgent message to proceed to Teop Harbor.

Brockman submerged as they sped up the coast, believing it essential to approach the area undetected. In the afternoon they raised a radio mast and received further details of the rescue plan. Later, orders came in to clear the area until the thirty-first to give the evacuees time to reach the harbor. Never one to waste an opportunity, Brockman took advantage

As *Nautilus* prepares for her fourth war patrol, sailors load boxes of Kellogg's Corn Flakes and Durkee's Mayonnaise, December 11, 1942. U.S. NAVY.

Nautilus taking on provisions prior to departing Pearl Harbor, December 11, 1942. Note the huge six-inch caliber deck gun. U.S. NAVY.

of the extra day to run north to Buka Island and patrol Cape Hanpan, however, he found nothing for his efforts. At 1939 on the evening of New Year's Eve, *Nautilus* surfaced just three miles from Teop Harbor under dark, overcast skies. Lynch, Porterfield, and Killgore were ready and scrambled topside to prepare the ship's boat and rubber raft. The extra time afforded by the delay allowed Lynch and the crew to gather equipment for the operation as well as supplies and gifts for the Australians remaining on the island. The trio was equipped with compass, a toolkit, binoculars, weapons, field rations, and a walkie-talkie to help manage their way in and out of the harbor. Also, to leave ashore, they brought food (a six months' supply enough for one man), batteries, half of the ship's medical supplies, some brandy, and a cornucopia of gifts collected from the crew. These included cigarettes, tobacco, clothing, and toiletries. The crew was so eager to help the Australians the captain had to call a halt to the collections before the cargo became too heavy for the boat.

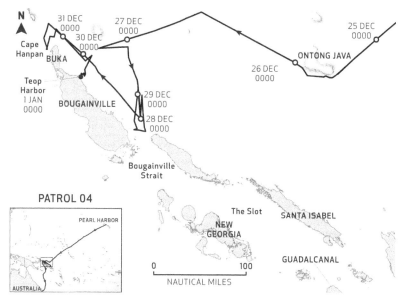

The submarine was detailed to rescue civilians, including Catholic mission-aries from Teop Harbor just ahead of Japanese occupation. ILLUSTRATION BY BETHANY JOURDAN.

Lynch, Porterfield, and Killgore set off into the darkness at 2148, aim-ing for a pair of beach fires set as prearranged signals. The boat returned in minutes with a broken rudder. It took a half hour of lost time to make the repairs. At 2229 they set out again, motoring toward the beach. Brockman gave them two orders before departure: be back no later than 0430 and if they were unable to return or be picked up that night, the submarine would return at 2100 each night to look for them. Flashlight signals were arranged to supplement the radio communications. As the boat drew away, Brockman yelled, "If you're not back by daylight, I'm leaving!"[3] He had all machine guns on the bridge manned and ready for action.

Moe Killgore was "volunteered" for the operation because he was an excellent mechanic and was not married. Porterfield felt the mission was too dangerous and risky for a recently married man. Moe's other asset was his mastery of four-letter words, notable even among a crew of

---

3. Interview with Floyd "Red" Porterfield, February 2000.

submarine sailors. He had the opportunity to employ this skill early in the trip to shore as Lynch drove the motorboat directly into a reef and capsized them about two hundred yards from the beach. Tumbling into the shallow water, Kilgore let go a string of invective at Lynch that apparently impressed even Red. For his part, Lynch absorbed the deserved verbal abuse with grace as the men righted the boat and started bailing water with their helmets. "Just shut up and bail!" Red finally yelled back at Killgore. The ruckus was heard as far away as the shore, where Lieutenant Read was anxiously waiting. Grabbing a native's canoe, he paddled out to investigate and found the *Nautilus* men struggling to pull the boat off the reef. With the help of several natives, they righted the launch and considered how to proceed. At that point, midnight was upon them, and Porterfield reached into the cache of supplies they were bringing in and pulled out a brandy miniature. "Happy New Year!" he declared, and passed the bottle around for a nip.

The encounter with the reef had again broken the boat's rudder, so maneuvering near shore was ill-advised. Read and Lynch talked things over and decided to shuttle the supplies in and passengers out on canoes, while Porterfield rigged the rubber boat, which would be towed behind the launch. At some point, Read realized that there were more refugees ashore than originally promised, a total of twenty-nine men and women. More than could be accommodated in the boats. It was agreed to take women and children first, and then (assuming Brockman agreed) come back for the men. Red started pumping air into the rubber boat while Read organized the loading of supplies into canoes and headed back to gather his flock ashore.

On the beach, fourteen sisters and plantation owners Edie Huson and Chris Faulkner gathered in the canoes with their bags and suitcases. In their charge were three children, Clara, Theresa, and Josephina Pitt, daughters of plantation owner Bobby Pitt who would remain on the island with his wife and two boys. Fathers Allotte and Morel joined the first group, while Mrs. Campbell stayed behind with her husband.[4] They

---

4. There is disagreement among sources as to who was in the first party. The deck log records the people listed. Brockman's patrol report says "seventeen ladies, and three children plus one man," with Mr. and Mrs. Campbell in place of the two priests. Regardless, the others came on the second trip.

quietly paddled out to the boats and waited while Porterfield finished pumping up the rubber boat. The silence was finally broken by Red, commenting in his Oklahoma drawl, "These things sure take a lot of air!" Sister Hedda said it was the most welcome sound in the world. Finally, the refugees began piling into the launch and raft while the men loaded their bags. As Edie Huson was climbing aboard, Lynch made a comment about "excess baggage." Without a word, Huson tossed the larger of her two suitcases overboard and took her seat stoically. Through it all (and to Red's surprise), Moe Killgore was said to have used "impeccable language" while in the presence of the sisters.

Finally, they were on their way. A native in a canoe guided them through the reef. With a broken rudder, Red steered the boat by standing in the stern and shifting his weight from side to side. Lynch flashed his light from time to time, seeing nothing as they steered by compass into the darkness ahead. The waters were calm, but the women were apprehensive to be heading out to open sea at night in such a small boat. Lynch continued to signal to no avail, the tension palpable. Then the sharp-eyed native alongside in his canoe declared, "Em he stop!" and pointed into the gloom ahead. Lynch and the others saw nothing. Suddenly, the submarine loomed. At 0300, four and a half hours after the rescuers left *Nautilus*, passengers climbed aboard, the deck lined with men offering helping hands. Lynch saluted Captain Brockman and asked permission to refuel and return for eight more evacuees.

Brockman gave permission, but again warned Lynch to be back by 0430. Off they motored back to the harbor. Meanwhile, the sisters and others were welcomed aboard the submarine with open arms. Sister Hedda politely refused any offers to carry her diary, but the tired and hungry women accepted all other assistance at hand. The cooks were ready to serve a light supper in the crew's mess and the guests were entertained by officers and men not on watch. They were half starved, and the sight of a bowl of sugar, real salt, and fresh coffee was absorbed with awe and wonder.

Lynch's return was anxiously awaited. The 0430 deadline came and passed. Finally, at 0441, the launch returned, and the eight additional passengers scrambled aboard. Among them were Claude and Margaret

Campbell, Father George Guthrie, four plantation men, and Frederick Urban, an Austrian prisoner of war. The topside crew "worked like Trojans" to stow the boat, drain the oil from the boat's motor, remove the batteries, and get below before daylight. By 0535, all was in order and two minutes later *Nautilus* submerged, the sun already peeking over the horizon. It was a risky affair, but all twenty-nine were safely aboard and no longer in danger of the Japanese. The next day a message was received:

CONGRATULATIONS, NAUTILUS. YOU WERE JUST AHEAD OF THE SHERIFF. JAP DESTROYER ENTERED TEOP HARBOR SHORTLY AFTER YOU LEFT.

Brockman made his cabin, another officer's stateroom, the CPO quarters, and the wardroom available to the female visitors while the men were given crew's bunks as the crewmen slept on the deck. He told the visitors to "make the submarine your home," as they were served a delicious New Year's Day feast. The men scoured their lockers for spare toothbrushes, treats from home, and anything they could find to share with the civilians. Doc Potts tended to their medical needs, including a case of malaria. The crew organized a party for the children complete with presents (socks, sweaters, knick-knacks, and souvenirs donated by the men). In return, the planters shared what information they could about the area, such as tanker traffic, where ships tended to gather, and routine air reconnaissance schedules.

On January 4, *Nautilus* rendezvoused with a patrol craft off Tulagi to the east. The passengers were carefully transferred to the waiting vessel and bid a tearful farewell to their rescuers. Brockman noted, "Two of the ladies who were widows kissed two of the *Nautilus* crew good-bye." One of the sisters asked Porterfield if there was anything she could do for him. In his Oklahoma drawl Red asked if she could write a letter to his mother for him, which of course she was more than happy to oblige. The sisters and the others continued their long and perilous journey home via Guadalcanal, Auckland, and Hawaii before arriving in California at the end of the month. They left a heartfelt letter of appreciation that they all signed to "Captain Brockman and the Officers and Crew, U.S.S. *Nautilus*."

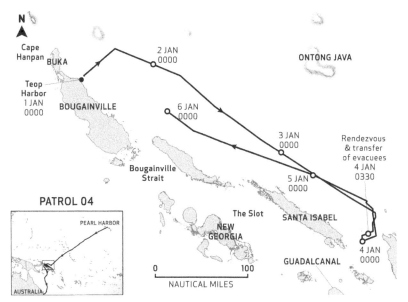

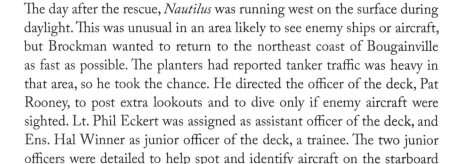

Nautilus transferred evacuees to a waiting vessel and returned to her patrol
area. ILLUSTRATION BY BETHANY JOURDAN.

The day after the rescue, *Nautilus* was running west on the surface during
daylight. This was unusual in an area likely to see enemy ships or aircraft,
but Brockman wanted to return to the northeast coast of Bougainville
as fast as possible. The planters had reported tanker traffic was heavy in
that area, so he took the chance. He directed the officer of the deck, Pat
Rooney, to post extra lookouts and to dive only if enemy aircraft were
sighted. Lt. Phil Eckert was assigned as assistant officer of the deck, and
Ens. Hal Winner as junior officer of the deck, a trainee. The two junior
officers were detailed to help spot and identify aircraft on the starboard
and port sides, respectively. An additional lookout, Yeoman Lawrence
Rossi, was posted aft.

At around 0730 Rooney went below to check the navigation on the
conning tower plot. He sent a sailor to go topside and climb the periscope shears to clean the lenses. In this confusing situation with extra

3 January 1943.

To: Captain Brockman,
          and the Officers and Crew,
          U.S.S. NAUTILUS.

The evacuees from Bougainville desire
to express to you all and to your Government
our sincere gratitude and appreciation of your
prompt and efficient response to our appeal
for help and for the wonderful hospitality and
friendship extended to us by all on board.

We shall never forget our unique experience and the very happy association with you
all.

We thank you most sincerely and can only
wish you Good Hunting and that we may be able
to meet you again some day "Apres la guerre".

Again our most sincere thanks for all that
you have done for us.

Letter of appreciation from Bougainville evacuees, January 1943. U.S. NAVY.

men on the bridge and the officer of the deck in the conning tower, Rossi called, "Clear the bridge! Plane on the port quarter!" Eckert stepped back to join Rossi and identify the plane, as instructed. The other men on the bridge scrambled below, including Ensign Winner. Not realizing there were two men still on the aft section of the bridge, he gave the order to dive while pulling the hatch shut behind him.

Meanwhile, after a few seconds failing to identify the plane, Eckert told Rossi to forget about it and get below. They headed for the hatch, about twenty-five feet away, when to their horror it banged shut! Within moments, the main ballast tanks began venting and they knew they were in big trouble. Eckert had thought about this situation and knew he had seconds to act. He yelled to Rossi, "We have to get off right now!" and led them down a ladder, climbed over a lifeline, and jumped into the sea. Rossi jumped as well and hit the side of the ballast tank, but washed clear. They swam frantically, Eckert hampered by a raincoat and heavy binoculars hanging from his neck. In moments, the dark hull passed, and Eckert saw the stern and letters USS NAUTILUS (SS-168) slip into the sea. They were safe from tangling with the propellers or being sucked down with the hull, but were alone in the vast ocean.

Captain Brockman's strict policy that every man wears a life jacket when on the bridge probably saved their lives. Eckert doffed his raincoat and without a second thought cast his expensive Zeiss binoculars to the deep. He helped Rossi blow up his life jacket, then his own. Their next concern was sharks, especially the lieutenant with bare legs and khaki shorts. Rossi, at least, was wearing dungarees. Eckert wrapped the discarded raincoat around his legs to make less of a tempting target for the feeding denizens. Meanwhile, fury was about to be unleashed in the submarine below as Captain Brockman appeared and wondered where his diving officer was, that being Eckert's watch station.

"Where's the diving officer?" Brockman growled. Ens. George Davis clearly heard him as he was shaving in his stateroom. Moments later the question was repeated in a booming voice heard as far as the forward torpedo room, "Where's the goddamn diving officer?!" In seconds everyone realized what had happened. Brockman was livid and threatened Rooney and Winner with courts martial. The captain ranted for minutes as the submarine leveled off at 175 feet and the other men in the room quietly stared at their equipment. Into this scene stepped the unflappable Lynch. He managed to cool down the captain, who finally said, "How will we get them back, Ozzie?" Lynch calmly replied, "Very simple, Captain. We will turn around, blow all main ballast, battle surface near point X, and pick them up."

Point X referred to the spot on the plotting table that marked the position of the ship when they dove, and the submarine's course and speed was continuously fed into the device, tracking their movements. They just had to maneuver back to that point. They reversed course as Lynch directed, and returned to periscope depth. In the water above Rossi saw the periscope emerge and shouted, Mr. Eckert! They're coming back!" Lynch spotted them through the periscope, the boat surfaced, and five minutes later the men were hauled back aboard, about a half hour after the dive. The plane that spurred the action was nowhere in sight.

Curiously, the ship's log simply records, "Surfaced on course 289°T." No mention of the incident appeared there or in the patrol report.[5]

Nautilus spent the next several days lurking around Bougainville Strait hoping to find enemy ships slipping through. Finally, in the wee hours of January 9, they were rewarded with a sighting of two large merchant ships escorted by a destroyer. As the submarine approached, the destroyer began sweeping the area with a searchlight, forcing a dive. The cloudy night was extremely dark and Brockman could not locate the target through the periscope except by training it on the bearing reported by sonar and waiting for the occasional flash of lightning that illuminated the sky. By these means he was able to get a firing solution and launched three torpedoes. Two hits sent one of the merchants, judged to be a 9,600 ton vessel, to the bottom.[6] The destroyer discouraged further pursuit of the second merchant with a dispirited depth charging, but none of them were close.

---

5. This story was published in an article by Phil Eckert in *Shipmate*, the Naval Academy alumni magazine in June 1989. Bob Burrell corroborated it in a December 2000 interview.

6. *Nautilus* was credited by Adm. James Fife, commander of Task Force 42, with the "probable" sinking of a 9,300 ton transport. JANAC did not recognize this.

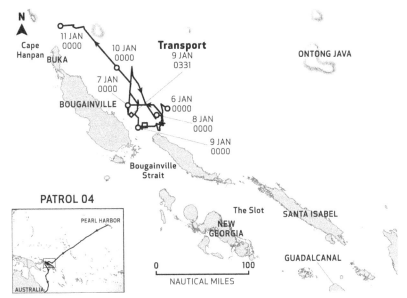

Nautilus attacked a transport vessel on January 9. ILLUSTRATION BY BETHANY JOURDAN.

Brockman was losing patience with the slim pickings at the strait, so he headed north along the coast and around Cape Henpen to the west side of Buka Island, where destroyers had been sighted. After unsuccessfully chasing several ships too far away to approach, he took a good look inside Queen Carola Harbour, but found it empty. He decided that Bougainville Strait offered the best opportunities after all and reversed his path around Henpen and headed back south along the northeast coast. On January 14, while en route on a very dark night, the submarine's radar picked up a pair of contacts ahead, about five miles distant. Brockman went to flank speed to gain position ahead of the targets, setting up for a submerged periscope approach. A perfect setup was achieved, and three torpedoes led to two hits on what was judged to be a 10,385 ton tanker of the *Kurosio Maru*-class. The second contact was a destroyer, and after a quick setup, Brockman fired one torpedo, which missed. He continued swinging around for a stern tube shot at the tanker, which was listing, but being empty, didn't sink. Two more torpedoes and another hit failed to sink the vessel, which was by then making eleven knots with the destroyer leading it to safety. Brockman concluded, "An empty tanker is difficult to sink!"[7]

Continuing south, *Nautilus* tangled briefly with a submarine, which was suspected to have picked up its ample silhouette in the bright moonlight, and approached when a fortuitous rain squall foiled the attack. Once discovered, the enemy submarine moved away at high speed.

On the early afternoon of January 16, *Nautilus* was cruising the south end of Bougainville Strait, submerged, when a ship was sighted. Ozzie Lynch was officer of the deck.

"Captain, I have a contact ahead, a lone cargo vessel, about six-five hundred yards." Brockman immediately made his way to the conning tower. Eye to the periscope, he said, "Go to battle stations torpedo, Mr. Lynch. Down scope. This is bad periscope weather."

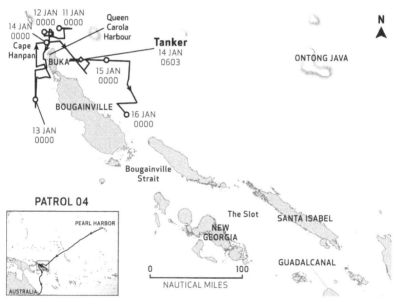

Nautilus attacked and damaged a tanker on January 14. ILLUSTRATION BY BETHANY JOURDAN.

---

7. Fife credited *Nautilus* with damage to a 10,380-ton tanker.

"Aye, sir," Lynch replied, and gave the order that set the men of *Nautilus* to action. After being in a lull for some time, this patrol was becoming busy. "I hope he didn't pick up the periscope!" The seas were calm with a modest swell, making it easy for a sharp-eyed lookout to spot danger nearby. As the submarine approached, the ship began to slowly change course so that the situation became more favorable for attack. After a few quick observations, Brockman was ready.

"Final bearing and shoot," he called. Just then sonar reported, "Echo ranging coming from the target!" As three torpedoes left the tubes, the target maneuvered.

"Echo ranging?" said Lynch, puzzled. "I don't see an escort."

As Lynch and Brockman considered this, the target turned toward them and continued echo ranging. Though looking like a merchant ship, it was acting like a destroyer.

"We may have run into a Q-ship," said Brockman. "Take her deep, Mr. Lynch. Rig for depth charge!"

Sure enough, the enemy vessel ran right overhead and dropped a frighteningly accurate depth charge barrage.

"Make your depth three-three-zero feet," ordered Brockman. This was deeper than the boat's design operating depth of three hundred feet, but worth the risk. Over the next hour the enemy vessel made repeated depth charge attacks and expertly tracked the submarine, cleverly using the confines of the entrance to the strait to thwart an easy escape. At 1403, five more charges came down directly overhead, detonating just a bit too shallow to cause serious damage.

"This guy must be the brother of the fellow who worked us over last patrol," commented Brockman with grudging respect.

Q-ships were merchant vessels converted to carry heavy armament and sonar gear. They were designed to lure unsuspecting submarines to attack, only to then find themselves facing the equivalent of a destroyer. The German navy employed a number of these vessels in World War II. The particular vessel facing *Nautilus* was maneuverable and equipped with active sonars and some means of projecting depth charges. After a half hour lull in the attacks, Brockman inched slowly to periscope depth to have a look. After several peeks though the periscope, he consulted the recognition guide.

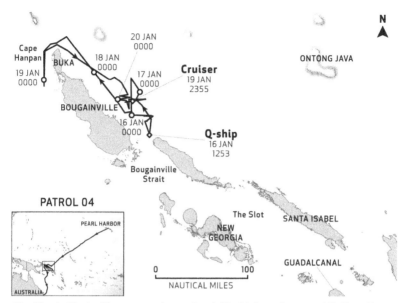

Nautilus battled with an armed merchant (Q-ship) on January 16, then three days later damaged a *Mogami*-class cruiser. ILLUSTRATION BY BETHANY JOURDAN.

"This looks like the *Hitari Maru*," he commented. Brockman's assessment of the situation may have been accurate, but the only official Q-ship built by the Japanese was *Delhi Maru*, which was sunk on its maiden voyage in January 1944 by the submarine USS *Swordfish*. Later, Brockman raised the periscope again and saw nothing. They headed northwest to explore Kieta Harbor farther up the coast. Prowling around the strait with an armored merchant in the vicinity was not a good idea. The next several days were spent moving around the area. They followed orders first to go back around Henpen to Buka Strait, then to stay to the east to avoid encountering other US submarines that might be there (namely *Swordfish* and *Gato*), and were briefly considered to be sent south to New Georgia to bombard Japanese positions. On the nineteenth, sounds of extended depth charging in the distance made Brockman wonder if *Gato* had tangled with the Q-ship. That evening, the action resumed with Ens. George Davis manning the bridge on the surface. At 2337, a sharp-eyed lookout reported, "Ship sighted to the east, bearing zero-seven-seven, range one-eight thousand!"

The captain was summoned to the bridge. Brockman called for full speed to close the range and manned battle stations. Radar picked up the target at five miles, now believed to be a destroyer. As the distance decreased to four miles, the ship turned and headed directly toward *Nautilus*, making twenty-six knots. The seas frothed from her bow as the warship bore down on the submarine.

"Submerge the ship!" called Brockman. "Right full rudder, steady course north! Ready tubes five and six!" With the enemy ship approaching at high speed, the captain was hoping to get off a stern shot before he got too close. To the attack party he said, "We'll start swinging left as we work on a firing solution and then let him have it with the bow tubes. Make ready tubes one, two, and three." Men throughout the ship set to work readying torpedoes, securing spaces for action, and tracking the enemy with sonar and sightings through the periscope. Brockman ordered left rudder to begin a gradual turn to bring the forward tubes to bear as soon as the stern shot was fired. At 2355 the range was down to seven hundred yards and Brockman could wait no longer. "Final bearing and shoot!" Two torpedoes left the stern tubes and sped to the looming vessel. "Left full rudder!" he called, still on the scope, watching for any result of the shot. "He's turning toward us again; probably can see our periscope!" Thirty seconds later the captain got the result he was hoping for.

"A hit!" he called excitedly. She's swinging away from us. I can see her whole broadside . . . it fills my entire field of view! Rudder amidships. Final bearing and shoot!"

Three more torpedoes sped toward the target. Unfortunately, the range was too short and they passed under the target harmlessly, failing to arm.

"Damn," cursed Brockman.

"Propellers stopped for a minute," reported sonar, "but they've started up again."

Midnight struck as Brockman realized he was up against a bigger target than he bargained for.

"That's no destroyer . . . that's a cruiser! Looks like a *Mogami* class. She's firing at us! Left full rudder!"

At point-blank range of just two hundred yards, machine guns and heavier caliber armament let loose in the direction of the periscope. Men throughout the submarine reported hearing scraping sounds against the hull. Brockman maneuvered away as best he could, trying not to be rammed or shot and opened the range so he could fire another torpedo. Meanwhile, the stricken cruiser was struggling to regain speed as a series of explosions erupted on board. After a half hour, the enemy, making ten knots and zig-zagging, managed to withdraw. *Nautilus*, forced to slow down for risk of exhausting her battery, started a new approach, but by then the cruiser was well clear. A half hour later the submarine surfaced and headed south in the general direction of the wounded vessel, and though they encountered a heavy oil slick, they were unable to catch up with the withdrawing ship.

"I thought we had that cruiser in the bag!" lamented Lynch.[8]

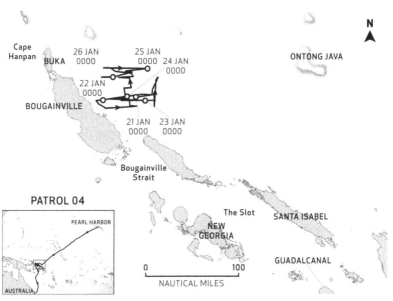

Nautilus continued patrolling the east coast of Bougainville without success.
ILLUSTRATION BY BETHANY JOURDAN.

8. Admiral Fife credited *Nautilus* with damaging a ten thousand-ton *Mogami*-class cruiser.

The next week was less eventful as *Nautilus* confined her patrols to areas bounded by *Gato* and *Swordfish*. Other submarines reported convoys passing through, but Brockman was not able to locate them, or they were too distant to catch. As its patrol was ending, *Nautilus* was ordered back to Henpen and the Buka Strait. On January 28 smoke was sighted, and a merchant vessel appeared. After a deliberate approach, with three torpedoes ready to launch, a destroyer was seen. One minute later, at 0852, three torpedoes sped on their way toward the merchant vessel. Brockman turned his attention to the destroyer. Two hits were scored on what was judged to be a *Palau Maru*-class vessel at 4,495 tons, last seen to be heavily damaged on the stern. Meanwhile, Brockman turned away from the destroyer, now bearing down on the submarine, and fired both stern tubes before heading deep. The shot down the throat of the enemy ship discouraged its attack briefly, but shortly it returned, and the inevitable depth charge attack began. Twelve charges "shook us more than a little," according to Brockman, but at three hundred feet they escaped serious damage, and after nearly three hours were able to slink away.

The long patrol was beginning to wear on the ship and her crew. Besides the regular litany of damage to fittings and equipment, the ship was suffering from external air leaks that released bubbles to the surface that were potentially visible to aircraft. Habitability was a serious concern on account of inadequate air conditioning. Two cases of heat prostration were noted and nearly the entire crew suffered from prickly heat and other forms of skin irritation. The temperature and humidity in the ship were uncomfortably high every day, with the highest temperature recoded in the engine room at 124 degrees and humidity at 98 percent in the conning tower. On the twenty-eighth Brockman noted, "Practically all hands are just about to pass out from the extreme heat and I have no desire for further trouble."

Trouble, however, was afoot. The next day smoke was sighted, and *Nautilus* began yet another approach. At 0235 a large supply ship with destroyer escort were seen, but visibility was poor and Brockman could not get a good periscope observation. With only two torpedoes remaining in

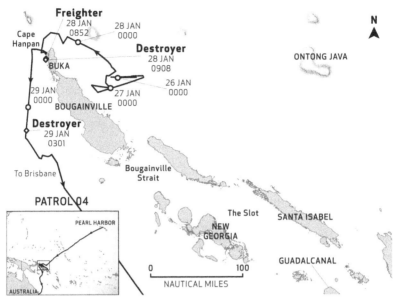

Nautilus engaged in several attacks as her patrol came to an end, sinking a destroyer on January 29. ILLUSTRATION BY BETHANY JOURDAN.

the forward tubes, he decided to close enough to shoot forward then turn to bring the stern torpedoes to bear. Further looks identified the destroyer as a *Minekaze* class. At a range of 3,500 yards Brockman took his shot, but a poor firing solution led to a miss of the supply ship. To her great misfortune, the destroyer took one of the torpedoes instead and began to sink. *Nautilus* tried to line up the stern shot on the supply ship, but the vessel turned tail, spewed out a smoke screen, and sped away.[9]

Finally, on January 30, *Nautilus* received orders to proceed to Australia, thus ending another eventful patrol. She arrived at Brisbane at 1047 on the morning of February 4 after a quiet transit. Her return was well received by Admiral Fife, who endorsed Brockman's patrol report with the words, "*Nautilus* is to be congratulated for the successful accomplishment of the difficult and hazardous task of rescuing twenty-nine civilians who were being gravely threatened with capture by the enemy." Besides

---

9. Fife credited the submarine with the sinking of a *Minekaze*-class destroyer of 1,000 tons, the only officially recognized sinking of the patrol. JANAC later upgraded the tonnage to 1,500.

the sinking of the destroyer, he credited the ship with probably sinking a transport and cargo ship, and damaging a tanker and a *Mogami*-class cruiser. None other than Adm. William F. "Bull" Halsey, commander of the South Pacific Force, commended *Nautilus* for the rescue and for "damage inflicted on the enemy." Brockman was eventually awarded a third Navy Cross for "extraordinary heroism in the line of his profession."

Among the crew specifically cited for outstanding performance were radiomen Bruce Fox and Buzz Lee for working day and night to make the balky radar work properly. Brockman wrote, "Too much credit cannot be given these two men for their interest and devotion to duty displayed by them during this cruise."

While *Nautilus* was battling with enemy warships and transports off Bougainville in mid-January, two momentous events rocked the US Submarine Force. The first involved her sister ship *Argonaut*, patrolling nearby in the area between Bougainville and New Britain. Commanded by Lt. Cdr. John Pierce, on January 10 the submarine attacked a convoy of five freighters escorted by three destroyers. The action was witnessed by the crew of army aircraft returning from a bombing mission. They reported that one of the destroyers was hit by a torpedo while the other two counterattacked. Apparently damaged by depth charging, *Argonaut* broke the surface and was set upon by the enemy gunships, which fired round after round into the submarine. Finally, she disappeared, taking 102 crewmen with her, the worst loss of life for an American submarine during wartime. This tragedy hit the men of *Nautilus* hard, as a number of crewmen came from *Argonaut* and six men who previously served on *Nautilus* were among those lost. Foy Hester, in particular, cited eight men who were former shipmates, and a chief radioman who was a close friend.

The second event was the loss of the commander of the Pacific Submarine Force, Adm. Robert English, who was killed along with eighteen other passengers in the crash of a civilian Pan American flight in California on January 21. English was planning to tour submarine support facilities at Mare Island and take an opportunity to visit family. Though his death sent shockwaves through the Submarine Force, his legacy as commander of the Pacific force was not particularly distinguished. Not well regarded by his skippers, many of whom received very harsh reviews or were summarily dismissed if they did not please him, English failed to make the best use of the assets at his disposal. Many submarines were dispersed to missions in remote theaters that produced little result. He persisted in ignoring problems with the standard Mark-14 torpedo, instead blaming the captains for poor shooting. Regardless, for his efforts to whip a peacetime submarine fleet into an aggressive fighting force, English was posthumously awarded the Distinguished Service Medal. His duties were temporarily assumed by Rear Adm. John "Babe" Brown while Admiral King considered a replacement. After some juggling of commanders King selected Rear Adm. Charles Lockwood, who was soon promoted to vice admiral and served in that position through the end of the war until 1946.

PART II

CONQUEST OF THE PACIFIC

WITH THE TIDE OF WAR TURNED AND THE INITIATIVE ON THE SIDE OF the United States and its allies, the long, bloody conquest of the Pacific began. Battles on Guadalcanal were ending as the Japanese evacuated troops to defend other islands in the Solomon Islands and protect their naval base at Rabaul in New Britain. Allied forces continued their push to the northwest toward Bougainville and eventually isolated and neutralized Rabaul, destroying large amounts of Japanese naval and air strength in the process. Fighting in the Solomons would continue through the end of the war while General MacArthur's troops moved on to New Guinea.

Meanwhile, as part of the Allied two-front strategy, a central Pacific campaign was launched to capture the Japanese held Gilbert Islands, beginning with Tarawa in November 1943, followed by the Marianas campaign beginning in June 1944. The first order of business, however, was to oust enemy forces from occupied US mainland territory, specifically Attu Island in the Aleutians.

USS *Nautilus* played a key role in these battles, deploying troops to attack Japanese strongholds, conducting surveillance of enemy coastlines, and aggressively attacking enemy ships wherever they might appear. Sailing repeatedly into harm's way, the submarine time and again risked the fate that befell *Argonaut* and fifty-one other US boats lost during World War II. Nearly 3,500 US submariners perished during the war, more than 20 percent of those who sailed on war patrols. This was the highest casualty rate for any branch of the US military.

CHAPTER FIVE

Attu

Nick Bruck and Jerry Gross sat in the tiny messroom, mugs of tepid coffee in their fists. Foy Hester sat nearby, pen in hand, quietly writing a letter home, to be mailed when they reached the next port. The deck rocked gently as *Nautilus* cruised on the surface, Australia's Sunshine Coast twenty miles to the west. Nick wore a dour expression; Jerry glumly stared at his mug, not particularly enthused with the contents. After a month in the warm, friendly environs of Brisbane, the sailors were not eager to head north to frigid spring seas and enemy action.

Jerry finally broke the silence. "That was a time, that kangaroo hunt," he offered.

"That it was, Jerry, that it was. Though I don't remember seeing anything but kangaroo tracks. And rabbits. Lotsa rabbits." A rueful smile crossed his face. "Lucky we're better shots with torpedoes."

"Yeah," replied Jerry. "Japs would be laughing their butts off if they saw us blasting away at those little furry bastards. We couldn't hit a one." He chuckled, then his glum expression returned. "Shit, Nick, back to sea again we go."

"What do you want—an egg in your beer? You just had a Navy-paid vacation, sheilas with heat waves everywhere, eager to show a Yank some gratitude for saving Australia from the Japs. It's time we get back to work!"

Bruck's words to his shipmate were not delivered unkindly. He was trying to shock them both back to reality. After four grueling patrols, their extended stay in Brisbane was a chance to make repairs to aging and

185

battle-damaged equipment, and also the first real chance for crew R&R. Two floors of a local hotel were reserved for the exclusive use of American submariners returning from war patrol, and the sailors were treated as valued guests. With many of the local men off fighting the Japanese in New Guinea, or serving with the Allies fighting in Europe, there was a surplus of women, referred to by the Aussies as "sheilas" or "jillaroos." Many were working as civilian volunteers providing humanitarian service, or supporting wartime industries. Eager for companionship, and truly appreciative of their American Allies, girls were seen everywhere arm in arm with sailors.

One day some of the crew were invited to go on a kangaroo hunt. Climbing onto a rugged weapons carrier suitable for transportation into the outback, the group jounced for miles along a rutted cattle trail and into a dense wood. After a jaw rattling trip, they emerged into a large clearing and were astonished to see a medieval castle looming ahead! The replica castle and outbuildings were the site of a camp for disadvantaged youth run by a group of Catholic priests. Sleeping quarters were assigned to the visitors, who were then armed with M-1 rifles and carbines. A local led the sailors to an area covered with fresh kangaroo tracks, where they were left to fend for themselves. After several frustrating hours, the hunters gave up searching for kangaroos and tried their luck on the ubiquitous rabbits. Having no success at hitting the rapidly moving targets, they unleashed their ammo on some giant (but stationary) ant hills and called it a day. Upon return to the castle, any disappointment of their failure to bring home game was relieved by a delicious dinner of wild kangaroo tail, home grown vegetables, and fresh baked bread slathered with cream and honey.[1]

On March 4, 1943, R&R finally came to an end. *Nautilus* got underway with orders to sail to a remote base in the New Hebrides called Espiritu Santo (located on what is now the Republic of Vanuatu). There they would spend a few weeks training Marines in amphibious operations before returning to Pearl Harbor to prepare for the next war patrol.

---

1. An account of the kangaroo hunt and other tales of the Brisbane visit from *Silently We Served*, courtesy Jerry Gross (2007).

Arriving on March 9, Jerry, Nick, Foy, and the rest of the crew were surprised and pleased to be reunited with Lieutenant Colonel Carlson and the Marine Raiders they hosted on their second patrol. The Marines greeted their old shipmates warmly and treated them to a feast of the best chow the mess could rustle up. Jerry said it was much appreciated, though he admitted the food was inferior to navy submarine standards.

The crew and Marines spent a few weeks practicing amphibious operations from submarines, with troops debarking on rubber rafts as they had done at Makin Island on the second patrol. These exercises were both for the benefit of those who would be called upon to assault a future enemy beach, as well as the *Nautilus* crew who would be expected to transport them. When they were at Makin, it had been difficult to clamber into floating rafts tethered to the side of the hull on pitching seas in the dead of night, so the rafts were loaded on the broad, ample deck of the submarine. When all equipment and personnel were securely loaded, the boat slowly submerged allowing the rafts to float away. This technique seemed to work much better and would be used in future operations. The crew did not yet know it, but they would be employing these lessons in a matter of weeks.

The *Nautilus* crew bid farewell to Carlson's Raiders and got underway for Pearl Harbor on April 5. Nick and Jerry found themselves back in the messroom, clutching mugs of coffee, griping about going to sea again.

"Was great to see those saltwater cowboys," said Jerry. "I was glad to be rid of their asses after lugging them around taking up space, but it was sure good to see them again."

"Fewer of them than when we picked them up," mused Nick, referring to the casualties the Marines took on Makin. "Glad I'm not in their line of work."

"Yeah, but look at us. Bunch of sorry pig boaters. What do you think's in store for us after Pearl?"

"No idea, Jerry. You know they don't tell me where we're going until we get there. Ask Mr. Eckert—he probably don't know either. But you know there's something coming up to look forward to."

"What's that? Clue me in."

"You know we're crossing the equator Thursday night. We've got a few polywogs came on board in Brisbane. You want to be on the entertainment committee?"

"Why not! Should be fun!"

Sailors of all ilk find unique ways to divert themselves from the boredom of long days at sea. One enduring tradition is the initiation of a sailor who has never crossed the equator—a "pollywog"— into the company of the "shellbacks." "Crossing the Line" ceremonies are nearly as old as seafaring itself. Our modern practice is believed to have evolved from Viking rituals, executed upon crossing the 30th parallel, a tradition that they passed on to the Anglo-Saxons and Normans in Britain. In modern times, the ceremony usually involves the most senior shellback presenting to the captain of the vessel a list of slimy wogs to appear before him. This summons does not exclude anyone because of rank; even admirals must go through the ceremony if they are not yet shellbacks. The day of the crossing has the pollywogs performing a number of embarrassing or disgusting tasks, ranging from a talent show to crawling through garbage, usually ending by kissing the "royal baby" (usually the fattest chief on board) on his grease-slathered belly. Finally, "King Neptune" (sometimes accompanied by other colorful characters such as "Queen Amphitrite" and "Davy Jones") pronounces the man to be a shellback, and presents him with an official certificate. Most of the *Nautilus* crew who were not already shellbacks had achieved the honor during the previous war patrol, which concluded in Brisbane. A few new men who had not crossed the line by sea (flying over it didn't count) would be the subject of the festivities.

The rest of the voyage to Pearl Harbor was uneventful. *Nautilus* arrived on April 15 and began a short but intense refit, including a dry docking and renewal of main engine pistons and heads, jobs which could not be done at the facilities in Brisbane. Just five days later, on the twentieth, the boat left the friendly environs of Pearl Harbor and headed north. Destination: Dutch Harbor, Alaska.

The two thousand nautical mile voyage to Dutch Harbor (nearly the distance across the continental United States) was a difficult journey. Foremost were the conditions. For a crew accustomed to the sultry South Pacific climate, having experienced cases of heat stroke in the prior patrol, the cold and damp of early spring arctic waters were a shock. Besides, the weather was awful. As recorded in Captain Brockman's patrol report, "North of 34°N the weather became erratic. On April 23 and 24 a hurricane was near our track. Green water came down the main induction into the engine room in such quantities at one time that the throttleman on the port side stopped the engines thinking we were diving, and he had failed to hear the signal. The after lookout was lashed to the radar mast with an airplane safety belt. He was spun completely around by one wave. Our boats[2] were again destroyed. Subsequent days were rough and

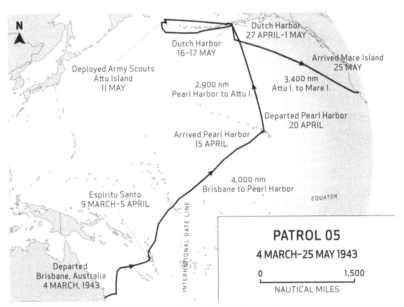

Her fifth patrol saw *Nautilus* travel from Australia to Alaska, eventually ending in California, covering more than eleven thousand nautical miles. ILLUSTRATION BY BETHANY JOURDAN.

2. Small wooden utility boats carried in the superstructure.

overcast with abnormal and sudden changes in the barometer readings. Winds would shift quickly from one direction to another. One star fix was obtained in three days after the hurricane, and sun sights were few." And later, "Ninety percent of the crew had chest colds at one time or another during this cruise."

In spite of the weather, Captain Brockman held day and night battle surface drills, where the crew fired the massive six-inch deck guns and other weapons for training. This necessary, but hazardous, activity led to two men receiving small wounds when a projectile in a 20-mm gun barrel exploded and burst. According to reports, the gunners failed to remove an oiled wooden slide used to house the gun in its waterproof container topside before test firing the weapon. Fortunately, the injuries were not serious, but worth noting in the patrol report.

On April 27, *Nautilus* negotiated the treacherous Unimak Pass and entered the Bering Sea. Severe weather and powerful tidal flows are common in the nine-mile-wide waterway among the Fox Islands, with occasional sudden blasts of wind descending from the mountainous coast to the sea, which are known as williwaws. Safely through, the submarine headed southwest to the naval base at Dutch Harbor on Unalaska Island. Arriving in the afternoon, they were cordially welcomed by the base commander, who made available all facilities and even issued winter clothing to the crew.

Nautilus had made the more than six thousand nautical mile voyage from Australia's tropical coast to frigid Dutch Harbor to embark a company of army special troops from the 7th Scout Company, otherwise known as the Alaskan Scouts. Comprised of Aleuts, Eskimos, sourdough prospectors, miners, hunters, trappers, and fishermen, these rugged outdoorsmen conducted reconnaissance and intelligence-gathering missions and spearheaded amphibious assaults during the campaign in the Aleutian Islands. They were specially trained in use of camouflage, survival skills, small unit tactics, and operations from rubber boats so they could deploy from PT boats, PBY flying boats, destroyers, and submarines. Half of the company (105 men), including their commander, Capt. William

Willoughby,[3] had just arrived on *Nautilus*'s sister ship, *Narwhal*, direct from San Diego. An additional 109 men, along with rubber boats and other equipment, were transported on the vessel *President Fillmore*. Along with 165 men of the army's 7th Cavalry Reconnaissance Company to be deployed from the destroyer USS *Kane*, this would form the Provisional Battalion. Their assignment: to land behind enemy lines and help retake the island of Attu, occupied by the Japanese in June of 1942.

Though Brockman may have been pleased with his reception at the base, he was far from pleased that the army troops were not ready for training when he arrived. By 0900 the next morning, with still no sign of the Scouts, Brockman had enough. He summoned his 1st lieutenant, Phil Eckart.

"Mr. Eckart, I want you to assemble a working party and head over to the *Fillmore*. Have the Scouts' commanding officer report to me with his key men so we can discuss procedures and get the training started. Time is not on our side!"

"Aye, aye, sir," Phil replied. He scurried off to find Chief Porterfield and gather several men. When they arrived on board *Fillmore*, they set to work stripping their rubber landing boats of useless gear to the consternation of the Scouts. By midafternoon ten boats and thirty Scouts were on board *Nautilus* and started indoctrination into submarine egress procedures. With only two days remaining before getting underway, Brockman was worried that the army troops would not have a chance to learn the hard-earned lessons of the Makin Island assault and would not be ready for their mission.

"Captain Willoughby, reporting as ordered, sir!" With a crisp salute, the commander of the Scouts stood before Captain Brockman, who had a reprimand at the ready.

---

3. A note on rankings and seniority: a captain in the army or Marines is the rank equivalent to a navy lieutenant. The commanding officer of a naval vessel is normally referred to as "captain," regardless of actual rank. Captain Willoughby, the commanding officer of the army Scouts, was therefore subordinate to Lieutenant Commander Brockman, the commanding officer of *Nautilus* (with the equivalent army rank of major). *Narwhal* was commanded by Lt. Cdr. Frank Latta, who was junior to Brockman. Thus, Brockman was in charge of the operation and *Nautilus* was the senior vessel; however, Captain Willoughby was embarked on *Narwhal*, which led to some confusion.

"Mr. Willoughby, I don't know what experience you have with submarine operations, but deploying on rubber boats at night is not duck soup. Your men need to practice procedures and get used to working with our crew, or this operation will fail before it starts!"

"Yes, sir! My men will all be present in the morning and ready to work, sir."

"And another thing," Brockman continued, "I am not happy that you are planning to ride on *Narwhal*. The troop commander should be on the senior vessel."

"Yes, sir," replied the army Scout. "But I was ordered to berth on *Narwhal*, and my company staff is there with me."

"Yes, so I gather." Brockman was somewhat mollified by Willoughby's professional demeanor and enthusiasm. He was expecting something of an attitude from a bunch of ragtag, backwoods, independent-minded, self-proclaimed heroes. What he was seeing was promising. "Well, we'll have to make the best of the situation, and a couple of days of training will have to do. By the way," said Brockman, changing his tone with a new topic, "I understand you played some football?"

"Ah . . . yes . . . at UCLA." Willoughby was surprised by the softening of Brockman's stern demeanor.

"Well, I heard you were pretty good. I played a little myself." Brockman was big enough to play football on the offensive line at the Naval Academy, part of what made him such an imposing figure. "I also understand you get things done. Must not be easy keeping discipline with the gang you're in charge of?"

"Sir, you will be impressed with the Scouts. They know what they're doing, and they'll follow orders." Sensing an opening, he ventured, "Captain, the men needed a little break after ten days on *Narwhal*. I promise you they'll be ready in the morning." The trip from San Diego had not been particularly eventful, but still was draining for troops not used to confined quarters, pitching decks, and foul air. They faced another submarine voyage, and then a night assault on an enemy held beach. A day of rest ashore was not unreasonable.

"OK, Mr. Willoughby, let's do our best to get the men ready for action. We learned a lot working with the Marines on Makin and Santo, and I want to make sure you learn it, too. Dismissed!" The army officer saluted and ducked out of the cabin, eager to get back topside in the Alaskan daylight. He joined his troops already working with Eckert and Porterfield on deck.

Problems were compounded overnight while charging air banks with compressed air needed to fill the rubber boats. One of the two vital air compressors suffered a "major casualty." Brockman was forced to take advantage of the base commander's offer of support, and workers began rebuilding the machine with little time for such major work.

In spite of the poor start, the army troops proved to be willing, able, and eager to work as a team with their navy counterparts. The next morning the entire Scout contingent was present and working with a will. *Narwhal*'s captain observed the training and began conducting similar drills of his own. That evening the ships held night landing exercises with excellent results. In the end, Captain Brockman had nothing but praise for Captain Willoughby's men, stating in his patrol report, "It was a pleasure to have the army Scouts on board. They cooperated in every way with the *Nautilus* personnel. This was one time when army and navy coordination could not have been better. The commanding officer is likewise

Nautilus at Dutch Harbor on April 30, 1943, training US Army Scouts in preparation for their landing on Attu. U.S. NAVY.

proud of his officers and crew. They went out of their way to make the army feel at home. Men gave their bunks to the army as well as some of their clothes. Likewise, the army gave our men some of their clothes." *Narwhal* got underway on the evening on April 30, and *Nautilus* at 2000 on May 1, after air compressor repairs were completed. Immediately, the boat ran into heavy seas "much to the discomfort of the army Scouts." Though the hardy troops were accustomed to harsh environments, it is not hard to imagine the feeling of helplessness when confined to cramped quarters, foul air, and a violently pitching deck with no stable visual frame of reference. Even some seasoned sailors find submarines disconcerting, and it takes days at best to overcome the intense queasiness of motion sickness. Some unfortunate individuals just cannot get used to it; *Narwhal*'s patrol report states on April 29 that two crewmen were transferred to the base in Dutch Harbor as "chronic seasickness cases." Besides mal de mer, the addition of 109 men to a vessel that normally carried fewer than one hundred presented some serious habitability challenges. During the night, the ship could ventilate spaces with fresh air while on the surface, but during most of the day while underwater, the air purification system could not keep up. Air became foul with diesel fumes, body odor, the stench of vomit, and cigarette smoke. Oxygen levels dropped such that it was added most days from a supply compressed in on-board tanks. The men tolerated the foul odors as best they could. They survived with oxygen levels so low that a match would not light. However, one thing that could not be tolerated was the high concentration of carbon dioxide.

CO_2 is present at levels around 0.04 percent in everyday air;[4] the recommended CO_2 limit for continuous safe breathing is 0.5 percent. The way of dealing with CO_2 buildup on *Nautilus* was to use a dry chemical (lithium hydroxide), which absorbs the gas. Each day the ship was using twice as many cans of the absorbent than normal, but CO_2 continued to rise. As levels approached 1 percent (twenty-five times the normal atmospheric level), many on board became irritable, developed headaches,

---

4. As of this writing, atmospheric CO_2 levels stand at 410 ppm (0.041 percent) and rising from a pre-industrial level of 280 ppm.

fatigue, and in more extreme cases, nausea. But CO_2 continued to rise, at times as high as 3 percent. All army passengers and off-duty crew were encouraged to sleep, which reduced oxygen consumption and exhalation, and smoking was prohibited after midafternoon each day. Things got worse on May 7 as the Scouts began to make ready for their disembarkation, continuously moving and breathing heavily. Captain Brockman stated, "To climb from control room to conning tower was worse than running a hundred yard dash." CO_2 pegged at 4 percent "and there was much panting." To the great consternation of all on board, owing to poor weather the assault was postponed, and *Nautilus* remained submerged ten miles offshore.

Other less serious but vexing problems included berthing. Torpedo storage skids were rigged with three bunks each, mattresses were placed on decks, and bunks had to be shared among crew and soldiers. One extra cook and one extra baker were added to the crew, each performing their difficult tasks admirably. Brockman commented, "The food was up to submarine standard, and many compliments were received from the army personnel." Head facilities were a problem as sanitary tanks would quickly fill. A recurring headache for the diving officer of the watch involved the twenty tons of crew and passengers walking about the ship, causing no end of noisy trim pump operation to keep the vessel stable. Operations in such cold water were a new challenge to the warm-water crew as condensation was ever present soaking people, clothing, and equipment. Electrical shorts to ground in equipment were common.

For the next several nights the submarine stood out thirty or forty miles from the island and surfaced to charge batteries and ventilate the ship, while each day they crept underwater close to the beach to reconnoiter the coast and prepare for landings. Because of continuing poor weather, the assault was postponed further so that the Scouts spent ten dismal days on the submarine before landings were finally called on May 10. By then, the air was so foul and the Scouts so miserable that they were more than eager to go ashore and face whatever the enemy could offer.

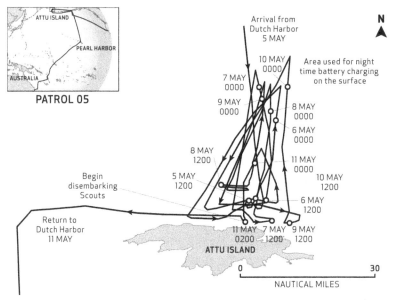

ATTU ISLAND

PEARL HARBOR

AUSTRALIA

PATROL 05

Arrival from
Dutch Harbor
5 MAY

N

10 MAY
0000

Area used for night
time battery charging
on the surface

7 MAY
0000

9 MAY
0000

8 MAY
0000

6 MAY
0000

8 MAY
1200

11 MAY
0000

Begin
disembarking
Scouts

5 MAY
1200

10 MAY
1200

6 MAY
1200

Return to
Dutch Harbor
11 MAY

11 MAY 7 MAY 9 MAY
0200   1200   1200

ATTU ISLAND

0   30

NAUTICAL MILES

Poor weather delayed the landings at Attu for several days. *Nautilus* stood offshore each night to charge her batteries and would submerge to reconnoiter the shoreline each day. ILLUSTRATION BY BETHANY JOURDAN.

Nautilus crept toward Blind Cove and Scarlett Beach in frigid fog and drizzle, calling for *Narwhal* using an acoustic underwater telephone called the QC to no reply. It was late afternoon, and the Scouts were to go ashore at 0200 in the morning. Brockman was annoyed that Captain Willoughby was not on board *Nautilus*, which was the command vessel. The Scout commander's plan was to send two lightly equipped rubber rafts from each submarine ten minutes ahead of the rest of the troops, but with no contact from *Narwhal* this could not be coordinated. As midnight approached, the submarine reached the rendezvous point and began circling, calling her sister ship repeatedly.

"Well Ozzie," Brockman said to Lynch, his experienced executive officer, "what we have here is a regular SNAFU.[5] And we haven't even started."

"Yes, sir. We're used to that, sir."

---

5. Situation normal: all fouled (or fucked) up.

"Right. And we knew it would happen, with Willoughby on *Narwhal* and us in charge. Well, we're in charge, so we'll take charge. Ozzie, roust the army and give them their battle breakfast. Let's get this operation under way!"

"Aye, sir," Ozzie replied. He called down to the galley to prepare a hearty meal of steak and eggs, the traditional breakfast given to troops before a combat operation. Just after midnight radar contact was made with *Narwhal*, but still no communication. Taking matters into his own hands, Brockman ordered the Scouts to the gun hatches at 0145 and called to *Narwhal* that they were disembarking troops and ordered her to complete their own operations by 0300. No reply was received. Unknown to Brockman, their companion vessel had likewise detected *Nautilus* with radar, and Captain Latta was making his own preparations to disembark troops according to plan.

Using the method rehearsed with Carlson's Marines on Espiritu Santo, and practiced with the Scouts, the submarine crews dragged the rubber boats topside on the after deck and inflated them with compressed air. They loaded them with equipment and helped the army troops clamber aboard. The sailors went below and secured the hatches, leaving the troops on deck.

From the bridge, the officer of the deck gave the order, "Open vents, aft main ballast!" As air rushed out of the aft ballast tank vents, water flooded in, and the stern gradually settled. Soon the rubber boats were floating free, and the Scouts began the long paddle to shore. This was no easy feat, as the soldiers had to paddle two and a half miles through thick fog and 20-degree temperatures at night, accompanied by wind and drizzle. Captain Brockman watched the two hour ordeal on radar and by infrared light, maintaining position offshore. In time, all 214[6] of Willoughby's Scouts were safely ashore. Now *Nautilus* detected a radar contact at 9,300 yards. Surmising this to be USS *Kane* with the Recon Company, Brockman decided to retire so as not to cause *Kane* any added worry. He took his boat slowly westward away from shore, keeping close

---

6. Sources vary as to the number of Scouts deployed from the submarines, with numbers stated as high as 244. The patrol reports are quite clear that there were 109 men on *Nautilus* and 105 on *Narwhal*.

watch of the beach for any signals. Soon, the 165 man Recon Company was ashore, and Willoughby's entire force of 379 trained commandos, designated the Provisional Battalion, prepared to leave the beach and face their first objective: the summit of a three hundred foot cliff at the head of the cove, guarding the valley beyond.

Fortunately, the last place the Japanese expected a landing was in Blind Cove. The submarine and destroyer-embarked force was able to get ashore and begin their march with no opposition. Their initial enemy was the cold, wet, and fog. One of Willoughby's men commented, "It was easy to get completely turned around in the thick-moving mist that made everything vague." To make matters worse, the force could not establish communications with headquarters or any of the other units landing on Attu. Malfunctioning equipment not suited for the harsh Alaskan conditions and the loss of vital communications gear at the main beachhead cut the battalion off from other commands.

With dawn came a new and unexpected development. Aircraft from the escort carrier USS *Nassau*, supporting the invasion, flew down the coast. Seeing the army rubber boats bobbing near shore, and assuming they were enemy equipment, the navy pilots felt compelled to strafe and sink them. Like it or not, the Provisional Battalion was on its own, with no option to retreat back to sea.

With poor maps, just one and a half days' rations, dense fog, awful weather, and some of the worst terrain ahead of them, Willoughby and his men turned their backs to the sea and began to climb.

In the late afternoon of May 11, 1943, 2,200 men of the US 7th Infantry Division came ashore on a wide, sheltered beach called Massacre Bay, on the southeast side of the Aleutian island of Attu. The locale was so named on account of the killing of fifteen island natives by Russian fur hunters in 1745. In spite of the ominous moniker, the invading force landed unopposed and without casualty. The biggest problem to that point was the harsh Aleutian weather; the assault had been planned for May 7, but strong winds had forced a delay. The invading ships retired to sea, returning on the tenth, but a dense fog demanded for further postponement.

A collision between two destroyers in the impenetrable haze further delayed the following morning's landings on the southern beachhead, so that the first troops did not come ashore until 1630. Regardless, the entire force, vanguard of an invading army of 12,000 troops, was landed and the beachhead declared secure by 2200. Within the hour, Maj. Gen. Albert Brown established his headquarters ashore and the force prepared for the next morning's advance up the valley to the northwest.

The bay and valley were flanked on both sides by sharp mountain ridges rising over a thousand feet. Detached platoons scaled these peaks to clear the high ground and protect the advancing main body from enemy flanking attacks. The discovery of recently abandoned guns covering the beach that had never been fired deepened the mystery of why the Japanese failed to challenge the landings in Massacre Bay. Several Japanese soldiers were seen hurrying deeper into the hills, and a recently deserted camp was found, left burned and smoking. Other than occasional and ineffective sniper fire, the first day passed without incident. Up to that point, all was going according to plan. That Japanese plan, that is.

Col. Yasuyo Yamasaki, commanding the 2,400-strong Japanese garrison, had developed a sound defensive strategy based on deception and excellent use of the dramatic terrain of Attu. The main Japanese camps were set on Holtz Bay and Chichagof Harbor on the northeast side of the island. They were heavily defended with well-prepared positions and plans put in place for successive withdrawals to nested fortifications. Batteries of dual-purpose guns, effective against both aircraft and ground troops, guarded key locations. Defensive positions on the south side of the island were either absent or heavily disguised; dummy positions were constructed at other locations to tempt a landing on the sheltered beach of Massacre Bay. From hard-won experience, the Japanese knew that the invaders would not be able to easily move equipment, artillery, and supplies through the mountainous terrain and soft tundra, which quickly churned to mud under the wheels and tracks of vehicles. Allied air support would be limited by incessant fog and rain. Yamasaki planned to lure the Americans into the valley at the head of Massacre Bay and into a narrow pass two miles from the beach. At that point, the Japanese would engage the attackers from high ground on three sides and hope to annihilate them or force their withdrawal.

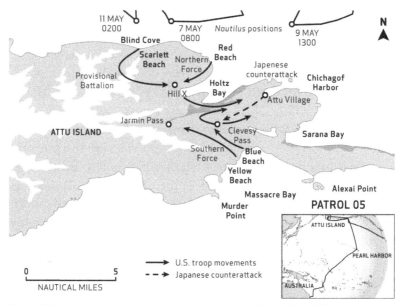

Major US and Japanese troop movements during the Battle of Attu. ILLUSTRA-
TION BY BETHANY JOURDAN.

General Brown's forces made little progress. Japanese observers in the
fog-shrouded ridges watched their every move. Sporadic small arms fire
from the heights intensified as troops neared Jarmin Pass at the head of
the valley. American artillery, mired in the soft tundra near the beachhead, made little impression on the defenders. Repeated attempts to force
the pass were beaten back as US casualties began to mount. The landing
craft used to bring supplies ashore were being lost at an alarming rate to
the weather, grounding in uncharted waters, and enemy fire; by May 18
only three of the original ninety-three remained in operation. Supplies,
ammunition, and casualties had to be carried up and down the rugged
cliffs and across boggy tundra. Soon, more men were carrying supplies
(and returning with casualties) than were fighting. Communications were
impaired by poor resistance of field radios to moisture, snow, and ice.
Most of the headquarters communications gear were lost when a supply
ship ran aground.[7] General Brown was unable to relay information to

---

7. The ship, USS *Perida*, was pulled to safety and eventually unloaded, but not for several days.

the joint commander, Vice Admiral Rockwell, and he could not call for reinforcements from the afloat reserve. Though heavily outnumbered, the Japanese held commanding positions and fought with great determination, forcing the infantry advance to grind to a halt, just six hundred yards from the pass. In spite of all efforts, the main American force remained bottled up in Massacre Valley for the next six days.

Attu is the westernmost island of the Aleutian chain, less than 650 nautical miles from the World War II Japanese base of Paramushiro on the Kurile Islands (today part of Russia), and 1,200 nautical miles from Hokkaido, the northernmost of Japan's main islands. It is thirty-five miles long by twenty miles wide with eternally snow-covered peaks that reach nearly three thousand feet and dominate the island. Some on both sides of the conflict (including legendary US general Billy Mitchell) considered the Aleutian Islands to be of great strategic importance. The Japanese sought to occupy Attu and neighboring Kiska Island to prevent an American strike across the North Pacific and also to base potential attacks of their own on the West Coast of the United States. In spite of this, neither side sought to garrison large numbers of troops or develop substantial installations on such remote and inhospitable locales.

The Doolittle Raid on Tokyo, launched from the aircraft carrier USS *Hornet* on April 18, 1942, was a factor in Japanese war planning. Unable to imagine that B-25 light bombers could be deployed from carriers, the Japanese concluded that the planes must have been launched from an Aleutian airbase. That led to Operation AF, the attack on the US. Navy base at Dutch Harbor on June 3 and landings on Attu and neighboring Kiska on June 6–7, which took place simultaneously to the larger Operation MI, the attack on Midway in the Central Pacific. This was the first and only time that US territory was occupied by an invading army.

When Japanese troops stormed ashore on Attu on June 7, they found it absent of any American military presence. In fact, the only inhabitants of the island were some forty-five native Unangax Aleuts, along with Foster Jones, a radio technician and weather station operator, and his wife, Etta, a schoolteacher, both in their sixties. During the attack, several Unangax were killed, and Jones and his wife were taken and separated. Foster was either killed or died by his own hand, depending on accounts. Etta and the forty-two surviving natives were taken as captives and sent to prison camp in Japan. On Kiska, the invaders found a ten-man US Navy weather station detachment, which they quickly overwhelmed. Over the next year, the Japanese occupied the islands, built installations and defensive positions, and made plans for an airstrip, which was never completed. Resupply and reinforcement of the garrisons was interrupted in March 1943 when a two-cruiser US force met a Japanese naval squadron escorting supply ships in the Battle of the Komandorski Islands. Though facing a superior force of four cruisers, the Americans forced the Japanese to withdraw, preventing further reinforcement of the Aleutians. Future supplies arrived only by submarine.

The slow progress in constructing a Japanese airbase on the islands was largely attributed to the wretchedly inhospitable weather. Though the climate was not of arctic severity, conditions were typically a cold, damp, fog, with temperatures not much above freezing, even in the summer months. The sun appeared less than one full day per month, with full overcast skies on average twenty-five days. One could expect two weeks of rain out of four, and steady winds. Even in May, during the Allied invasion, temperatures during battle were reported as low as 10 degrees. Ironically, above-freezing daytime temperatures led to softening of the tundra, which hindered movement of vehicles and equipment. Combat operations on Attu relied almost entirely on the foot soldier, who could expect little support from advanced technologies of warfare.

Members of the US 7th Infantry Division may have been surprised to learn they were chosen for the operation to retake Attu, as they had been formed and trained for motorized desert operations in North Africa. With the German field marshal Erwin Rommel in retreat, troops were reassigned, and January 1943 found the 7th redesignated from a motorized unit to a light infantry division. An intense period of retraining commenced, including a few weeks of amphibious landing exercises. The soldiers were not well equipped or prepared for the severe conditions of Attu, but in a few short months found themselves engaged in fierce combat in a harsh environment. As the battle for the island stretched from days to weeks, men began to succumb to frostbite, trench foot, and exposure from the harsh elements in large numbers.

The Allied plan to retake Attu, otherwise known as "Operation Land Crab," called for a naval bombardment of the Massacre beachhead, but this was prevented owing to severe fog. Battleships USS *Idaho* and USS *Pennsylvania* (in its first action since suffering damage during the December 1941 Pearl Harbor attack) instead shelled the Japanese base at Chichagof Harbor. Likewise, air support by Canadian reconnaissance and fighter-bomber aircraft was limited by weather. The twelve thousand troops of the 7th Light Infantry Division were largely unsupported by sea or air. Owing to the landscape, operation of heavy tracked vehicles was impossible, and even artillery pieces had to be drawn into position by hand. By the end of the first day of battle on May 12, US troops were held up in a narrow canyon without air or naval gunfire support, limited supplies and failed communications, and soaking wet in the freezing cold. The Japanese held the high ground with well-prepared positions and could not be pushed out despite repeated attempts over the ensuing days. It was a dire situation.

However, there was another element to the Allied plan. Anticipating the challenge of attacking through a valley with the main body, a smaller force of a single infantry battalion with supporting units was to make a daring landing on a tiny one hundred-yard beach on the western arm of Holtz Bay. It was code-named "Red Beach," and located just three miles from the Japanese base. Landing craft had to negotiate a winding course through submerged rocks and could approach no closer than a thousand yards from the beach. From there, soldiers had to climb into small whaleboats and row ashore under heavy fog. This maneuver was completely unanticipated by the defenders, and owing to surprise and the poor visibility, 1,500 troops came ashore unopposed by evening of the first day. Under waning twilight, the battalion advanced along the western shore of Holtz Bay toward their initial objective, a group of peaks designated "Hill X." From this location, the northern force could overlook the Japanese base at the head of the harbor from a commanding position.

At this point, lack of a good survey of the island hindered the advance. Owing to fog, growing darkness, and poor maps, the lead troops were ordered to halt and establish defensive positions short of Hill X and await the dawn to occupy the heights. A small group of enemy soldiers were surprised by the Americans, and two of them escaped to warn the base. The Japanese promptly sent troops to occupy Hill X and defend the high ground. The initiative had been lost, and the northern force spent the next few days in a bloody struggle to take the hill and continue their advance.

This task might have proven impossible but for a third element of the Allied plan. Further to the west of Holtz Bay, just offshore of a small inlet with a spit of sand called Blind Cove, lurked the submarines USS *Nautilus* and her sister USS *Narwhal*. Captain Brockman was anxiously watching for signs of trouble as Captain Willoughby and his Provisional Battalion of highly trained special force troops moved inland, assigned to strike east into Holtz Bay behind the Japanese opposing the northern force.

The main force was held up in Massacre Valley, and the northern force was stalemated at Hill X. The success of Operation Land Crab was now in the hands of the small band of submarine commandos.

Upon landing in Blind Cove, Captain Willoughby attempted to contact his commanders, but had no luck. On its own, the Provisional Battalion headed up the valley behind the enemy's rear lines, according to plan. At first, the Americans were unopposed, and progress was swift. Expecting a quick linkup with the northern force just on the other side of the ridges they faced, the cold and hungry troops consumed their limited rations with no thought of a prolonged battle. By the middle of the first night after landing, the battalion had entered the valley to the west of Hill X; unknown to them, the northern force was stalled on the opposite side. On the morning of May 12, the Japanese finally reacted to the forces behind them and pinned the troopers down with withering fire. The advance came to a sudden halt.

Over the next two days the battalion continued to pressure the Japanese, clawing their way yard at a time to the high ground to the west of Hill X. By May 14 Captain Willoughby's battalion was in bad shape. They had chosen to carry extra ammunition in lieu of rations, and they had not eaten for days. Attempts to drop supplies had been thwarted by weather and difficult terrain. Mortar rounds were exhausted, and small arms ammunition was low. Fighting was continuous, day and night, with little chance for sleep. The freezing conditions had taken more of a toll on the troops than the enemy, and half of the force was dead, wounded, suffering from exposure, or frostbitten. Still, they fought, having no choice but to press up the valley behind Hill X and try to link up with the northern force, stuck on the other side. In spite of their hunger and fatigue, they fought so ferociously that one Japanese officer estimated he was facing an entire division.

As the battle wore on, the Japanese found themselves in an untenable position, able to hold off the main forces of Americans from the north and south, but also facing determined pressure from Willoughby's men from the west. On May 15, fearing their positions on Hill X would be cut off, Colonel Yamasaki ordered his forces to withdraw to the east, around Holtz Bay to their base at Chichagof Harbor.

The forces facing the Provisional Battalion suddenly evaporated, and a linkup with the northern force was finally achieved. Of the 379-man force that had landed in Blind Cove four days earlier, combat casualties tallied eleven men killed[8] and twenty wounded; however, many more had suffered cruelly from the conditions with severe frostbite and even gangrene such that only forty of the troops could walk. The others crawled, or were carried.

The Japanese retreat from Hill X exposed the defenders at the head of Massacre Valley to attack from the rear. On May 18 they likewise withdrew toward Chichagof Harbor, allowing a linkup of the northern and southern forces. Thanks to the valiant efforts of Captain Willoughby's Scouts and the Recon Company, the stalemate was broken.

8. One of the men lost in the action was Capt. Emory A. Austin, commander of the Recon Company. Later, Blind Cove was renamed Austin Cove in his honor. Also, the valley west of Hill X was given the name Scout Canyon.

Captain Willoughby's most severe casualties were evacuated, and the remaining 165 men, fewer than half of the original force, were sent to bivouac at the rear of the American lines with an engineer battalion to recuperate. The rest of the 7th Division pushed into Chichagof Harbor over the next few days. The situation was dire for the Japanese, who had fought courageously and had made excellent use of well-prepared defenses, but were outnumbered five to one at the start of the battle and had suffered serious attrition over the first week of fighting. Imperial headquarters recognized that their position was hopeless and ordered an evacuation of as much of the force as possible by submarine. Colonel Yamasaki's men continued to resist US forces using an intricate network of fighting positions linked by trenches, hoping to gain time to allow their submarines to reach the harbor. But the days wore on, and no submarines appeared; Admiral Rockwell's naval blockade was impenetrable.

Finally, by May 28, Yamasaki had lost 70 percent of his force and was down to just seven hundred battle weary men, with supplies and ammunition nearly gone. Evacuation was impossible. Surrender was not an option. As he saw it, the only path to success lay in a counterattack through the weakest point in the American lines to reestablish a defensive position to the southwest and hope for resupply there. It was a desperate plan with little hope. The Japanese commander sent a final message to headquarters, burned all documents, and ordered six hundred hospitalized men who could no longer fight to die by their own hand. Those who could or would not were given morphine overdoses. The focus of Yamasaki's plan of attack was to have his men charge into American lines and attempt to punch through a gap later named Clevesy Pass. In their path were US artillery positions that he hoped to capture. Battalion engineers, artillerymen, cooks, support troops, and the bivouacked Provisional Battalion lightly defended this area. Captain Willoughby's battle was not yet over.

Just after midnight on May 29, the Japanese attack appeared out of the fog and slammed into the unsuspecting American lines. The US positions were quickly overrun, and troops retreated to high ground in disarray. As the spearhead neared Clevesy Pass, the sounds of approaching battle spurred the men there to throw up a hasty defense. A group of sixteen officers, Captain Willoughby among them, absorbed the first blows. Eleven were killed, and the Scout commander was wounded in the face and hit by hand grenade fragments. The Japanese swept on toward the artillery positions, intending to turn the guns on the Americans and cover their movement into the valley beyond. Colonel Yamasaki's desperate gamble was succeeding.

At this point, bolstered by the remaining men of the Provisional Battalion, resistance from the rear echelon troops stiffened. Many Japanese had been killed in the initial charge and in their first attack of the pass, but they regrouped and stormed into the American defenses, many without ammunition. Fierce hand-to-hand combat ensued, US troops facing a desperate enemy with little hope of survival and no thought of surrender. The line held. Colonel Yamasaki died in the assault, and a group of his men, facing capture, committed suicide with hand grenades. Remaining small groups of Japanese, refusing to surrender, were killed. The next day, the Americans moved into Chichagof Harbor and the battle for Attu was finally over.

In the end, only twenty-eight prisoners were taken of the nearly 2,400 defenders. US losses numbered 3,829: 549 killed, 1,148 wounded by the enemy, and more than 2,000 casualties to the elements. By some measure, this was the second deadliest US battle of the Pacific War (behind Iwo Jima). Captain William Willoughby was evacuated and survived the war, eventually achieving the rank of colonel. The Alaskan Scouts and the 7th Reconnaissance Company were awarded Distinguished Unit Citations for their actions.

The retaking of Attu, though a costly victory, taught the US military valuable lessons in amphibious assaults, cold-weather operations, and logistical support of a far-flung battlefield. The engagement was also costly for the widely stretched Japanese forces, which could ill afford the loss of troops and equipment. Japanese ships were diverted from Truk to attempt to evacuate Attu, leaving other Pacific areas vulnerable. For example, Rendova, in the central Solomons was left largely undefended, and the island was taken with ease by US Army and Marine troops in June, providing a base of operations for the New Georgia campaign.

Threatened by the loss of Attu, the Japanese withdrew their garrison at Kiska Island at the beginning of August. Two weeks later, more than thirty thousand American and Canadian troops landed to find the island abandoned. Although there was no enemy to fight, the hostile environment of the Aleutians led to more than three hundred casualties, some by booby traps or mines left by the Japanese, a number by friendly fire, but many from accidents, disease, and frostbite. With the retaking of Kiska, the Aleutian Islands campaign came to an end after fourteen months of fighting.

A particularly sad bit of history in this affair involves the fate of the Aleuts from the Aleutian Island chain and the Pribilof Islands (located in the Bering Sea, about three hundred miles north of the Aleutians). After the Unangax Aleut people of Attu were taken as prisoners by Japan, the US government decided to evacuate the remaining villages in the region, ostensibly for their own safety. In short order, some 881 Aleuts from nine different island villages were transported to abandoned salmon canneries in the eastern panhandle of Alaska near Juneau, almost two thousand miles from their homes. In some cases, they were given a scant hour to pack, and were allowed to take but one suitcase of belongings. Under the jurisdiction of the US Fish and Wildlife Service, the internees were housed in leaky, rotting buildings with limited facilities. Kept there for the duration of the war long after US forces had secured their home islands, they were largely neglected. According to *Alaska's Forgotten War* by Kortnie Horazdovsky (2018), some 118 Aleuts perished from lack of warmth, food, and medical care during the interment. Nazi prisoners in a nearby POW camp were treated far more humanely.

The forty-two Unangax Aleuts, captured by the Japanese when they first invaded Attu, did not fare better. As many as twenty-two of them died in captivity (some sources quote numbers as low as sixteen, still quite a sad outcome). Mrs. Etta Jones, also sent to prison camp in Japan, was liberated at the end of the war and lived in Florida to the age of eighty-six. In 1988, forty-two years after returning to their villages, the US government recognized that the constitutional rights of the Aleuts had been violated. Subsequently, Congress passed the Aleutian and Pribilof Islands Restitution Act, which paid $12,000 to Aleut surviving victims of the US internment camps.

Nick and Jerry found themselves again back in the *Nautilus* messroom, mugs of coffee in hand. After deploying the Scouts, the submarine was sent around the island to patrol, looking for enemy shipping approaching from the southwest. However, seas were so rough that they could not run at periscope depth, and visibility so poor that little could be seen. Surfacing in heavy seas, the ship was directed to proceed to Dutch Harbor, where it arrived for a brief refueling stop on the evening of May 16. Departing the next afternoon, they headed south, back to Pearl Harbor. Though happy to be leaving the Aleutian cold behind, the crew was not eager to face another arduous mission.

"Well Nick, I guess we can look forward to sweating again." Jerry looked down into his mug. "I never thought I'd be wishing for heat."

"Yeah. What am I gonna do with this army jacket? I sure was happy to get it, but it'll just be taking up space down south," replied Nick.

"Maybe you can trade it in Pearl for something useful. Anyway, it was big of those Scouts to give us some of their extra gear. I wonder how those poor mud eaters are doing?" Jerry couldn't have known that by this time Willoughby and his men were limping along to link up with the northern force, having succeeded in pushing the Japanese off of Hill X.

"They were sure cool hands. Not a gink in the lot of 'em. Wonder if we'll ever see them again?" Nick sighed. "Well, what's next for old *Nautilus?*"

Just then, Red Porterfield stuck his head in. "You guys hear the scuttlebutt?"

"No, what is it?" they asked in unison.

"It's true! We're headed to Mare Island for overhaul!"

"No shit!" exclaimed Jerry. "Frisco, here we come!"[9]

Phil Eckert appeared behind Chief Porterfield and grabbed his shoulder. "That's not all," he said with a grin. "This here salty old sailor is getting a promotion!"

Nick declared, "Whoa! What do chiefs get promoted to? King?"

Red smirked, "Naw, they're actually going to *de*mote me. Down to ensign."

"Well, congratulations anyway, Chief!" They all stood and shook his hand. "Well deserved!" Jerry's smiling face suddenly dropped. He said anxiously, "Does that mean you're gonna leave us?" Red was a popular figure on board; a great leader and mentor.

"Not sure, Jerry. I've asked to stay. We'll see what the navy says."

"We'll try to keep him," said Eckert. "If I have anything to say about it. Which I don't. Anyway, we need a rookie ensign on board, so we lieutenants have somebody to boss around!"

The crew was pleased with the change of plans, and Brockman noted in his patrol report that "morale increased one hundred per cent."

Nautilus turned her bow to the southeast and headed for safe and sunny California.

---

9. Mare Island Naval Shipyard and submarine base was in Vallejo, California, on the northeast shore of San Pablo Bay in the San Francisco-Oakland Bay area. It was the first US Navy base established on the Pacific Ocean, and *Nautilus* was the first submarine built there. The shipyard built and overhauled submarines and other vessels until it closed in 1996.

CHAPTER SIX

Tarawa

The worn and battered *Nautilus* and her weary crew spent the summer in Mare Island, California, undergoing an extensive yard overhaul. Major repairs included welding around rivet heads to make fuel tanks tight, replacement of all air flasks, installation of new battery elements, and installation of new deck torpedo tubes. Crewmen had a chance to enjoy some R&R, visit family, and attend training schools. Thirty fresh crewmen came aboard, and two new officers, most notably Cdr. William Irvin, the new commanding officer. Bill Brockman was relieved after five markedly successful patrols and three Navy Cross awards, among other accolades. He went on to command a submarine division, briefly taking charge of USS *Haddock* (SS-231) for a patrol after the boat's captain was injured in a jeep accident. Brockman finished the war commanding the oiler USS *Cahaba* (AO-82), providing the vital but dangerous task of fueling vessels in combat, dodging submarines, and defying kamikaze air attacks. Brockman continued his successful naval career after the war, advancing to the rank of rear admiral upon retirement.

Shipmate Red Porterfield said that Brockman was "not the smartest person I ever met, but he was very aggressive in combat."[1] He was blunt, detail oriented, and a "lead from the front" captain. Buzz Lee described Brockman as "an excellent commanding officer, very demanding, always on the job, very aggressive. When the general alarm sounded on *Nautilus* the crew knew Brockman would be taking them into harm's way."

---

1. Interview with Floyd "Red" Porterfield, February 2000.

Yeoman Bob Burrell recalled that the crew "loved and trusted him and would go anywhere with him. He promised he would take us there and bring us back. And he always did."[2]

Brockman found success in civilian life in his hometown of Baltimore, Maryland, as a chemical company executive. He achieved further fame appearing on the back cover of the February 1955 edition of *The Saturday Evening Post*, posing in an advertisement for Camel cigarettes. Standing behind a globe, a sextant, a model of his famous submarine, and other nautical memorabilia, Brockman cast a dashing and confident figure, a sly and knowing hint of a smile brushing his lips. A bejeweled nautilus pin decorated his tie. The accompanying quote was, "In twenty-four years I've tried 'em all. Nothing beats Camels for flavor . . . and the more years you smoke 'em, the more you appreciate their mildness!"

Irvin came to *Nautilus* as an experienced submariner, but would have large shoes to fill. Fortunately, most of the wardroom remained intact, with veterans Lynch, Foster, Eckert, Davis, and Winner staying aboard, joined by the experienced Red Porterfield, a newly minted ensign. Irvin would rely heavily on those men, particularly Lynch, in the patrols to come.

While the boat was in overhaul, the Submarine Force was abuzz with major news. On April 18, 1943, a flight of eighteen US Army Air Forces twin engine P-38 Lightning fighters attacked a bomber carrying Japanese admiral Isoroku Yamamoto, commander of the Imperial Japanese Navy and architect of the Pearl Harbor attack. Yamamoto was on an inspection tour of forces in the Solomons, and navy intelligence intercepted and decoded messages detailing his itinerary, the type of plane he would be flying in, and number of escort aircraft. To avoid detection and guarantee a surprise attack, the mission entailed an over-water flight of a thousand miles round trip, requiring the long range P-38 fighters with extra fuel tanks added. In what was called Operation Vengeance, the Americans encountered Yamamoto's flight of two bombers (the second carrying his chief of staff) with six escorting fighters, and set upon them shooting down both bombers and a Zero. Yamamoto, his chief of staff,

---

2. Interview with Bob Burrell by Liv Schad, May 2004.

and seventeen other Japanese were killed. One P-38 with its US pilot, Lt. Raymond Hine, was lost. The news of this dramatic affair was first reported by the Japanese on May 21, raising the morale of Americans as details were covered in the US press over the coming days. The full story (including the code-breaking operation that directed the attack) was not revealed to the public until after the war.

June 1943 marked another revelation, this one of particular relevance to the submarine force. Up to this point in the undersea war, Japanese depth charges could be set for a maximum depth of two hundred feet, and American subs could hope to evade them by diving to their designed test depth of three hundred feet—or even greater. This tactic was effective in the early part of the war, allowing American submarines to eventually slink far enough away to escape detection by the attacking destroyer's sonar. *Nautilus*, in particular, almost certainly avoided destruction because of shallow-set charges on more than one occasion. This happy state of affairs lasted until Andrew May, a US congressman from Kentucky returning from a war zone visit in June 1943, revealed this vitally secret information in a press conference. Within months, the Japanese modified their depth charges and changed tactics, exploding their weapons at deeper depths. Admiral Lockwood, commander of the US submarine fleet in the Pacific said, "I hear Congressman May said the Jap depth charges are not set deep enough. He would be pleased to know that the Japs set them deeper now." The sinking of as many as ten boats (with loss of eight hundred American lives) may have resulted from Congressman May's disclosure. He was never prosecuted for his deadly breach of security, but was later convicted of bribery and war profiteering, and sent to federal prison.

These losses were felt at a personal level, at home and aboard ship. After the war, Foy Hester noted in his copy of *United States Submarine Losses, World War II*,[3] the names of thirty-four shipmates and friends who were lost on eighteen US submarines. Bob Burrell could remember every submarine lost with friends aboard sixty years later. Knowledge of the grievous losses and facing constant danger must have had a terribly

---

3. *United States Submarine Losses, World War II*, NAVPERS 15784 (1949).

draining effect on the men. However, a chance to rest and recover in California was the tonic the crew needed. Said Hester,[4] "It was after thirteen months at sea that we were back in Mare Island for another overhaul; I began to see it was possible to live through the war. I began to have hopes. Those thirteen months, in which we made five patrols, some of them were pretty rugged." In late August, a refurbished *Nautilus* and her revitalized crew set sail from Mare Island, heading to Pearl Harbor and another mission in the enemy-held Pacific.

Nautilus departed Mare Island on the morning of August 17, 1943, under overcast skies, light winds, and calm seas. The transit to Pearl Harbor was uneventful, arriving at the submarine base late afternoon August 31. The crew would spend two weeks primarily engaged in much needed training exercises. Twenty-six new men were integrated into the crew, which expanded the total to ninety-four; thirty-one crewmen, veterans of all five previous *Nautilus* patrols, formed a core of experience to mentor the rookies. In the wardroom, only Lynch and Porterfield had served on all five prior sorties. The training agenda was extensive, including torpedo transfer at sea, airplane and submarine fueling, boat handling and rigging, torpedo firing, and gunnery practice. The crew also rehearsed their upcoming mission by conducting reconnaissance drills at Barbers Point Beach.

Commander Irvin would be assigned a relatively easy mission for his first patrol, a special reconnaissance of the islands of Tarawa, Kuma, Butaritari, Abemama, and Makin in support of the upcoming Gilbert Islands campaign. Joining the wardroom for the trip were Marine Capt. James Jones and army Capt. Donald Newman, who would serve as observers. Jones would later lead an assault on the island of Abemama (then called Apamama). *Nautilus* got underway from Pearl Harbor on the afternoon of September 16 and headed southwest on a two thousand nautical mile transit. On September 25, the submarine crept close to the

---

4. Hester (2018) (from an entry in Foy Hester's diary written during the overhaul period in Mare Island).

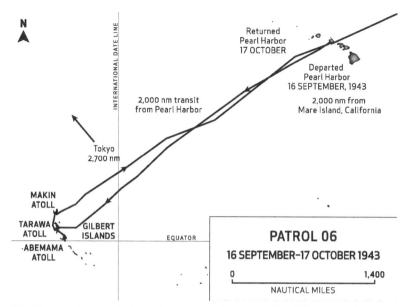

N

INTERNATIONAL DATE LINE

Returned
Pearl Harbor
17 OCTOBER

Departed
Pearl Harbor
16 SEPTEMBER, 1943

2,000 nm transit
from Pearl Harbor

2,000 nm from
Mare Island, California

Tokyo
2,700 nm

MAKIN
ATOLL

TARAWA
ATOLL

GILBERT
ISLANDS

EQUATOR

ABEMAMA
ATOLL

PATROL 06

16 SEPTEMBER-17 OCTOBER 1943

0   1,400

NAUTICAL MILES

Nautilus conducted photographic reconnaissance of the Gilbert Island chain during her sixth patrol. ILLUSTRATION BY BETHANY JOURDAN.

shoreline of Tarawa while Ozzie Lynch prepared his camera equipment and set up a tiny darkroom in the lower sonar space.

The first problem encountered was poor charts. *Nautilus* worked her way up the east shore of the atoll, discovering along the way that the planimetric charts provided for the mission had to be rotated by eleven degrees to match the actual coastline, among other significant errors. Irvin and his team took note of shore installations, vessels, landmarks, soundings, and water currents as Ozzie snapped photographs. The ship was provided with official navy photographic equipment, but Lynch had his own excellent camera, a German Prizma. According to Bob Burrell, the quality of the Prizma was far superior to the American-made issue, such that after their patrol, the navy sought civilian owners of the German cameras, asking the equipment be loaned for the war effort. Burrell said that as many as a dozen were received.[5]

---

5. According to Blair (1975), advertisements in photographic trade journals fetched ten Prizmas, which were used on all subsequent submarine photo missions.

After surveying the coast, the submarine spent two days "working" Bititu,[6] where most of the Japanese garrison was located and supported by an airbase. Approaching to within four thousand yards of the island and fighting two knots of swirling current, they observed many military installations as well as patrol vessels and a hospital ship in the lagoon. From time to time aircraft were sighted and *Nautilus* dove deep to avoid detection in the clear waters.

On September 30 a dispatch arrived from headquarters.

"Captain, a message." Buzz Lee handed Irvin a clipboard with the decoded missive. Executive Officer Ozzie Lynch was in the wardroom, having a bite before his reconnaissance work of the day. Irvin walked in and sat down.

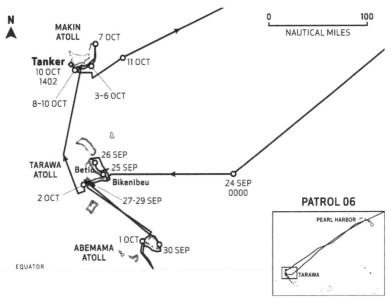

Nautilus surveyed several atolls in the Gilbert Islands, correcting charts and surveying prospective troop landing sites. ILLUSTRATION BY BETHANY JOURDAN.

---

6. Today known as Betio (pronounced Bes-she-o), part of the Republic of Kiribati (pronounced Kiribass), the island lies on the southwest corner of the atoll Tarawa and is the main center of population and major port.

"Ozzie, take a look at this." He passed the clipboard over and waited while Lynch read the document. After a few moments, he let out a low whistle.

"Survey the reef and take soundings?" He looked up from the document. "That reef is barely five hundred yards from shore!"

"Right," confirmed Irvin. "We'd have to surface at night and find some volunteers to paddle in on a raft. Right under those guns."

"Captain, sir, according to our information, those guns have a range of eighteen thousand yards, and the Japanese see real well at night. We'd be sitting ducks under those guns. Also, the currents are strong. We have some cool hands on this boat, and we've done some crazy capers, but this is a tough row of buttons to shine."

"You're right. I'd hate to ask for volunteers for something like this," agreed Irvin. He thought for a bit. "I'm not one to turn down a job, but this is too risky."

Irvin composed a reply to headquarters, noting the particular dangers associated with the assignment, including the fact that low tide occurred just after dark, and their battery would be low from the day's submerged reconnaissance. He concluded that they would conduct a high periscope observation of the reef rather than risk the ship and the greater mission.

One cannot fault Irvin for the decision, and it is the captain's prerogative to execute his orders with some latitude taking into consideration circumstances and risks. But as events unfolded, better intelligence about that reef might have saved many Marine lives in the eventual assault on Tarawa.

Nautilus continued her mission, heading south to Abemama. They circled the island and observed the two nearby islets, taking many photos. Again, the chart required a significant rotation to match reality. The crew did not know it at the time, but they (and Captain Jones) would be returning in a few weeks. Finishing the work at Abemama, the ship headed north and again ran close to Tarawa, this time checking radar targets and making further observations of the reef. Curiously, no distinctive radar returns were observed, leading Irvin to conclude that most every structure on the island was made of wood. With the periscope high, Irvin took a look at one of the observation towers and noted two

Japanese sentries gesturing with excitement. Clearly, it was time to leave. *Nautilus* went deep and headed north to familiar Makin Atoll (including Butaritari and Kuma). By this time the weather was deteriorating and overcast skies made for very poor light conditions. The charts had not been improved since the raid the previous August, and wicked currents made navigation hazardous. A bright half-moon was high in the sky at sunset, shortening the time the submarine could be surfaced close to shore. Making headway submerged against strong currents was difficult. The job they thought would be the easiest was turning out to be toughest, and after five days little had been accomplished. Conditions improved on October 9. A series of photos began to be taken only to be interrupted by the sighting of a floatplane. That night Irvin reported his mission was completed. However, as they rounded Ukiangong Point on the south side of the island, a ship was sighted.

A small interisland tanker was observed heading east toward the island at eight knots. With battle stations manned, Irvin set up a three-torpedo spread and fired at a range of two thousand yards. As the Mark-14 weapons sped to the target, the ship slowed as it neared the lagoon entrance and the torpedoes all missed their mark, but their wakes were prominent in the smooth seas and the tanker turned toward the submarine, increasing speed. At the same time a patrol craft approached from the southwest. Irvin fired one more torpedo down the throat of the approaching ship, a hasty shot with little chance of success. Another miss, but the shot gave *Nautilus* a chance to escape. Down they went as the patrol craft passed close above and depth charges began to fall. Aircraft joined in, dropping several large bombs, but none were close enough to cause damage. The submarine evaded at deep submergence and retired eastward. It surfaced at sunset, turned south, and began charging batteries. Just before midnight Irvin received orders to end the patrol, and they headed northeast at full speed.

Nautilus returned to Pearl Harbor on the morning of October 17, having collected a wealth of valuable information that would support future Pacific operations. Irvin (with Lynch's input) made a number of suggestions regarding cameras, exposure settings, special equipment for improving operations, and procedures that would aid future submarine reconnaissance efforts. Admiral Lockwood commented that "the mission was efficiently and thoroughly conducted and much valuable information was obtained," adding kudos to the new commanding officer, officers, and crew.

Ensign Red Porterfield and former *Nautilus* executive officer and navigator, Lt. Cdr. Pat Rooney were enjoying a beer in the Officer's Club at the Pearl Harbor submarine base, reminiscing about old times, and imagining adventures to come. Rooney had detached from *Nautilus* before her fourth patrol to take command of the new *Gato*-class submarine USS *Corvina*, SS-226, then under construction. He commissioned her in August 1943 and had arrived in Pearl Harbor just four days before his old ship returned from her reconnaissance mission. *Corvina* was set to get underway on her first combat sortie in early November, assigned to patrol the heavily guarded Japanese stronghold of Truk. The two men had sailed together on three harrowing patrols, with Porterfield serving as chief of the boat. The senior chief on a submarine represents the crew and works closely with the executive officer on matters of discipline, morale, and training, and the two had formed a special bond. Red had a high regard for his former shipmate, and Rooney needed someone with Porterfield's experience to round out his wardroom. He came right out and asked him.

"Red, how would you like to transfer to *Corvina*? We're leaving in three weeks."

Porterfield was not surprised at the offer, and did not hesitate. He was eager to sail on a new boat, and was not too sure about Irvin, his new captain. He knew he could count on Rooney to be a good leader and solid commander.

"I think I'd like that, Pat. I'd be proud to call you skipper!" They shook hands on the deal, and Rooney promised to follow through and have orders cut for the transfer.

A week later, they met again, and Red was hopping mad, employing language distinctly unbecoming of an officer.

"Cool down, Red," said Rooney. "This wasn't my doing. One of your yeomen caught wind of it and told Irvin. Apparently he doesn't want to lose you!"

"But this is a chicken-shit move!" growled Red. "I've done my part. . . . I don't deserve this!"

"Well, sorry Red, I'm disappointed too. But there's nothing I can do about it. Commander Irvin outranks me." The two men groused about the situation for a while longer, but in the end, they agreed they had to accept navy orders.[7]

"Well, Pat, you have a good one. Maybe I can transfer after we get back and I can join you for the next mission." Porterfield and Rooney bid farewell and the new commander left to make final preparations for his first patrol.

Corvina got underway from Pearl Harbor on November 4. She made a brief refueling stop at Johnston Island and headed to Truk. She was never heard from again. It is believed that she was sunk on November 16 by the Japanese submarine *I-176*, the only American submarine to be sunk by a Japanese submarine in the entire war. Rooney and his crew of eighty-two were confirmed lost on March 14. Thanks to a nosey yeoman, Red Porterfield was not among them.

On November 8, *Nautilus* embarked a Marine detachment, the Amphibious Reconnaissance Company of the 5th Amphibious Corps consisting of eight officers and seventy men under the command of the aforementioned Captain Jones. Included in the company was Australian army Lt. George Hand of the Ocean Island Defence Force acting as a native interpreter. Slated to land on Abemama Island south of Tarawa, their objective was to capture the atoll for use as an air base to support the planned Marshall Islands campaign. Besides transporting the assault troops, *Nautilus* was assigned to make weather observations and serve as rescue vessel for downed aviators supporting the main attack on the Japanese island base at Tarawa. At the same time, a separate force would assault Makin Island, where *Nautilus* had landed Carlson's Raiders the previous August.

---

7. This anecdote was told in a February 2000 interview with Floyd "Red" Porterfield.

The parade of men detaching from the ship for other duties continued as new men came on board. Among the notable departures were
Jerry Gross, Wane Campbell, and Buzz Lee, along with seven others who
sailed on the first six *Nautilus* patrols. Eleven crewmen were replaced by
fifteen new sailors, so ninety-eight bodies squeezed into the submarine
along with nine officers and the seventy-eight Marines. The wardroom
experienced some turnover as well, with Lt. Ben Jarvis, Lt. (jg) George
Strong, and Ens. Charles Cummings Jr. replacing Lieutenant Commander Foster and Lieutenant Mason. With just three weeks between
missions, the new men would have to learn quickly. Fortunately, veterans
like Lynch, Porterfield, Bruck, Sabbe, and Hester were ready and able to
assist, and training was aggressive.

The ship got underway from Pearl Harbor on the morning of
November 8 and developed trouble from the start. Vital air compressors
failed, the stern planes had problems, and cracked cylinder liners in the
diesels remained a headache. Irvin requested a stop at Johnston Island,
a remote Pacific atoll about seven hundred nautical miles southwest of
Hawaii that was used as a refueling and repair stop as well as an air base.
Arriving on the morning of November 11, *Nautilus* met a small boat,
handed over parts needing repair, and spent the day cruising just off
the island. Late in the afternoon, the boat returned with mended parts
and two large fish in a box of ice, a gift from the commanding officer at
Johnston.

The rest of the two thousand mile transit to Tarawa Atoll was marked
by a number of sightings of US aircraft, mainly B-24 bombers. Submarines were not supplied with operations orders for other units (lest they
be captured and fall into Japanese hands), but clearly major events were
afoot, and *Nautilus* was sailing into harm's way yet again. At dawn on
November 16, the ship entered her assigned patrol area and sprung a leak
when she dived to test depth to judge the underwater sound conditions.
Nine tons of water rushed in through a failed main induction valve gasket
before Irvin could get his boat to the surface. A new gasket was prepared,
and men crawled up into the tiny space to replace the failed bit of rubber.
There was no mention of what the seventy-eight Marines thought of this
incident, but it was noted that CO_2 had risen to 2.1 percent by the time

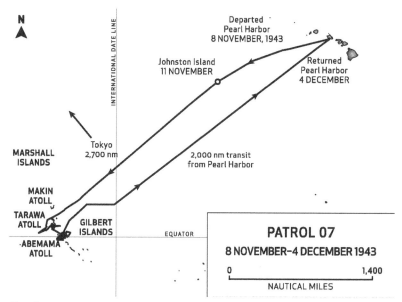

Nautilus supported landings at Tarawa and Abemama on her seventh patrol.
ILLUSTRATION BY BETHANY JOURDAN.

of surfacing. Much of this was attributed to the fifteen minute period that smoking was allowed.

On November 17, the ship arrived at her assigned patrol station west of Tarawa to observe and report weather conditions, which were ideal for air operations. While submerged the boat had become lighter and lighter so that over time, more than seven tons of ballast had to be added to keep the boat in trim. Investigations revealed that a blow valve had been leaking high-pressure air into one of the ballast tanks. As a temporary measure Irvin decided to cruise with the ballast tank vent open, wasting pressurized air, and leaving a trail of bubbles on the surface. Regrinding of the valve seat would have to wait until operations permitted. Old *Nautilus* would stick to her mission. The next day Irvin moved in on Tarawa to watch for downed aviators. He noted in his diary at 1019, "From about dawn until now there has been an almost continuous parade of aircraft from the southwest to Bititu [Betio] and return. Jap air appears to be non-existent and we have been unmolested except for a curious photographer who evidently wants one for his Brownie album." They surfaced and passed between Tarawa and Maiana Islands, just twelve miles south of the upcoming target of a major Marine assault. The assault was planned for high tide on the morning of November 20, just thirty-six hours hence. In the meanwhile, naval air attacks were joined by surface forces to begin a massive bombardment of the small island fortress to destroy defensive positions and weaken Japanese resistance. *Nautilus* had a ringside seat to the big show.

At dawn on November 19, the submarine was cruising on the surface just south of Betio about twelve thousand yards (six nautical miles) from the beach. They were again assigned to rescue downed aviators, and at sunset they were to run in close to shore to report damage. In the meanwhile, they marveled at the amazing display of American firepower as the day's bombardment began. Irvin invited small groups of Marines

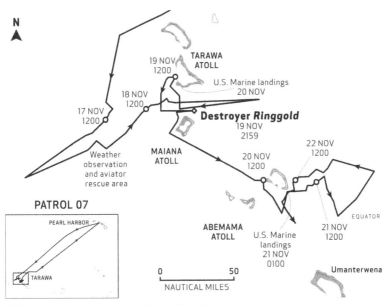

While observing Tarawa landings, *Nautilus* was mistakenly fired upon by the destroyer USS *Ringgold*. The submarine was badly damaged but continued her mission, landing troops on Abemama twenty-six hours later. ILLUSTRATION BY BETHANY JOURDAN.

to the bridge, five or ten at a time, to observe the action. In the clear conditions they could see lines of heavy ships on the horizon sailing up from the south and bombarding the western end of the island, with another group coming from behind. The invasion force was the largest yet assembled for a single operation, including seventeen aircraft carriers, a dozen battleships, an equal number of cruisers, and scores of destroyers and transports. Thirty-five thousand men of the 2nd Marine Division and the army's 27th Infantry Division were embarked. Six of the battleships were of the newer *North Carolina* and *South Dakota* classes, which could each lob nine tons of sixteen-inch projectiles over twenty miles in a single salvo. Irvin and the men topside closely observed the fall of shot and noted guns on the island booming in reply.

Ozzie Lynch was stationed below in the conning tower. As executive officer and the most experienced officer aboard, he keenly felt the responsibility of looking after his ship and inexperienced captain. Irvin was only on his second patrol in command, and he did not see much action on the first one. The captain relied on Lynch heavily, and had a great deal of respect for his skill and leadership. "I have never met a better one," Irvin later said of his exec.[8] He also noted the man was always professional, proper, and courteous. "The most polite individual I have ever, in my life, encountered. Always, 'Yes, sir,' 'No sir, captain,' to the extreme. He deferred to my judgement in everything and he never argued about anything I ever said to him." As it turned out, this day would see a notable exception to that norm.

Irvin was concerned that they stay close enough to be in position to make the assigned observations of the beach before dark. Lynch was worried that they were running too close for comfort. He stuck his head up through the conning tower upper hatch below Irvin's feet and said, forcefully, "Captain, you're too close. Turn away!"

"I don't think so, Ozzie," replied Irvin. "Those island defenders are too busily engaged to be concerned about a submarine." They continued to watch the impressive display of fireworks, the blasts echoing across the water. Geysers of dust, mud, and spray burst above the palm trees. Ozzie's

---

8. This and other Irvin quotes from an oral history recorded by the US Naval Institute in 1980.

head popped up again. "Captain, sir, we're too close!" Irvin replied, "I don't think we're too close, looking at it from up here." Another group of Marines made their way topside to get some fresh air, sunshine, and a taste of the action.

Yet again, Lynch appeared at the hatch and said, "Captain, you're too close. Roll out!" Irvin told him to check his charts again. This scene continued until, finally, the captain had second thoughts. He sent the Marines below in case a quick dive was necessary.

Lynch appeared again. This time, in desperation, he pleaded, "Captain, I beg you. You're too close. Roll out just a little!"

"Well, if you think we're too close, I'll turn away for just a short time," he replied, continuing with the obvious, "but we must stay in close to the beach so when the sun goes down, we can do our observation without having to run too far." Irvin called to the helmsman, "Right standard rudder," and gave a new course to the east to open the range to the enemy base. As they began to turn a lookout reported, "Guns on our side of the island are firing, sir!" Batteries on the southeast corner of Betio started spitting fire in their direction. Suddenly, a sound like that of a racing freight train was heard by those on the bridge. The men felt their chests pound—thump, thump, thump—as three projectiles flew directly overhead and landed just 150 yards beyond. Fountains of water shot into the sky as the eight-inch shells exploded on contact.

"Dive! Take her down fast!" screamed Irvin. With that, Lynch stuck his head through the hatch and yelled, "You stupid bastard! I told you we were too close!!"[9] Suitably chastened, Irvin forgave Lynch his uncharacteristic outburst and chose to spend the rest of the day safely submerged and make further observations through the periscopes. At sunset, he maneuvered in as close as he could get to the beach, working in toward a position nine hundred yards south of the west end of the reef. With fifteen feet of periscope jutting above the waves, Irvin observed the surf on the west side of Betio. He noted that since their observations a month earlier, the Japanese had built a six to eight foot wall along the seaward beaches, commenting, "It looks formidable." A few buildings appeared to

9. Irvin told this tale in his 1980 US Naval Institute oral history.

be damaged, but most were not touched. Small guns of about 40-mm size were trained around and depressed at the periscope but did not open fire. The heavy caliber guns appeared to be undamaged. Irvin retired to make his report. It did not bode well for the troops landing on those beaches in the morning.

In the evening, *Nautilus* surfaced and made her way along her assigned route northeast of Maiana Island, and then south to land her troops on Abemama the next morning. She was under no circumstances to go west of Tarawa, as the main carrier task force was still there. The waters south of Tarawa would be busy in a few hours with a fleet of transports, minesweepers, and landing ships escorted by destroyers converging on the small island of Betio. Irvin reported difficulty making this passage owing to the currents running a strong two knots to the west. He was also concerned with strengthening radar interference from what appeared to be US ships to the east. As he later noted in his patrol report, "The submarine has no friends" and he did not want to tangle with warships that might easily take him for a hostile vessel. Hoping to clear Maiana and head south before getting too close to the ships ahead, he called for full speed, postponing the battery charge to put all engines on propulsion. They were making good headway when at 2130 Bob Burrell, manning the radar watch, reported a contact ahead.

"Conn, radar. Contact at 10,900 yards, bearing zero-nine-four true." The ships were barely five miles away and much too close.

"Very well," he acknowledged. After a brief pause, he turned to Lynch and ordered, "Officer of the deck, man battle stations!" Standing with him on the bridge was Porterfield, who was holding a flare gun. "Ensign Porterfield," said Irvin, "recheck that we have the right signal." Red dropped down in the conning tower and was back up in a moment. "I checked again, sir. The green flare means we're friendly," confirmed Porterfield. "And you're sure you have a green flare in there?" Irvin did not want any mistakes. "Yes sir!" replied Red. "Very well. Stay right next to me. If I slap you on the back and yell 'fire,' shoot that flare!"

Radar continued to track the contact, which at first did not seem to react. Irvin tried to keep his distance, but by then the Maiana reef was just four thousand yards away to the south and the island was looming large. The situation further deteriorated with the urgent report, "Conn, radar. Contact has turned toward us and is speeding up!"

Nautilus was in a bad way. Irvin believed the ships (there appeared to be two or three) were friendly but they were behaving very belligerently. The battery was low from the day's submerged operations. If they dived, they would be hard pressed to keep off the reef at submerged speed with strong currents setting in that direction. Since they had clearly been detected, it was time to announce themselves.

"Porterfield, fire that flare!" called Irvin, slapping Red on the back. Porterfield pulled the trigger, and into the sky shot a blazing red light as the flare burst forth.

"It's red!" cried Irvin in dismay. At that moment the flare reached its apex and exploded into a brilliant green, but to that point it had clearly showed red, the wrong signal. At the same time the lookout reported, "Lightning on the horizon!" as the destroyer USS *Ringgold* opened fire with radar-guided five-inch guns. A second later a tremendous jolt rocked the ship as the first salvo landed. It was a perfect shot striking the base of the port side of the conning tower. The projectile entered through superstructure plating leaving a clean hole, then sheared the blow lines to the after and middle ballast tanks and plowed through a part of the auxiliary engine air induction opening leaving a ragged hole about one by two feet. The still moving shell blasted through a superstructure frame before hitting the conning tower itself, where it made a foot-long gouge nearly an inch deep but did not penetrate it. It ricocheted through a main strength frame tearing it away from the pressure hull, bent the periscope well, and came to rest against the pressure hull knocking out a few rivets. Somehow, the shell failed to explode, which saved the submarine from certain doom. Another shell landed close by the port side and did explode, the concussion from the near miss rupturing cooling water lines to the port main motor. Seawater rushed into the motor room.

"Dive! Dive!" screamed Irvin as everyone scrambled below. "Make your depth three hundred feet. Rig for depth charge!" *Nautilus* began to submerge as *Ringgold* and the light cruiser *Santa Fe* pumped round after round in their direction, the larger ship firing six-inch ammunition. By some accounts more than one hundred cannon shells and two torpedoes were thrown at *Nautilus*, but luckily only the first shot hit, and it was a dud. Dud or not, the impact (along with the other shell's near miss) caused serious damage and major flooding in the conning tower and motor room. Irvin reversed course and headed west to evade the attacking ships, the current carrying them to the other side of Maiana and away from their assigned route. Lynch took charge of damage control, as is the duty of the executive officer in an emergency. He and Chief Signalman Jim Peirano quickly located the source of flooding in the conning tower. Apparently, a voice tube used for communications from the bridge had been damaged leaving a two-and-a-half-inch hole. As they dove deeper the pressure rose, leading to water gushing faster. With no other way to slow the leak, a sailor on duty in the space stuck his elbow in the voice tube, reminding everyone of the story of the little Dutch boy and the dike.

By then, a substantial amount of water had flooded in amidships and aft and continued to flow in faster than it could be pumped out. The diving officer called for speed and an up angle to give some lift to the hull as the ship reached ordered depth and continued to descend. Irvin ordered full speed in spite of the waning battery charge, and with an extreme six-degree up angle depth was held at 310 feet.

Seawater continued to flow into the conning tower and spill into the control room, where it was drenching the gyro switchboard. Chief Hester grabbed some canvas and tried desperately to deflect the deluge without success. "Mr. Lynch!" he called, "If we can't stop this water, we're going to lose the gyro!" Submerged, near a reef, in high currents, with warships all around, the gyro was essential to safely navigate their way out of trouble. "We're trying, Chief!" Ozzie called as he wrestled with depth control, having taken over the diving station. But Foy had another idea.

"Sir," he said in his usual calm and quiet manner, belying the urgency of the situation, "If we can't stop the water from coming in, if you could just put a list on so when the water comes down the hatch, instead of flowing on the switchboard it will flow over to the side and we can save the gyro."[10] So while he was trying to keep the ship afloat Lynch set to work moving ballast to one side, putting a list on the ship so the waterfall spilling into the control room missed the switchboard.

At this point, Ozzie did not realize that the motor room was flooding, adding weight to the stern. He kept pumping ballast water out of the after tanks until they were dry. "Engine room, check spaces for flooding aft!" he ordered. After a few minutes he got the report that the ruptured motor cooling line was dumping water into the bilge. His pumps were busy dewatering the midships bilge and controlling the list, but he needed to move weight forward. He came upon and simple, yet effective solution.

"Engine room. Form a bucket brigade to move water from the motor room bilge to the engine room!" The engine room watch acknowledged and soon a line of men was passing water from the motor room through the hatches and forward to the engine room and the next compartment. Meanwhile, machinists worked on stemming the leak in the cooling lines. With effort they managed to slow the inrush of water so that buckets and pumps could begin to win the battle. As the minutes passed the ship lightened and Ozzie called for one-third speed, greatly slowing the drain on the battery. All this time, attention never waned from the threat above, as three vessels appeared to be tracking them, alternately getting closer and farther but staying off the beam. Inexplicably, the expected depth charge attack was not forthcoming.

Soon, Ozzie regained full depth control and Irvin eased the submarine up to two hundred feet as echo ranging from the surface ships began to fade. The captain thought it was a good time to see how the Marines were doing through all of the action and made his way forward. The entire company was camped out in the torpedo room, as much to be out of the way as to help ballast the ship with the extra weight forward. Irvin took a lighthearted approach as he explained that things were under control and there was nothing to be concerned about. The Marines were stoic

---

10. Foy Hester, along with Ben Jarvis, James Peirano, Joseph Goodman, and Myles Banbury were later awarded Bronze Star medals for their actions on this patrol. Ozzie Lynch was awarded a Silver Star for this mission, along with a Navy Cross and other decorations during his storied military service.

but were unanimous in the attitude that they would much prefer a rubber boat on a hostile beach to their present predicament. One sergeant said, "The only thing I've got to say, Captain, is that this is a hell of a place to have to dig a foxhole!"

With echo ranging distant, at 2355 the ship came to periscope depth after a two-and-a-half-hour ordeal. No contacts. Firing up the radar, which took a while owing to excessive moisture, they found the area clear. At 0053 on November 20 they surfaced and took stock of the damage. The first problem they encountered was the inability to normally blow the port main ballast tanks because some of the air lines had been carried away by the shell. The ship started to roll over and Irvin was forced to submerge again. As he later reported, "I almost had a mutiny!" After some head scratching, they deduced the problem and realized they could shut off the ruptured lines and blow tanks using just high pressure air. The repair to the air compressors at Johnston Island turned out to be critical. Ozzie and the crew worked out a procedure for diving and surfacing, though it would require more time than usual. Other damage included flooding and wetting of a number of motors and electrical panels, including the periscope motors. The main induction supplying air to the diesel was flooded, so air had to flow directly though the main hatch, which was less efficient but workable.

Nautilus cautiously worked her way around the west side of Maiana, careful not to drift too far west and risk tangling with more "friendly" forces. Irvin reported the incident of the previous night, including damage and location of the attack, saying that they were delayed but capable of carrying out their assigned mission. Landing on the twentieth in coordination with the Tarawa assault was no longer possible, so it was pushed to the early morning of the twenty-first. As the submarine made her way south to Abemama, Irvin took the opportunity to celebrate Thanksgiving early so that the Marines could have the traditional feast before leaving the ship.

The bombardment of Tarawa resumed at dawn on November 20, battle-ships pounding Betio with fourteen- and sixteen-inch shells. The island's eight-inch Vickers artillery, purchased from the British and encased in concrete bunkers, were no match for the huge battleship guns. One shell, probably from USS *Maryland*, penetrated the ammunition storage of one of the shore batteries, setting off a huge explosion as the ordnance went up in a massive fireball. Three of the four big guns were eventually silenced. Minesweepers entered the lagoon on the north shore of the islet protected by nothing more than a smoke screen as they cleared a path for landing craft. Destroyers, including the aforementioned USS *Ringgold*, accompanied the minesweepers and slugged it out with smaller shore batteries. Taking several serious hits, the destroyer remained in the lagoon to provide close gunfire support for the troop landings that were to follow.

Both sides understood the strategic significance of Tarawa, the point driven home to the Japanese with the Carlson raid on nearby Makin the previous August. The base at Betio was heavily fortified over the fol-lowing year with the efforts of a construction battalion including 1,200 conscripted Korean laborers who built some five hundred concrete rein-forced defensive positions supported by forty artillery pieces and fourteen tanks. Larger coastal defense guns, including the four eight-inch Vickers and ten other pieces, were meant to guard the approaches to the beaches, particularly on the lagoon side where an attack would likely materialize. The islet, less than four hundred acres in area, was manned by nearly five thousand defenders (including the Koreans) and commanded by Rear Adm. Keiji Shibazaki who boasted, "It would take one-million men one-hundred years" to capture Tarawa. Makin Island to the north had been reoccupied and was likewise reinforced with a garrison of close to one thousand men protected by concrete fighting pits, coastal defense guns, and smaller artillery.

The first wave of a force of eighteen thousand troops of the 2nd Marine Division under the command of Maj. Gen. Julian Smith came ashore as the bombardment ceased at 0900, just after high tide. The attackers expected the reefs that ringed the beaches to have five feet of water over them, sufficient to float the shallow draft Higgens boats and bring the Marines ashore quickly with some protection. Unfortunately, *Nautilus* had been unable to survey those reefs to confirm their depths back in September, and battle planners failed to consider that the island was experiencing a neap[11] tide. Warnings by a New Zealand liaison officer who had experience on Tarawa went unheeded. Objections by the staff of the amphibious assault force were overruled in favor of assertions by sea captains and former island residents that the water would be deep enough. As the assault began, the tide rose to barely three feet, and the four foot draft landing craft were unable to clear the reef. The boats dropped their ramps and the Marines waded ashore under withering fire. In spite of the awesome bombardment, many of the shore defense guns (including one of the Vickers) were able to fire and most of the fighting pits were intact. An airstrip running down the center of the island allowed Admiral Shibazaki to reposition troops to meet the incoming threat, determined to crush the invaders on the beaches.

Many of the Marines faced wading five hundred yards before they could reach the defensive seawall, itself a difficult position to breach. Tanks could not easily come ashore, many hit by gunfire as they tried to traverse the shallows or ironically sinking into pits caused by the naval bombardment. Only tracked amphibious vehicles known as LVT "Alligators" could climb across the reef and bring a few Marines at a time to shore. The intrepid drivers of the LVTs attempted to shuttle troops back and forth from the reef, but many of the unarmored vehicles were too badly holed to remain afloat. Those that could reach the seawall were unable to climb it, leaving the men pinned down on the beach in front of it. Throughout this grim morning, the commander of the landing forces, Col. David Shoup, rallied his men and directed attacks on defended positions. With nowhere to go but forward, surviving Marines began to move up the beach and past the seawall. A few tanks and guns were put ashore and accurate naval gunfire from destroyers operating just off the reefs was effective. In particular, a five-inch round from either *Ringgold* or her companion USS *Dashiell* landed among a group of defenders moving

11. Neap tide occurs just after the first or third quarters of the moon when there is least difference between high and low water. Thus, it is not as high as during a full or new moon, known as the "spring" tide.

between command posts and killed Admiral Shibazaki in the midafternoon. Communication lines between the Japanese positions were cut by the naval bombardment so that commanders could not coordinate defenses. By the end of the day, five thousand US troops had come ashore at the cost of 1,500 casualties and had gained a toehold on the beaches. Unable to organize a counterattack, the Japanese consolidated defenses and awaited the morning. Floating in the lagoon and faced with spending the night in their crowded Higgens boats, most of the second wave of Marines was unable to come ashore.

To the north, elements of the US Army 27th Infantry Division numbering nearly 6,500 troops commanded by Maj. Gen. Ralph Smith, came ashore on Butaritari Island of Makin Atoll in much the same location that Carlson had raided the year before. As at Tarawa, the assault was preceded by air and naval bombardment, and likewise the landing troops had trouble crossing the surrounding reefs due to the neap tide. On Makin, however, the Japanese chose not to strongly oppose the landings, but rather to fight it out from fortified strongpoints along the island. Much of the first day was spent taking out these positions one by one, with snipers in the palm trees harassing the attackers.

In contrast to the dramatic action to the northwest, *Nautilus* spent a quiet day transiting to her objective at Abemama as the embarked troops prepared for their belated assault. Part of the day was spent on the surface charging batteries, replenishing air banks, and rehearsing makeshift procedures for diving with damaged equipment. Submerging in the afternoon, they got a chance to observe the beach by periscope, then retired to the south to charge batteries. Captain Irvin noted, "Touched the Equator, but King Neptune was too tired to hold court." Crossing the line ceremonies would have to wait for another day. As midnight approached, the submarine neared the beach and at 0100 on November 21. The Marine company left the ship in rubber boats without incident, other than failure to get two of their six outboard motors to start. Two others quit on the way to shore, so the men improvised by towing and paddling. They made slow progress fighting the current, rough seas, and surf, but by 0330 they were safely ashore without opposition. The troops brought with them some equipment and forty-eight-hours' worth of rations and supplies. *Nautilus* was to land the rest of the equipment the next night once a beach was secured farther up island in a location designated Hospital Area. The submarine would maintain communications by radio or, failing that, signaling using an arrangement of banners made from mattress covers.

Nautilus retired to let the Marines do their work. The banner arrangement signaling "situation satisfactory" was displayed throughout the day. That evening, seeing no change of status or sign of any Marines in the Hospital Area, Irvin tried to communicate with the troops ashore to no avail. At 2022 a radar contact close by sent the ship to battle stations. The mysterious contact, thought to be an enemy submarine, closed to barely more than a mile before it disappeared. Nothing further was seen nor heard. Irvin continued to make attempts to contact forces on the island, but with no indication that the beach was secure he did not try to land equipment that night. As was learned from later reports, when the men reached shore, they discovered that winds and currents had taken them farther to the west then planned, coming close to missing landfall altogether. They found themselves on a different islet, nearly two miles from the intended landing beach. Encountering no opposition, they set up a command post and moved toward the channel to the adjacent islet. As they moved stealthily forward, two islanders were seen approaching along a path nearby. Staying hidden, the Marines waited until the natives were almost upon them, then Lieutenant Hand (the Australian interpreter) sprang up and greeted the natives in their own language. To everyone's astonishment, the islanders grinned and replied in English, "Why Mr. Hand. My word! I am glad to see you, but were you wise to visit us just now, Mr. Hand? The Sapanese are here!"[12]

The islanders had suffered from the oppressive Japanese occupation and the men were only too happy to help the Americans. They provided details of the enemy emplacements, numbers, and weapons. This information was of immeasurable help, but it was also fairly grim news. Though outnumbered, the defenders were well entrenched and amply

---

12. Quoted from the United States Marine Corps Amphibious Reconnaissance Battalion Wikipedia page. Note that in the Gilbertese language "j" is pronounced like "ss" in English, which carried over in spoken translation.

supplied. And they knew the Marines were coming. Captain Jones and his men spent the next day skirmishing with enemy forces as they advanced before reaching an unfavorable position with the Japanese dug in on high terrain with unseen machine gun nests. Jones tried to communicate with the submarine to no avail. Exhausted and hungry, they set up defensive positions and waited for morning to arrive.

Meanwhile on Tarawa, the attackers were having a rough go of it as they tried to push the thin line, held on the northern beach, inland against new Japanese firing positions set up during the night. At the same time, a wave of reinforcements landed on the western beaches, supported by accurate naval gunfire. By noon, heavy machine guns were brought ashore that were capable of countering enemy positions. By that afternoon, Marines were able to cross the airstrip and gain the south side of the island along with the western section as the Japanese retreated. Additional Marine landings on the adjacent islet of Bairiki acted to block the withdrawal. By evening of November 21 much of the island was in US control, though resistance was far from quelled. The third day of fighting saw banzai charges and pockets of resistance as Marines advanced across the island. The atoll was not completely secured until November 28. In the end, US casualties numbered 1,009 killed and more than 2,000 wounded against the death of almost the entire 5,000-thousand man garrison of Japanese. Just 17 enemy soldiers and 129 Korean laborers were captured.

Significant progress was also made on Makin, and after the second day of heavy fighting Japanese resistance evaporated with the loss of 395 men, including most of the regular troops. American army forces suffered 66 men killed and 185 wounded while taking the island, but more grievous casualties were incurred by the sinking of the supporting escort carrier USS *Liscome Bay* by the submarine *I-175* with the loss of 644 sailors.

The situation on Abemama was less clear. On November 22, *Nautilus*, on the surface, cruised by the Hospital Area trying to make visual or radio contact with the beach. There was no sign of activity, no light, no banners, no fire, nothing. They had not landed fresh supplies as previously arranged and it was presumed that the Marines ashore were needing provisions, but there was no point in landing on a beach that might yet be held by the enemy. Irvin briefly thought about asking for volunteers to go ashore, but feared he might lose them too. A vessel was glimpsed through the palm trees on the other (west) side of the island. Irvin could not be sure it was the repair ship he had earlier requested or a Japanese ship bearing reinforcements. He decided to circle back around to the south side of the island, both to investigate the sighting as well as to see if he could make contact with the Marines at the initial landing beach. At 1920, he was finally able to communicate with Captain Jones who told him that their progress to the Hospital Area had been blocked by Japanese barriers, and they were in dire need of supplies. *Nautilus* crew proceeded to load food and ammunition onto the ship's boat, and with the aid of Marines in rubber rafts, deliver the cargo ashore. Just after the job was finished, they learned that the vessel sighted earlier in the day was the tug USS *Clamp*, sent to help repair damage to the submarine.

The next evening, November 23, *Nautilus* again made contact with the shore party near the initial landing beach and were asked to take aboard two wounded soldiers and send additional blood plasma. PFC Harry Marek and Cpl. John King were ferried out to the submarine at 2008. King was not seriously hurt having suffered a hernia, but Marek was shot though the chest by an accidental discharge of his weapon and was clearly dying. The wardroom table was cleared, and he was brought down below. Pharmacist's Mate Joe Potts tried to save him while Bob Burrell held his hand, but their efforts were in vain. Burrell was trying to give the dying man a sip of water when he expired at 2215. The men put him in a canvas bag, added a six-inch shell for weight, covered him with an American flag, and placed him on Captain Irvin's bunk pending an opportunity for burial the next day. Potts and Burrell sat with him all night. At 0450 on November 24, the submarine stood offshore in the darkness and brought the dead Marine topside and held funeral services. Pvt. Harry Marek was committed to the deep. He was the only man to die aboard *Nautilus* during the war.

Captain Jones had also arranged for fire support from *Nautilus* to help his troops break through Japanese positions the next day. He and Irvin worked out a communication system and a plan for the bombardment. At 0810, *Nautilus* opened fire at five thousand yards and closed to

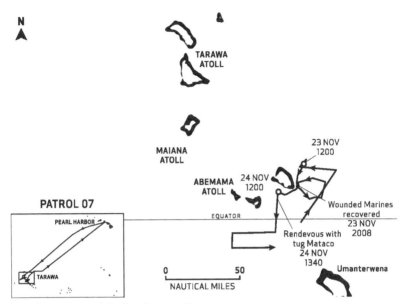

Nautilus supported the landings on Abemama. ILLUSTRATION BY BETHANY JOURDAN.

three thousand yards, targeting a grove of palm trees marking the enemy position. The ammunition used had quick fuses that triggered on impact with the trees, and made for very effective fire. A Marine radioed spotting information back to the ship, asking for slight adjustments. This worked quite well, though on a couple of occasions the spotter yelled, "You stupid jackass! I said to the right! You shot to the left and you almost hit me!" Close fire support indeed! Irvin also noted that one of the guns had a problem with its elevating mechanism so that sometimes it would squat on firing and shoot high. Those rounds soared over the island and out of sight. They learned later that the salvage vessel USS *Mataco* was in the vicinity and had no idea who was shooting at them! After about an hour and seventy-five rounds, the Marines called for a cease fire. Captain Jones later reported that the position was utterly destroyed, and they were able to move past it.[13]

---

13. Other sources suggest that the *Nautilus* bombardment was only effective for enemy troops out in the open, and that naval gunfire from the destroyer *Gansevoort* finished the job.

After the bombardment, Irvin headed around the southwest side of the island to rendezvous with what he thought was the tug *Clamp*, expecting help from a welder and also hoping to transfer their remaining wounded Marine. As the submarine approached, the vessel turned tail and began to retreat at top speed. *Nautilus* kept flashing recognition signals, and after a chase was finally able to convince the vessel, which was *Mataco*, to stop. Confusion ensued as the ship had no welding equipment nor did the crew know anything about wounded men. Evidently, they were sent to escort the stricken *Nautilus* out of the area. Fortunately, the hospital ship *Relief* was nearby, and Irvin was able to arrange to transfer the patient off his submarine.

On Abemama, Captain Jones made contact with the destroyer USS *Gansevoort* (DD-608) and was able to evacuate two more wounded men as well as arrange for additional fire support. The Marines continued to push forward against weakening Japanese resistance until finally, on the morning of November 25, a native reported the enemy had withdrawn. In the afternoon, the Japanese command post was reached where the men found twenty-three dead defenders surrounded by hundreds of rounds of ammunition, weapons, grenades, food, and other supplies. This mysterious situation was explained by an English-speaking Apamamese boy who had observed the command post from a secluded position. He said the garrison commander had assembled his troops and was urging them to "Kill all Americans!" brandishing a samurai sword in one hand and waving a pistol in the other. During one particularly violent gesture he accidentally shot himself, fatally, in the stomach. The remaining defenders, demoralized, committed suicide.

That evening at 1850, *Nautilus* closed the beach and Irvin was able to make contact with Jones who reported that the enemy was gone, the island was secure, and no further help was needed. Irvin wished them a Happy Thanksgiving and retired southward. The next day an occupation force was landed and the battalion was relieved. Marine losses on Abemama tallied two killed (Corporal Marek and another man, PFC William Miller, hit during the fighting) and three wounded. The entire garrison of twenty-five Japanese was wiped out, many by their own hand.

In time, an airstrip capable of supporting heavy bombers was constructed on the atoll to help further the Pacific campaign.

Nautilus loitered south of Abemama for another day, waiting for an escort to help the damaged submarine wend her way through the flotillas still teeming around the islands. On the morning of November 26, she sighted cruisers, then the flagship of Task Force 53, USS *Maryland.* The commander directed *Mataco* to escort *Nautilus*, and together they headed northeast to make the two thousand mile transit back to base. The submarine safely arrived in Pearl Harbor on the morning of December 4 after a short, but frightening, twenty-six day patrol. Bob Burrell recalled, "We returned to Pearl Harbor with the five-inch shell, and although it was a direct hit and the nose of the shell was smashed, it was a miracle that it didn't explode and put all of us on the bottom. It just wasn't our time to go."

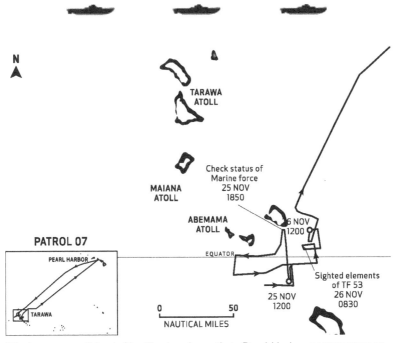

Mission accomplished; *Nautilus* heads north to Pearl Harbor. ILLUSTRATION BY BETHANY JOURDAN.

Irvin and his crew were greeted with fanfare and accolades when they returned to Pearl. The squadron commander, Charles "Swede" Momsen,[14] endorsed Irvin's patrol report with the comment, "The magnificent spirit and performance of all hands in successfully completing their mission under the most difficult circumstances sets a standard of achievement for all forces. The Squadron Commander again commends the Commanding Officer, officers and men on their aggressiveness, teamwork, and professional capability."

Irvin was eventually awarded the Navy Cross for his patrol, the citation reading in part, "Charged with an extremely perilous mission, Captain Irvin courageously remained on station after his ship had been severely damaged by hostile shellfire and, with valiant determination, successfully landed a detachment of Marines on Apamama [Abemama] Island." For his part, Irvin wrote about his crew, "They are very proud that their ship stopped a five inch shell. The bombardment of the shore positions was the high spot for the crew from a morale standpoint. They always like to shoot the six-inch guns."

As for that five-inch shell, it remained embedded in the submarine superstructure for the duration of the patrol. During the transit to Pearl, Irvin had a team of men climb under the deck where they found the round and managed, with effort, to pry it loose. After arrival in port, Admiral Lockwood came aboard to discuss the events of the mission, and the topic of the shell came up. Irvin told him that he had removed it from under the deck, and the admiral expressed relief that he had gotten rid of it. Irvin replied, "Well, sir, we didn't get rid of it. We put it in a deck locker."

Lockwood said, "You mean you carried it in the deck locker from the time you pried it loose?" Irvin acknowledged the fact. It had not occurred to him that it might yet explode. Lockwood asked where it currently was, and the captain sheepishly allowed that it was in the deck locker he was standing on. Irvin thought the admiral would jump off the ship. He

14. Momsen was a pioneer in deep sea diving and led the navy experimental diving unit before the war. His group conducted experiments and developed procedures for safe breathing of mixed-gases under high pressure. He was famous for inventing the Momsen lung for submarine escape, and led the salvage of the submarine USS *Squalus*.

left immediately and told his staff to have the bomb disposal unit fetch it ASAP.

Shortly after their meeting, the bomb disposal unit arrived and Irvin handed over the shell. Before they left, he wondered what would become of it. The sailor in charge replied, "Well, once we defuse it and get the powder out of it, then anybody can have it." The captain asked if it could be given to the Officer's Club. But what about the fuse itself? That had to go to the Bureau of Ordnance for further analysis. Irvin asked if he could see it before it was sent away, and the sailor promised he would bring it by.

When in due course the man came back with the fuse, Irvin took it in his hand to inspect it and turned his back. He made a show of fumbling with it and, plop! It went over the side and into the harbor! "Oh, that was clumsy of me!" said Irvin. "But, regrettably, your fuse just went over the side!" The bomb disposal man was livid, and fussed that he never should have brought it back and never should have let Irvin handle it. The captain was apologetic, but said, "Well, you know, it was just an accident. It's too bad it slipped and went overboard."

The man left, grumbling and grousing. Irvin went below and placed the fuse, which he had palmed, on his desk. Some handy bit of scrap metal had actually gone over the side. The fuse remained the captain's souvenir.

The shell itself did make it to the Pearl Harbor Officer's Club, mounted on a table where it remained for a decade or longer. At some point it disappeared, and Irvin suspects it was stolen, possibly by one of the officers who sailed on that patrol.[15]

---

15. This tale was related by William Irvin in a 1980 interview with the US Naval Institute.

CHAPTER SEVEN

Philippine Sea

CAPTAIN IRVIN WAS SITTING AT THE BAR IN THE PEARL HARBOR SUB-
marine base Officer's Club pumping his fellow skippers for last minute
dope about Japanese operations in his coming patrol area. He and his
Nautilus crew would be departing the next day, Christmas Eve, and he
was eager to learn all he could, particularly about new enemy radars. He
was deep in conversation about using his equipment in receiving mode
to pick up emissions from radars used on Japanese battleships when the
base fire alarm blared.

"Who do you think that's for?" wondered Irvin, distracted from the
bull session.

Someone came running in and said there was a fire on the pier.

"Which pier?" inquired Irvin. The sailor told him and Irvin jumped
up and yelled, "My God, we're tied up there!" He dashed out of the building and raced down to the docks, which were alive with fire apparatus.

Nautilus was burning. The forward battery compartment was in
flames and there was serious danger that the battery would overheat. A
hydrogen explosion could ensue, which would destroy the ship. Moreover,
the fire had spread to a nearby ammunition magazine whose sprinkler
system didn't respond. What dozens of Japanese warships, with hundreds
of depth charges, had failed to do was about to happen in safe harbor.

After the damage suffered during her last patrol the ship had
required extensive repairs. In the process, the fuel tanks were pumped
dry. Normally, fuel tanks are completely filled with a combination of fuel
oil and seawater. The oil floats on top. Empty tanks were properly first

filled with seawater, then fuel was added allowing the water to be safely expelled. Because the submarine was to get underway in the morning, there was not enough time to essentially fill the tanks twice, so Irvin decided to have the dry tanks filled with fuel, releasing the air through vent pipes throughout the ship. The fuel man intended to check the vents and shut them as each tank filled, but he neglected a vent pipe in the captain's stateroom near a light fixture. Fuel vapors gathered and ignited from the heat of the light, starting the fire.[1]

The crew wisely waved off firefighters who were prepared to quench the flames with water, which when encountering the battery would only increase the production of explosive hydrogen. The only way to squelch the conflagration was to flood the space with carbon dioxide. CO_2, the bane of submarine sailors during extended submergence, was about to be a lifesaver. CO_2 was fed into the affected spaces through a salvage air piping system, filling the compartments and replacing the oxygen. Without oxygen, fire could not be sustained and soon was out. *Nautilus* was saved; however, damage was extensive and sailing the next morning was out of the question. The submarine would go back into the repair yards, and the crew would have Christmas ashore after all. Though not in the manner Irvin would have preferred.

A full month passed before the submarine was again ready for sea. Besides repair of the battle damage suffered during the prior patrol and the compartments gutted by fire, the ship received new equipment. Though the updated radar and torpedo data computer were welcome enhancements to her fighting ability, much enthusiasm surrounded the air conditioning unit installed in the conning tower. The ten men crammed into the sweltering space during battle stations would have some measure of relief, especially while operating in tropical waters.

As usual, there were comings and goings of the crew. Three new officers came aboard: Bob Holloway, Ruel Whitcher, and Stan Slawsky, all ensigns. George Strong detached, but the bigger hole would be left

---

1. This explanation is found in Irvin's 1980 US Naval Institute oral history. A slightly different version was offered by Bob Burrell in a December 2000 interview. Burrell related that a sailor inspecting the leaky fuel vent accidentally broke the light, setting off sparks that ignited the oil vapors. To complicate matters, the ship was being painted and fresh paint vapors were present.

by the departure of the executive officer and veteran of all seven *Nautilus* war patrols to date, Ozzie Lynch. He went on to command the submarine USS *Seawolf* (SS-197) and later USS *Skate* (SS-305) on which he won the Navy Cross for valor on patrol in the Sea of Japan, sailing into the shallow waters of an enemy harbor and sinking five ships. After the war Lynch, in time, advanced to rear admiral and served with the Joint Chiefs of Staff. His final assignment saw him coordinating the successful recovery of the first unmanned *Apollo* spacecraft on November 9, 1967. Daughter Kathy Richardson said that when her father would write home from far-flung duty stations, he would always sign his letters, "Ever Strive." Admiral Ozzie Lynch died of a heart attack while on active duty and "departed on eternal patrol" on January 19, 1968, at the age of fifty-three.

Lt. Ben Jarvis advanced to executive officer and would distinguish himself in that position over the next five patrols. The crew lost a dozen men including Bob Burrell, who decided after the fire it was time to move on to a newer boat. Eleven new men came aboard for a complement of ninety-seven enlisted and ten officers. Hester, Bruck, and Porterfield were among the eighteen men making their eighth *Nautilus* war patrol.

After the loss of *Argonaut*, submarine command recognized that patrol of Japanese home waters was no place for the pokey, slow to dive, noisy cruiser subs *Nautilus* and *Narwhal*. The danger was compounded by Congressman May's revelations resulting in new depth charge tactics by enemy escorts. While many of the newer boats were sent to patrol the hazardous waters of the Sea of Japan and the East China Sea, *Nautilus* was to patrol a five hundred mile swath of the Philippine Sea with the objective of interdicting shipping aiming to resupply forces in the Marshall Islands, now beset by the American central Pacific thrust. She finally left Pearl Harbor on January 24, 1944, and headed west for the waters north of Palau, 3,600 nautical miles distant.

On January 31 the submarine crossed the International Date Line at latitude 19°N. At the same time, Marines of the V Amphibious Corps stormed ashore the island of Kwajalein, about one thousand miles to the southwest. The atoll and its close companion, Roi-Namur, were an integral part of the Japanese perimeter defense, and the huge lagoon and its

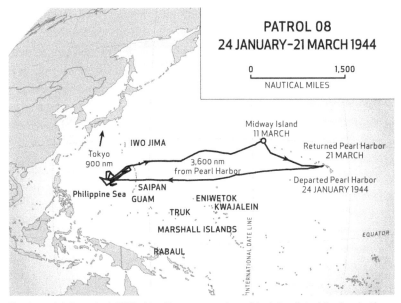

PATROL 08
24 JANUARY-21 MARCH 1944

0   1,500
NAUTICAL MILES

Midway Island
11 MARCH

IWO JIMA

Tokyo
900 nm

3,600 nm
from Pearl Harbor

Returned Pearl Harbor
21 MARCH

Departed Pearl Harbor
24 JANUARY 1944

SAIPAN
Philippine Sea   GUAM   ENIWETOK
          KWAJALEIN
    TRUK

MARSHALL ISLANDS

RABAUL

INTERNATIONAL DATE LINE

EQUATOR

For her eighth patrol, USS *Nautilus* was assigned to interdict shipping in the Philippine Sea. ILLUSTRATION BY BETHANY JOURDAN.

ring of islands was home to a naval base and an airfield. The hard-won lessons of Tarawa were applied as a preinvasion bombardment by naval gunfire, naval aircraft, and bombers, based on recently won Abemama, used improved tactics and closer-range fire. Enemy air bases in the region were attacked, suppressing Japanese airborne resistance. An over-whelming force of two divisions and several regiments of Marine and army troops numbering more than forty-six thousand strong established a beachhead on the main island of Kwajalein and quickly moved across the narrow island. The force simultaneously attacked Roi-Namur and the lightly defended island of Majuro to the east. This time the American troops were able to cross coral reefs in amphibious vehicles and come ashore quickly on the lagoon's beaches; the strongest defenses were fac-ing the ocean side where the attack was expected. The eight thousand or so stunned defenders on the three islands put up resistance and fought nearly to the last man, but within a few days the battles were over. American casualties numbered 348 killed on all three islands, a grim toll but far fewer than the cost of Tarawa.

On February 3, *Nautilus* passed north of the action as American troops were securing the islands. She continued west making two-thirds speed, conserving fuel for the long transit ahead, time on station, and return. On the evening of February 6, trouble struck as number two main engine fell silent.

"Chief Bruck!" called Lt. (jg) George Davis, officer of the deck. "Report status of main engines!" The ship slowed to five knots as number one main engine was also secured. Bruck replied, "We have a problem with number two. Shut down number one to investigate. Three and four still running."

After assessing the situation, Bruck was able to report the grim news. By then Irvin was back in the engine room.

"Sir, main engine number two has a broken crankshaft. We have no spare and no way of repairing it. I'm afraid it's OOC,[2] sir."

This was a major disappointment to Nick Bruck, who was proud of his skills and had worked tirelessly to keep the balky diesels running over the course of his two and a half years on board *Nautilus*. Buzz Lee said, "Bruck knew everything about those engines. They were our way home."[3]

Irvin had a tough decision to make. By now they were nearly three thousand nautical miles from home base in Hawaii and less than nine hundred miles from their patrol area. *Nautilus* carried four diesel-generators, two big 16-cylinder, 1,600 horsepower engines that could each produce 1,200 kilowatts of power to drive two electric motors, which in turn drove two propeller shafts. Two smaller auxiliary engines, rated at 400 horsepower, could generate 300 kilowatts each. The flexible diesel-electric propulsion scheme used on most American submarines allowed these engines to power the shaft motors or charge batteries in any combination. Therefore, *Nautilus* could continue to operate with one main engine gone. However, for the rest of the patrol her surface speed would be reduced to 11.5 knots (from a maximum of fourteen knots), and only nine knots

---

2. Out of commission. Broken.
3. Told in a March 2004 interview with Harold "Buzz" Lee.

when charging batteries. The initial charging rate would be cut almost in half and a quick charge would no longer be possible. Another concern was reliability. Loss of another main engine would put the submarine in a difficult position indeed. This point was driven home the following evening when number one main engine shut down. Speed dropped to five knots. The battery was low, but starting a charge would reduce speed further. Fortunately, Bruck was able to get the engine running again in short order, but the consequences of losing power were clear.

Irvin continued west, running at reduced speed on two engines to save fuel when possible. *Nautilus* had a fuel capacity of about 147,000 gallons (530 tons) of diesel fuel, which gave her a range of more than nine thousand nautical miles at ten knots cruising speed. With the long transit and orders to spend thirty days in their assigned patrol area, they would have to make compromises, and their engine problems only made matters worse. On February 12, as they entered their patrol area, Irvin met with Lieutenant Jarvis and Chief Bruck to discuss options and strategies.

"Bruck, what's the status of the engines?" enquired Irvin.

"Well, sir, number one, three, and four are all running fine. I'm afraid there's nothing I can do out here about number two."

"OK, that's what I expected. Mr. Jarvis, what do you have on fuel?"

Jarvis had been checking oil consumption and performing calculations. He referred to numbers and notes scribbled on a yellow-lined pad.

"Captain, our transit out here has cost us 51,945 gallons. If we stop at Midway to refuel on the way home that will take about 37,500 gallons at the same rate. Keeping 10 percent in reserve, that gives us 42,800 gallons available on station." He paused as Irvin looked at the numbers, and after the captain nodded his understanding, Jarvis continued.

"So, as I see it, if we run on the surface at two-thirds speed during the day and one-third at night, we can stay on station in our patrol area for seventeen days."

"But that's not much more than half our assigned time!" protested Irvin.

"Sir, why do we have to go two-thirds speed during the day?" asked Bruck. As a machinist mate concerned with engines, he spent little time in the control room or bridge.

"Well, Chief, you see *Nautilus* takes a while to dive, and a *long* while if we're going slow. If we're poking along at one-third speed, it could take us five minutes to submerge. When a Jap plane is bearing down on us, we need to dive faster than that!"

"Right," agreed Irvin. "Two-thirds speed during daylight hours is mandatory. So, Mr. Jarvis," he continued, "what if we run submerged during the day?"

"Well, we'd use no fuel during the day and could charge at night at one-third speed or maybe a little better. I'd expect we'd use less than half the fuel," replied the executive officer.

"Of course we'd cover less ground, but at least we could stay out here," said Irvin. "Let's see . . ." he paused while jotting some figures on Jarvis's pad. "If we run submerged during the day for the first twenty-one days, then surfaced at two-thirds speed during the day for the last nine, we can cover all thirty assigned patrol days."

They all agreed that was a good plan.[4]

Nautilus continued west until the fifteenth, then reversed course and headed southeast for a couple of days, then northeast at higher speed for two more days, covering a five-hundred-mile long swath of the Philippine Sea. Other than a hint of gunfire over the horizon on one occasion, nothing was seen. A flurry of messages about potential contacts, including a possible sortie of the superbattleship *Yamato* from Guam, sent them fruitlessly back and forth about the northeast corner of the area for several days before Irvin continued back down to the southwest. The three working engines continued to run smoothly.

Fifteen hundred nautical miles to the southeast, Admiral Nimitz and the US Marines were continuing their conquest of the central Pacific, assaulting the next Japanese island base in the Marshalls, a large coral formation known as Eniwetok Atoll.[5] About 3,500 Japanese troops and civilian workers manned the outpost occupying the islets of Engebi, Eniwetok, and Parry, which served as an aircraft refueling base. The attack began with a massive air strike on the Japanese fleet anchorage at Truk

---

4. This exchange was based on details in the patrol report as well as Irvin's oral history. Though meetings like this probably took place, the details of the roles of Jarvis and Bruck are speculative.

5. Also spelled Enewetak or sometimes Eniewetok.

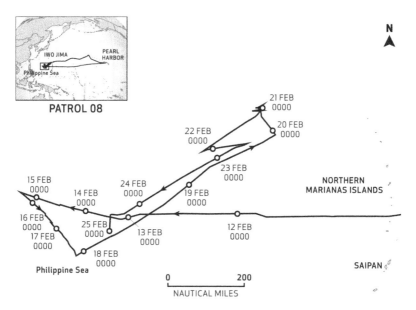

With engine troubles and poor intelligence, *Nautilus* spent fruitless days patrolling sea lanes. ILLUSTRATION BY BETHANY JOURDAN.

Atoll[6] some six hundred nautical miles to the west. Known as Operation Hailstone, on February 17 and 18, 1944, a force of nine US aircraft carriers, attendant battleships, and other warships hammered the island base and the ships anchored there. Between air and surface ship attacks over the two days, the Japanese lost some 250 warplanes (with the irreplaceable loss of many experienced pilots) and about forty ships—two light cruisers, four destroyers, nine auxiliary ships, and about two dozen cargo vessels. Meanwhile, naval bombardment of Eniwetok Atoll began followed by Marine landings on Engebi and Eniwetok Islands on February 18. A regiment of the New York Army National Guard supported the Marines. Most of the fighting was over by February 20 with the loss of 122 American troops. More than two thousand Japanese fell defending the two islands leaving just a few dozen captured.

The third island of the atoll, Parry, was the headquarters of the island defense brigade and was more heavily defended. On February 22, the

---

6. Now known as Chuuk.

battleships USS *Tennessee* and USS *Pennsylvania*[7] and a pair of cruisers delivered a thorough bombardment of the tiny teardrop-shaped islet, the defenders finding scant protection in trenches and foxholes. Marines of the Engebi assault, who were given a couple of days rest afterward, came ashore at Parry later that morning. By the end of the day, the island was largely secured with the loss of another 73 Marines and more than 1,200 Japanese. Eniwetok Atoll became a base for the US Navy forward operations, including later attacks on the Mariana and Caroline Islands to the west.

As February waned, the ship was into her third week of patrol with absolutely nothing to report. Finally, on March 1, just before sunset, patience was rewarded.

"Sir! Ships dead ahead!" cried the lookout.

Lieutenant (jg) Winner, officer of the deck, peered to the northwest. The sun was poised on the horizon ahead of him, making it difficult to see, and easier for an enemy ship to see *Nautilus*. Squinting through his binoculars, he replied, "I see them. Submerge the ship, quick dive! Clear the bridge!"

Lookouts scrambled below in a flash as geysers of air shot from the main ballast tank vents and the ship began to settle. Winner jumped down the ladder after them and pulled the hatch shut overhead as he descended into the conning tower below. "Last man down, hatch secured!" he called to the men in the control room below.

"Mr. Winner, what do you see?" asked Irvin as he climbed the ladder into the conning tower from the control room.

"Looks like two ships, Captain." Winner was already on the periscope.

"Very well. Man battle stations. Ahead two-thirds." With a fully charged battery Irvin could afford to close the range quickly.

---

7. Both of these ships were hit during the Japanese sneak attack at Pearl Harbor. They were repaired and put back in service in a matter of months.

BONG! BONG! BONG! The general quarters alarm rang out. Men rushed to their stations, eager for some action after weeks of transit and uneventful patrol. In minutes *Nautilus* was ready for battle.

"Battle stations manned and ready," reported Lieutenant Jarvis, taking his place in the conning tower to serve as attack coordinator.

"Can you identify the ships, Mr. Winner?" Visibility was poor looking into the setting sun.

"No, sir," replied the young lieutenant. "But I have an estimated range based on our height of eye and distance to the horizon. About eighteen miles."

"Well, that's rough, but a good start. Let's get closer." After a quarter hour of studying the target in the waning twilight and consulting the recognition guides, Irvin concluded they were looking at two ships in column, both freighters, the lead resembling *Argentina Maru* followed by *Canberra Maru*. The ships were heading on a nearly reciprocal course to the submarine, making about fourteen knots. Adding the three-knot speed of *Nautilus*, the distance closed steadily. Unfortunately, the poor visibility made it impossible to get a good reading of the range, and sonar could hear nothing.

"Make ready tubes one through six," ordered Irvin. He remained submerged, choosing to make a periscope approach. He planned to allow the targets to close to about two thousand yards and shoot the forward tubes at the lead ship as they passed with a broadside angle. He would then reverse course and fire the stern tubes at the second ship. It was a good plan, but chance did not favor it. At about five thousand yards, the commander was watching as the lead ship zigged directly toward the submarine putting *Nautilus* "into an embarrassing situation" as he described it. With the target heading straight for them, a bow shot was out of the question.

"Ahead full! Left full rudder!" called Irvin. "Steady two-eight-zero. Down scope!" As the periscope slid into its well, he addressed the attack party in the conning tower. "Listen up! The target has zigged toward us. I very much doubt he saw the periscope in the darkness, but it's just bad luck. We'll run off his track for a few minutes then fire stern tubes at the lead ship." He turned toward the plot and continued. "Since we can't get a good range, figure fourteen knots directly toward our position before we turn. Quickly!"

The plotters set to work with just minutes to figure a solution and set up the shot. At 1903, all was ready.

"Final bearing and shoot! Up scope!" called Irvin. As the periscope lens broke the surface above, the target came into view.

"Bearing . . . mark!"

"Fire five!" called the TDC operator, followed in a few seconds by "Fire six!"

Two torpedoes slid from their tubes and sped toward the target. At twenty-nine knots, the new Mark-18 electric weapons were slower than the Mark-14s used in previous patrols, and they had a much shorter range. However, they were far more reliable and did not produce a wake of bubbles pointing back to the submarine firing them, especially important in daytime engagements. This was not a promising shot, however, with poor firing solution and close to a head-on angle. The torpedo run would be about 3,500 yards, nearly the maximum range of the weapon.

"Torpedoes running straight and normal," called sonar.

"Very well. Ahead two-thirds. Left full rudder, steady on one-three-zero." Irvin ordered to the attack party, "Setup tubes one, two, three, and four on the second target." At 1910 they were in position and four more torpedoes sped from the forward tubes, which had a much better chance, with range about 1,700 yards and a better angle.

"Rig for depth charge," ordered Irvin, anticipating a reaction from enemy escorts. In a few minutes, sonar reported, "Two torpedo hits!" followed immediately by the roar of depth charges.

"Make your depth three hundred feet," ordered Irvin. Depth charges continued to burst around them, in between reports of explosions from the direction of the targets. Irvin evaded by heading in the direction the ships had come from, and after three hours and eighteen depth charges sounds of the enemy faded. At 2212 Irvin came to periscope depth and saw nothing. A half hour later *Nautilus* rose to the surface, her crew confident that more Japanese military cargo would not reach its destination.[8]

---

8. Irvin listed a *Canberra Maru*-class ship as "damaged or probably sunk." Admiral Lockwood credited him with damaging the 6,480-ton freighter.

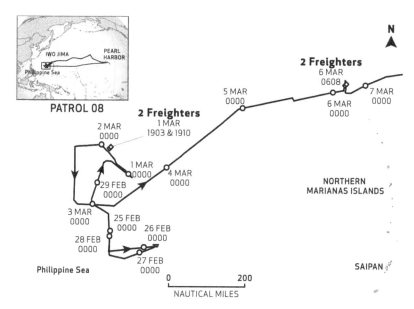

Nautilus ended her patrol early due to dwindling fuel but was able to attack two convoys. ILLUSTRATION BY BETHANY JOURDAN.

Nautilus continued her patrol, Jarvis and Bruck anxiously monitoring fuel oil levels. They had spent days running on the surface chasing phantom *Yamato* sightings, hoping to catch a convoy at the expense of more oil than planned. Finally, on the afternoon of March 3, Irvin had to admit that their dwindling fuel supply would not allow them to stay in the Philippine Sea any longer. Nine days short of the assigned patrol time, the ship turned to the northeast and headed for Midway Island.

As the submarine began her long journey home, the relentless march of Allied forces across the Pacific continued. Having wrapped up campaigns in the Gilbert and Marshall Islands, Nimitz and his naval and Marine forces were gearing up for the next major target: the Mariana Islands and the Japanese stronghold at Saipan. Meanwhile, General MacArthur and his army divisions were moving past the Solomon Islands and preparing to land on New Guinea in April. Fighting continued in

Bougainville (where *Nautilus* operated on her fourth patrol) with a major Japanese counterattack in mid-March that led to defeat and withdrawal inland of the bulk of enemy forces. MacArthur soon began withdrawing American troops to rest and refit, turning the Bougainville campaign over to the Australian army, which would continue to battle the Japanese on the island through the rest of the war. By the end, the Imperial Army would suffer terribly, losing more than 43,000 men (more than half to disease and starvation) out of the 65,000 troops originally sent to occupy Bougainville. Though Allied military casualties were relatively light, with more than 1,200 American and Australian soldiers lost, the toll on the civilian population was dreadful. Some estimates numbered local deaths at 25 percent of the prewar population of 52,000.

MacArthur wisely chose not to attack the Japanese fortress at Rabaul head on. The huge air wing and massive fleet anchorage would be neutralized by air raids and bypassed. Capturing of less heavily defended islands, such as the Trobriand and Admiralty Islands, as well as major air attacks from land-based bombers in Bougainville and carrier forces, met with great success and eliminated Rabaul as an effective base of operations. Many valuable Japanese aircraft and pilots were lost in defense of the stronghold, and although it held out until war's end, a huge garrison was trapped there, and the Allies did not have to fight it.

Meanwhile, *Nautilus* continued northeast. In the early morning hours of March 6, radar picked up a scent.

"Conn, radar. Contact bearing one-three-eight true, 23,500 yards, appearing to be four ships."

Lieutenant Davis, officer of the deck, did not hesitate.

"Man battle stations!" The general quarters alarm brought Irvin to the conning tower. Radar continued to track the convoy and saw that it was heading north, probably from Saipan heading back to Tokyo. Having picked them up to the southeast, *Nautilus* was in an ideal position.

"Mr. Davis, come left to zero-two-zero. We'll parallel their course and let them catch up to us."

"Aye, sir!" Davis gave the order. The chase was on. An hour later, just after 0400, the gibbous moon dropped below the horizon. The first light of dawn would not appear for another hour and a half, so *Nautilus* continued to close on surface in the darkness. At 0525, Irvin submerged and turned to the east. Minutes later sonar reported echo ranging from the northeast.

"Up periscope!" Irvin fixed his eye to the lens and peered into the brightening horizon. "I see two ships, the larger bearing . . . mark!"

"Three-three-three degrees relative," called the periscope assistant, reading the numbers off the bearing ring. *Nautilus* was heading due east, so that put the contact at 063° true bearing, to the northeast, consistent with the source of echo ranging.

"Very well. Down scope. Make ready all forward tubes. Right standard rudder, steady one-three-zero," ordered Irvin. *Nautilus* turned away briefly to slow the approach of the enemy ships as Irvin consulted the recognition guide. After several minutes, Irvin returned to course 090° and made another periscope observation.

"The bigger ship looks like the *Hokki Maru*, a freighter," Irvin told the attack party. "The second resembles *America Maru*. Could be a hospital ship. I see crosses on her funnels."

"She's in a military convoy," commented Jarvis.

"Right," agreed Irvin. A hospital ship, by the Geneva Conventions, must not be used for any military purpose or be in violation of legal restrictions. Still, according to the Conventions, such a ship should not be fired on unless first warned and given reasonable time to comply. From a practical standpoint, there were many loopholes in this obligation, including if diversion or capture was not feasible or no method to exercise control was available. Certainly, it was not feasible for *Nautilus* to sail into the middle of an enemy convoy and hail one of the ships to demand it comply with the Conventions! Violations could easily be considered grave enough to allow the ship to be classified as a military objective. Irvin did not give this matter too much further thought as the range closed to the targets.

"Come left to zero-seven-zero," he called. "We will fire tubes one and two at the larger ship. Then I'll take another bearing and we'll use three and four on the trailing ship." A chorus of acknowledgments followed the captain's orders as the men made final preparations. The range tracked to about two thousand yards.

"Final bearing and shoot! Up periscope!" Irvin marked the first target, and two torpedoes were on their way. A minute later he raised the periscope again and two more fish sped toward the second target. Expecting the first torpedoes to arrive momentarily, he left the periscope up and watched as two geysers rose from the side of the nearer ship.

"Two hits!" he called. Still mesmerized by the scene before him, he continued to watch as *America Maru* took two hits as well.

"Hit on the second ship, between after stack and mast. There are flames! Oh, wow, another hit, just about blew the stern off! No way she can remain afloat!"[9]

Irvin's attention was finally diverted by the sight of an escort destroyer bearing down on them, smoking heavily at full speed.

"Down scope! Make your depth three hundred feet! Rig for depth charge!"

Sonar reported hearing two more explosions and crackling sounds all around. At 0615 the first depth charges fell.

CLICK BOOM! CLICK BOOM! CLICK BOOM! BOOOOM!

These were close. A second Japanese escort destroyer joined the first and tried to get a good fix on the submarine. Fortunately for *Nautilus*, there was a strong thermal layer (change in sea temperature) at about 280 feet, which reflected sound waves and confused the attackers. The submarine lurked within this layer and tried to slink away. After an hour of probing attacks, one destroyer made a determined run, his screws heard very plainly throughout the ship as she passed overhead. Seven depth charges came down and detonated, deep, heavy, and close. Irvin reported later, "This placed him on the first team."

The escorts, possibly joined by a third ship, worked together, echo ranging, then stopping and listening, but they never appeared to get a good contact. Irvin changed course regularly and stayed under the cloaking thermal layer as the Japanese tried to make sense of the confused picture below. None of the twenty-one depth charges dropped on the submarine that day found their mark, but it was another narrow escape for *Nautilus*.

---

9. Lockwood and JANAC credited *Nautilus* with the sinking of *America Maru*, 6,100 tons. Lockwood also recognized damage to a *Hokki Maru* class.

"Captain," called Phil Eckert, the diving officer of the watch. "Having trouble holding depth. Have pumped auxiliaries dry and we're still sinking. Request speed!"

"They'll hear our engine noise if we speed up," worried Irvin.

"We don't have much choice," commented Jarvis, noting that they were slowly sinking. "We're down to 330 feet."

"Very well, we'll risk it. Ahead two-thirds!"

The electric motors spun the screws, which bit into the sea as the submarine picked up speed. Engine sounds, propeller beats, and flow noise emanated from the ship, telltale signs of a submarine. They could only hope the thermal layer would hide them. "Five degrees up!" called Eckert, adding lift to the ship. Depth held at 330 feet, but would not rise. "Seven degrees!" Finally, at a severe eight-degree up angle, the ship began slowly to rise.

"Three-two zero," called Eckert, reading off the depth in ten-foot increments. "Sir, at this up angle I can't get a suction on the trim pump," he said. "I can't get the water out until we level off!" He continued, "Three hundred, still rising."

"Very well," acknowledged Irvin. "We'll take her up to 280, then slow and level off."

At 280 feet depth, Irvin slowed the ship and Eckert eased the angle. Water was pouring into the motor room, a problem they had experience with. The motormen rigged a hose to pump motor room bilge water forward, from where it could be pumped to sea. This kept up with the water flowing in, but the ship slowly sank. When they reached 330 feet, Irvin had enough.

"Secure pumping! Ahead two-thirds! Mr. Eckart, get me back up!"

Eckert put an angle on the ship and slowly brought her up again, all the while sonar listened anxiously for echo ranging and tried to keep tabs on the enemy above. They repeated this procedure for the next several hours, hoping the leak would not increase and the destroyers overhead would not get a bead on them. Finally, at 1125, the sounds above faded. After another hour and a half, Irvin ventured a trip to periscope depth and saw clear seas all around. The rest of the day *Nautilus* remained submerged while the crew aft did their best to stem the leaks. Finally, well after sunset at 1934, *Nautilus* surfaced and set course for Midway.

Irvin was heading to his cabin for some well-deserved shuteye when a junior radioman appeared with a clipboard.

"What is it, son?" Irvin enquired as he tried to focus his eyes on the message. The radioman was silent as the captain read.

"What!" he cried. "A report??"

"What is it, sir?" asked Jarvis as he passed by on his way to the wardroom.

"It seems that the Japanese complained to Geneva that we sank a hospital ship. Geneva complained to Allied command who complained to Washington, and all hell broke loose." Reading on, he continued, "Washington wants a report from Pearl, who wants it from us!"

"Well, if that don't beat all!" Jarvis looked at his watch. "And in just twelve hours, all the way around the world! Wow!"

"Well, no use bellyaching. Get the logs and have Mr. Eckert meet us in the wardroom. We'd better get that report out tonight!" Irvin rubbed his eyes and headed for the coffee mess.

The details of Irvin's testimony and later investigations would exonerate *Nautilus* of any wrongdoing in the affair. Though *America Maru* had earlier served as a hospital ship, in January she had been chartered by the Imperial Japanese Navy and was operating as a belligerent vessel and fair game according to the Geneva Conventions. Regardless of the wartime propriety of the attack, the sinking of *America Maru* was a tragic case. Unknown to Irvin and his men, the vessel was sailing from Saipan to Japan with 642 persons aboard, including 511 civilian evacuees, mostly woman and children. The ship went down so quickly that only forty-three survivors were recovered.[10]

---

10. These figures were cited on the Imperial Japanese Navy Page (www.combinedfleet.com) by Bob Hackett. Other sources, including Blair (1975), suggest as many as 1,700 civilians were aboard.

Nautilus continued transiting east as Bruck watched the fuel level drop and Irvin vacillated between a refueling stop at Midway and the hope they might make the additional thousand miles direct to Pearl Harbor. On March 12, after some discussion with his officers and motormen, Irvin had to admit they'd never make it to Pearl, and even Midway was looking tight. But Bruck had an idea.

"Captain, we may be short on fuel oil, but we have plenty of lube oil," offered the chief.

"How does that help?" wondered Jarvis. "We can't burn lube oil. I don't get it!"

"We can't burn it straight, but we can mix some of it with the fuel oil. I would try a one-to-two proportion."

They discussed the idea for a while, but it seemed that they were running out of options. Irvin gave the go ahead. Bruck headed back to the engine room and set to work. By evening, they were running the engines on the mixture, and all seemed to be going well. Irvin was optimistic. "Commenced burning lube oil in proportion one to two to conserve fuel," he wrote in his diary. "At this ratio, we would have sufficient fuel to make Pearl provided we encountered no head seas." He changed course to head to Hawaii.

His optimism was short-lived. After a day or so the engines started to smoke. Soon, a long black plume trailed behind the submarine, stretching out for dozens of miles. A more obvious telltale sign of their presence could not be imagined. The crew were besides themselves with worry that a Japanese plane would find them. Lookouts kept an especially sharp eye. On the afternoon of March 14, number one main engine fell silent. A beleaguered Nick Bruck explained the situation to the captain, who went aft to investigate.

"Sir, I'm sorry, but we're having trouble with number one. The injectors are clogged with carbon deposits on account of the lube oil. My men are cleaning them, and we'll have it back in operation soon. But the lube oil is a real problem."

"I understand," said Irvin. "Do what you can. But as I see it, we're going to have to keep burning lube oil if we ever expect to make it even to Midway!"

Number four main engine was also showing signs of the deleterious effect of the lube oil. Irvin changed course for Midway, still six hundred nautical miles away. Followed by a smear of smog, *Nautilus* limped across the International Date Line on the afternoon of March 16, and the next morning (still the same day owing to crossing the Date Line) the submarine chugged into the Midway harbor with just about empty fuel tanks.

If any of the *Nautilus* sailors expected a short rest or a chance to hit the beach at Midway, they were sadly disappointed.

"OK, ladies, up and at 'em!" Ensign Porterfield briefly reverted to his former chief persona as he rousted the lounging men to their feet. "We have work to do!"

"What is it, chief—I mean, sir?" John Sabbe rolled out of his rack.

"You need to get these fish outta here," said Red. "We're offloading ten Mark-18's to make room for thirty-two warheads. Plus baggage."

"Baggage?" wondered Sabbe. "We taking tourists?"

Sabbe was joking, but it was no joke. It turned out that a vessel had sunk in the channel at Midway, and though everyone was safely rescued, the crew needed to get back to Pearl. *Nautilus* happened to be conveniently available. So besides offloading torpedoes, loading cargo, refueling, and taking on water, the crew had to find room for 102 officers and enlisted men for the trip to Pearl Harbor. By 1600 that evening, the exhausted crew, and grumpy passengers, headed back out to sea and continued east.

The trip was miserable, and no one was happy. *Nautilus* was directed to make the trip in four days, which meant they had to run on the surface day and night. The seas were rough, and there was no respite offered by submerged operations. It was crowded. The passengers were uncomfortable, and the crew was surly. Finally, at 1030 on March 21, the boat moored at the Pearl Harbor submarine base, completing a successful, but grueling, fifty-six day patrol covering nearly 10,800 nautical miles.

Squadron Commander Momsen and Admiral Lockwood were pleased with Irvin's patrol, noting the handicap of slow speed compared to newer submarines. They were also delighted with the performance of the new Mark-18 torpedoes. No one mentioned that the patrol was cut short. This would be William Irvin's third and last patrol, as he was detached on April 18. He was awarded the Bronze Star for meritorious service on the sortie, and served on the Pacific submarine staff for the duration of the war. He would go on to command Submarine Squadron Two in New London, Connecticut, after the war and later the cruiser USS *Northampton*. He eventually retired as a rear admiral.

The ship's incoming commanding officer, Cdr. George Sharp, embarked on April 2 to lead *Nautilus* into a new chapter of service and a new phase of Pacific conflict.

PART III

THE SPY SQUADRON

BOMBS BEGAN FALLING ON THE AIRFIELDS OF LUZON IN THE NORTHERN Philippines on December 8, 1941, the morning of the infamous Japanese attack on Pearl Harbor.[1] General MacArthur's Far East Air Force lost half its planes in the first forty-five minutes of hostilities, most of them caught on the ground by accurate bombing from crack Japanese pilots and relentless strafing by escorting Zero fighters. Allied air power was all but eliminated over the coming days as aging P-40 aircraft flown by inexperienced pilots were no match for the nimble Zeros. A few surviving bombers and fighters were withdrawn from the Philippine theater on December 20, their commander hastily evacuated. Meanwhile, the first waves of nearly 130,000 Japanese troops came ashore on Luzon in the north, Mindanao to the south, and Legaspi, less than two hundred miles from Manila. The US Asiatic Fleet offered little resistance. Beset by air attacks and with naval facilities on Cavite destroyed, the fleet withdrew. The 31,000 US Army and 120,000 Filipino troops[2] left to defend the island were scattered and ineffective, local forces hampered by lack of a common language and illiteracy among the noncommissioned officers. Many Filipino units lacked proper clothing and equipment. As

---

1. Being on the other side of the International Date Line, the date in Hawaii was December 7.

2. These numbers vary among sources depending on whether one counts reserve forces and civilians under arms. The US Office of the Provost Marshal General reported in November 1945 that sixty-five thousand American and Filipino fighting forces were present in the initial stages of the campaign. Thomas Huber (1991) in *The American Bataan Campaign* tallies Allied forces in the Philippines at 111,700 in a more detailed inventory.

the invaders approached Manila on the day after Christmas, MacArthur declared the capital an open city[3] and abandoned it to the Japanese. The remaining American and Filipino forces withdrew to the Bataan Peninsula while bombers continued to pound the city regardless of its open status, hitting military and civilian targets, in many cases simply rearranging the rubble of earlier bombings.

Through early spring, Allied forces held Bataan against withering attacks, retreating with backs against the sea. President Roosevelt ordered MacArthur to evacuate to Australia and take command of forces in the South West Pacific theater. MacArthur departed by PT boat with family and staff on March 11, later vowing "I shall return." The peninsula was surrendered on April 10, and the remaining forces, entrapped in the island fortress of Corregidor, surrendered on May 6, with all Allied forces in the Philippines officially surrendering on May 8. In what many consider to be the worst military defeat in US history, twenty-five thousand Allied soldiers were killed and some one hundred thousand captured.[4] Over the ensuing three and a half years, the latter were forced to endure harsh treatment in prison camps, many crowded into holds of "hell ships" with no water, food, or ventilation, and shipped to Japan to labor in factories and mines. As many as eighty thousand prisoners of war were transferred to camps under brutal conditions and wanton killings in what came to be known as the Bataan Death March. Some estimates suggest as many as eighteen thousand men, mostly Filipinos, lost their lives in that one episode alone.

In spite of the grim circumstances, many of the surviving defenders eluded capture and refused to surrender. Some were the remnants of formally trained army units who pledged to continue to fight the Japanese occupiers as a guerrilla force. Other bands of resistance fighters grew organically through the efforts of individual leaders who recruited members from the general population. These irregular contingents became

---

3. An "open city" is declared when all defensive measures have been abandoned, with the expectation that opposing military forces will peacefully occupy it and avoid harming civilians and destroying cultural landmarks.
4. The US Office of the Provost Marshal General (1945) suggests "at least 53,000 American and Filipino fighting men" were captured by the Japanese.

more numerous and soon began to inflict significant harm on the Japanese who were forced to form separate guerilla-fighting units aside from their regular army troops. By July 1942, these resistance forces came to be recognized by Allied command, and in December and the coming months, volunteers were sent to the Philippines to make contact with the guerillas. Notable among them was Filipino American pilot Capt. Jesús Villamor and businessman (holding a commission in the Naval Reserve) Lt. Cdr. Thomas "Chick" Parsons who established liaison with the men ashore and organized supply and evacuation missions. Most of these were conducted by submarines, informally known as the Spy Squadron, or Spyron. The first Spyron mission saw USS *Gudgeon* (SS-211) slip into the Sulu Sea in January 1943 and deliver Captain Villamor ashore on Negros Island where he began to set up a communications network.

The Philippine resistance continued to grow and thrive despite Japanese counterefforts, including reprisals against the helpless civilian population. Eventually, more than 250,000 persons were recognized as having fought in the resistance movement. Their efforts were so successful that by the time MacArthur and his army returned to retake the islands, more than half of the archipelago was already under control by friendly forces.

By mid-1944, the Japanese empire was in full retreat. In June, a massive naval fleet pounded Saipan, and in a costly battle that lasted until early July, the island was secured by US Marines. In an effort to blunt the Allied advance and force a decisive naval engagement, the Japanese fleet sortied en-masse from bases in the Philippines and elsewhere in Operation A-Go. Nine Imperial Fleet aircraft carriers and five battleships with dozens of cruisers and destroyers faced off against the American 5th Fleet, which outnumbered the Japanese in every category, most notably carrier aircraft. They met in the Philippine Sea west of Guam. In two days of pitched aerial battle, three of Japan's largest aircraft carriers were sunk along with other vessels sunk or damaged as opposed to damage to only one US battleship. The battle was nicknamed "The Great Marianas Turkey Shoot" by American aviators who destroyed hundreds of carrier and land-based aircraft, by some estimates as many as 750 planes. What was in 1942 the greatest naval air armada ever assembled had been reduced to an impotent force that would never recover.

This was followed by the capture of the nearby island of Tinian, which became an air base for B-29s of the Twelfth Air Force, sent to bomb the homeland of Japan. At the same time Guam was recaptured, completing the campaign in the Mariana Islands. Meanwhile, the American Submarine Force was striking a telling blow on enemy merchant shipping. By war's end, nearly three hundred US submarines were in operation and as many as five million tons of enemy shipping had been sunk. Most of the submarines in the US fleet were of the newer *Gato* and *Balao* classes, faster and deadlier, so the older *Nautilus* and *Narwhal* were assigned to transport or other special duties. They became the stalwarts of the Spy Squadron, with *Narwhal* conducting her first of nine Spyron patrols in November 1943. *Nautilus* would conduct her first foray into Japanese-controlled Philippines waters in June 1944, her ninth war patrol.

CHAPTER EIGHT

Mindanao and Leyte

"DID YOU HEAR ABOUT BANANAS?"

Nick Bruck, John Sabbe, and Foy Hester were relaxing in the chief's quarters as *Nautilus* headed southwest from Pearl Harbor, on the way to Brisbane, Australia, to begin her ninth war patrol. Nick Bruck had just heard the news that their crewmate John Peirano had been promoted to ensign.

"That would be *Mister* Bananas to you, Nick! That good-time Charlie is an officer now, believe it or not!" Sabbe chuckled with the rest of them. Peirano was a colorful character who had a reputation for carousing and telling tall tales.

"How did he get the nickname 'Bananas?'" wondered Foy.

"No one seems to know," replied Sabbe, "though it fits. Did you know he was a professional gambler before the war? At least, according to Buzz."

"Well, that explains how he always beats me at cards," mused Nick. Much of the lore surrounding Peirano had been supplied by Buzz Lee, himself a good storyteller. Peirano came aboard *Nautilus* on her fourth patrol, but Buzz claimed to have served with him before the war. According to Lee, their submarine was getting underway one day without Peirano, who failed to show up in time for sailing and had been declared AWOL.[1] As the vessel was leaving harbor, a speedboat was seen coming up astern. On board were Peirano and two women, presumably

---

1. Absent Without Official Leave, a serious offense.

his companions during the previous night. The boat raced alongside, and the delinquent sailor managed to scramble aboard. He claimed to have paid fifty dollars (a considerable sum at the time) to hire the speedboat.[2]

Apparently, the navy recognized Peirano's leadership abilities in spite of his flamboyant antics and, as with Porterfield, allowed him to stay on board. The freshly minted officer would join a remade wardroom led by the submarine's new commanding officer. George Sharp was the youngest commander in the navy in 1939 when as a lieutenant he captained the USS *Falcon*. The rescue ship with the new Momsen diving bell was famously used to save the lives of sailors aboard the sunken submarine USS *Squalus*. His next command was less than auspicious as he led USS *Spearfish* on patrol near Truk in June 1943. Alerted to a massive Japanese fleet of fourteen warships, including three aircraft carriers, he chose to make a conservative nighttime periscope approach. He fired torpedoes without hitting anything and was run off by an approaching destroyer without making further attacks. Admiral Lockwood was displeased by his lack of aggressiveness and relieved him. Sharp redeemed himself a few months later while commanding the rescue vessel USS *Florikan* with a daring salvage of another stricken submarine. His reward was a second chance at a submarine command.

Phil Eckert, survivor of the man overboard incident on the fourth patrol and expert diving officer, detached leaving Sharp and Executive Officer Ben Jarvis to lead a team of junior lieutenants and ensigns over the next few patrols. Porterfield and Peirano offered a significant degree of experience to the young wardroom. Eckert took the opportunity between postings to get married, and then became executive officer on USS *Sea Robin* (SS-407). He later took command of USS *Gar* (SS-206) days before war's end. In later years, Eckert penned articles in the US Naval Academy alumni magazine *Shipmate*, including one about his experience going overboard on *Nautilus* and another detailing the fates of the 375 alumni submarine officers lost during World War II.[3] There is

---

2. From an interview with Harold "Buzz" Lee, December 2001.

3. "Still on Patrol," September 1987 issue of *Shipmate* and "Left Overboard from a Diving Submarine," June 1989.

no report of him requisitioning an ammunition hoist to set up and abuse at his home in Maryland.

The crew lost a half dozen veterans of the previous eight *Nautilus* war patrols along with seventeen other men, replacements bringing the crew roster to ninety-nine enlisted men and eleven officers. The ship got underway from Pearl Harbor on April 25, 1944, arriving in Brisbane on May 14, where the crew loaded assorted cargo bound for the Philippines. On May 20, they left Brisbane and cruised to Darwin via a scenic inland passage of the Great Barrier Reef and Torres Strait. Unfortunately for the engineers, continued problems with main engine cracked heads, broken head studs, cracked liners, and broken clutch shafts kept them busy in the engine room, unable to sightsee. The ship departed with only three engines operating, and thirty-six hours of labor were required to place number two main engine back in commission.

At Darwin, the crew labored to unload fourteen torpedoes and all handling gear, making room for 192,000 pounds of cargo (including some loaded in Brisbane). By May 29, all was ready for the submarine's first Spyron mission. Just before getting underway Lt. (jg) John Simmons came aboard, aiming to be put ashore on Mindanao to liaison with the guerillas. *Nautilus* headed north into the Indonesian archipelago, wending her way through narrow island passages and shallow channels, always on the lookout for enemy ships and aircraft. Charts were dubious, currents unpredictable, and weather always a challenge. Jarvis, recently promoted to lieutenant commander, served as navigator, and certainly had his hands full.

Two days into the transit, trouble struck.

"What was that?" wondered Lt. (jg) Charles Cummings, officer of the deck. An explosion had rocked the boat and was felt throughout the ship, but no enemy was in sight. *Nautilus* had been making standard speed on all four main engines, but she immediately slowed. In moments, the call came to the bridge.

"Fire in the engine room!"

Captain Sharp was on his way to the bridge while Jarvis headed aft to take charge of damage control. In moments he reported that the fire was

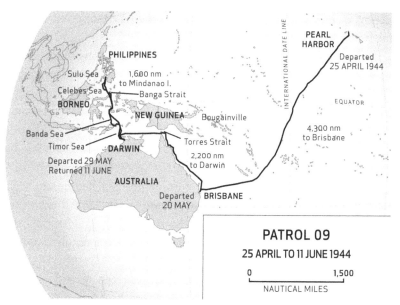

PATROL 09

25 APRIL TO 11 JUNE 1944

0   1,500

NAUTICAL MILES

Nautilus returned to Australia and was assigned to support the Philippines resistance as part of the Spyron program beginning with her ninth patrol.
ILLUSTRATION BY BETHANY JOURDAN.

out and requested ventilation. It took ten minutes of forced air to clear the smoke. The long-suffering Chief Bruck made his report.

"Sir, we had a crankcase explosion on number four," he said, mopping his sweaty brow with a dirty rag. "Thank God no one was hurt, though we have a few ears ringing." He continued, "All the outboard crankcase doors blew off and the blast started a rag fire in the bilges. We put that out right away."

"So where do we stand?" inquired Jarvis.

"Will have to get in there and see, sir. Right now, I don't know what happened and how much damage there is. Fortunately, the other engines seem to be OK, but we'll have to take number two offline while we're working on four."

"Very well. Do your best." Jarvis went forward to report to the captain. *Nautilus* continued on at reduced speed while the engineers got to work. The explosion was caused by either stuck or broken piston rings in one of the sixteen cylinders, and luckily the damage was confined to that single cylinder. Bruck and his men rebuilt the unit and remarkably had the engine running again ten grueling hours later. By the evening of June 1, *Nautilus* completed a transit of Banga Strait and entered the Celebes Sea, south of the Philippines island of Mindanao. The next morning, while cruising on the surface in glassy-calm seas, an enemy patrol craft was sighted, which immediately opened fire. All main engines cranked to full speed, but the patrol craft continued to close, firing continuously. Sharp ordered a quick dive, but kept tabs on the enemy through the periscope. The craft continued to approach, so *Nautilus* went deep and slunk away. Two days later as the boat nosed into Moro Gulf, three ships came out of a rain squall and caught *Nautilus* by surprise. Another deep dive avoided a pattern of five depth charges, and again she was able to evade.

The morning of June 5 marked the two year anniversary of the Battle of Midway, where *Nautilus* made her first war patrol. Fourteen of the current crew were on board that day, and the men regaled their junior crew members with their exploits. There was not much time for reminiscing, however, as the periscope watch saw signals from Coastwatchers on the beach near Tukuran on Mindanao Island. With the help of Lieutenant Simmons, Sharp was able to verify the proper security code and confirm the beach was clear to approach. While lurking just offshore in Illana Bay awaiting nightfall, sonar reported propeller noises on all three sets of sonar gear with a clear turn count of 125 revolutions per minute. Could a Japanese patrol be looking for them? The tension persisted for fifteen minutes until looks through the periscope confirmed the sounds to be nothing more than a nearby playful fish.

That evening at 1910, just before sunset, *Nautilus* approached to within a mile and a half of the beach. Red Porterfield had the deck and was on the periscope.

"Christ, will you look at this!" He let out a low whistle. "There must be a thousand men on the beach!"

"That's good, we'll need the manpower," commented Sharp. "Surface the ship!"

The submarine rose from the sea and cautiously nosed close to shore. A small launch flying American colors stood out.

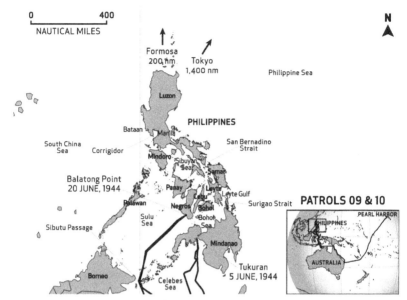

Nautilus delivered supplies at Tukuran on Mindanao Island on her ninth patrol. She returned to the area on her tenth patrol to deliver supplies at Balatong Point on Negros Island. ILLUSTRATION BY BETHANY JOURDAN.

"Open the hatches," ordered Sharp. "Mr. Porterfield, have the men begin striking cargo topside." The first lieutenant acknowledged the captain, and the crew began manhandling the ninety-six tons of supplies to the submarine's ample deck. There was no time to lose as such a large cargo would take hours to unload. The ship hove to at times as close as eight hundred yards from the beach. Col. Robert Bowler, commanding the men ashore, came aboard with a party of ten men to assist, and around thirty bancas,[4] outriggers, and rafts of all sizes came alongside to receive cargo. Annoyingly, they brought more Filipino men who came on board and stood about the deck, more in the way than helpful.

"This won't cut it," growled Porterfield. "We'll never get this crap off the boat in those pissant little canoes!" He set about to have the ship's motorboats launched, and gave orders to organize the working parties.

---

4. Also spelled bangka or panco, a small double-outrigger dugout canoe used in rivers and shallow coastal waters of the Philippines.

It proved to be quite a challenge, but the seasoned former chief petty officer was up to the task. Sharp later wrote: "Lack of organization or supervision of the working party from ashore was a serious matter. It was agreed that all work topside be done by the shore party, all work below decks by ship's force, but if we had waited for them to carry out that plan, we would be there yet." Under the watchful eye and sharp tongue of Porterfield, every available ship's officer and crewman set to work, loading most of the cargo into the boats. Each boat returned with a full load of Filipinos until the deck was so covered with standing or strolling men it was almost impossible to handle the cargo. The ship's motorboats carried much of the burden, loaded to many times their rated capacity with scant inches of freeboard. Amazingly, in just three hours all cargo was on the way ashore. Sharp commented, "The spirit of the ship's company was magnificent."

Besides the assigned cargo, Sharp directed the crew to hand over any unneeded supplies from the ship's stores. *Nautilus* delivered thirty-seven cases of 20-mm ammunition, 550 gallons of diesel oil, and a quantity of dry stores, including 210 pounds of white flour, all much appreciated by the ill-provisioned resistance fighters. The last trip delivered Lieutenant Simmons ashore. Boats were retrieved and stowed, and at 0247 *Nautilus* headed back out to sea, mission accomplished.

The trip back to Darwin was marked only by an encounter on the evening of June 7 with a belligerent schooner. Sharp manned battle stations and opened fire with six-inch guns, but at a range of more than six miles in growing darkness only near misses were observed. After a few salvos, Sharp broke off the attack as night fell. *Nautilus* arrived at Darwin on the morning of June 11 after a short, but successful sortie. Rear Adm. Ralph Christie, 7th Fleet commander, was pleased with the patrol and commented, "Enemy contacts were handled with sound judgement." Aggressiveness was not called for on a Spyron mission.

If the tired crew and aging submarine expected a respite for recuperation and repairs, they were profoundly misguided. Upon arrival in Darwin, the crew began immediately loading cargo for another Spyron mission. The next morning, four Filipino army enlisted men came on board bound for Negros Island north of Mindanao. At 1359, *Nautilus* was underway for her tenth war patrol, less than thirty hours after completing her ninth.

Three days later in the Banda Sea north of Timor, a two-masted schooner was sighted. Eager for action, Sharp called for battle stations and commenced firing with the main guns at five thousand yards. The sailboat crew immediately abandoned ship, but the gunners continued pumping round after round into the wreck. Finally, after twenty minutes and seventy-two shells of six-inch ammunition, Sharp called cease fire. A handful of survivors were observed, but with two lifeboats and land nearby the captain chose not to pick them up and let them fend for themselves. Regarding the prodigious expenditure of ammunition, he commented it was due to "excessive opening range, poor aiming, and my attempt to totally sink the craft."

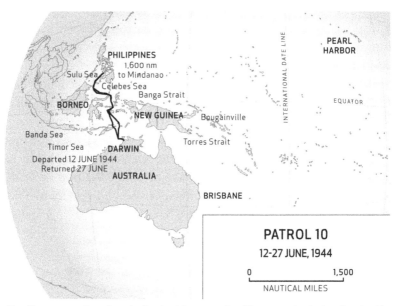

Nautilus encountered and attacked two small sailing vessels during her tenth patrol. ILLUSTRATION BY BETHANY JOURDAN.

Nautilus continued north. On June 17 she transited the narrow Sibutu Passage and entered the Sulu Sea, west of Mindanao, deep into enemy controlled waters. Aircraft sightings caused frequent dives, and radar interference was sensed all around. Heading northeast toward Negros Island, smoke was sighted over the horizon and Sharp bent on all engines making full speed. As the diesels hammered at high power, a serious knocking developed in number one. Bruck immediately shut it down, but upon stopping a violent crankcase explosion ripped through the space. As before, a fire started in the bilge and the room filled with smoke. Fifteen minutes later the fire was out, and smoke cleared, fortunately with no injuries. Sharp was forced to give up the chase as they could not close the contact at reduced three-engine speed.

Bruck and his beleaguered men set back to work on the damaged diesel. After some time, they discovered a failed bearing on one cylinder, which remained too hot to hold even after cooling for four hours. Adjacent bearings were damaged by the heat and explosion. Eventually, after four days of labor, Bruck was able to get the engine operating again by removing the entire piston and crank assembly and running the machine on fourteen cylinders. In the meanwhile, *Nautilus* limped toward her rendezvous at Negros on three diesels.

On the morning of June 20, a lookout sighted signals from Coast-watchers on Balatong Point, Negros Island. Sharp confirmed their authenticity and returned a reply, indicating they would stand offshore until evening. At 1940, the setting sun revealed a small fleet of sailboats, rowboats, and bancas heading for the submarine and Porterfield started the crew striking cargo topside. The boats came alongside and disgorged their passengers, led by Lt. Col. Salvador Abcede. As men began loading the small boats a parade of evacuees was taken aboard, including four women, one four-year-old girl, and twelve men and boys, among them a German prisoner of war. As the men worked with Abcede's well-organized force under ideal weather conditions in still waters, *Nautilus* hove to, 1,500 yards from shore. The four Filipino men embarked at Darwin went ashore. Sharp added to the assigned cargo 1,160 pounds of flour, sugar, coffee, powdered eggs, and powdered milk. By 0602, Colonel

Abcede bid farewell and returned to the beach, grateful for the vital supplies and a chance to evacuate a few civilians.

Nautilus retraced her route bound for Darwin, transiting the Sibutu and Banga Passages without incident. Sharp was surprised at the lack of Japanese surface patrols and aircraft. Returning to the Banda Sea on June 25, another sail was sighted, almost in the same location as the one attacked earlier. The vessel bent on all canvas, turned tail, and tried to run, but with all four engines back on line the submarine easily outpaced the sailboat. This time Sharp closed to 2,500 yards and dispatched the vessel with only nine rounds.

The water teemed with survivors and Sharp stood by to pick them up. The crew pulled aboard eighteen bedraggled Malaysians to add to their passenger manifest. Upon interrogation it was learned that the boat was bound for nearby Ambon under Japanese charter with more than twelve tons of pistol and rifle ammunition. The survivors also claimed that the Japanese shaved their heads and took most of their money. *Nautilus* continued south, now housing thirty-five evacuees and survivors placing extra work on the cooks and bakers. Regardless, Sharp commented that "all appeared to get a certain amount of satisfaction from feeding our half-starved passengers even to running a special menu for the children." The crew quartered the evacuees in the forward torpedo room and the Malaysian survivors in the aft torpedo room. The passengers were generally undernourished, and many suffered from malaria and tropical infections. A few of the Malaysians were treated for shrapnel wounds. Sharp concluded, "The wail of children and the stench of unwashed bodies was [*sic*] conquered by the men as are all obstacles by all good submariners."

The submarine, with her intrepid crew and grateful passengers, returned to Darwin on the afternoon of June 27. The 7th Fleet commander congratulated the officers and crew for another successful special mission, and recognized sinking of two schooners totaling 130 tons.[5]

---

5. JANAC did not credit such small sinkings.

During the middle of 1944, MacArthur and his armies were fighting their way across New Guinea with repeated amphibious landings and attacks through dense jungles, battling desperate and determined Japanese troops as well as disease, insects, heat, hunger, and exhaustion. US, Australian, Dutch, and British soldiers fought together, assisted by air attacks from the Australian mainland. Specially modified B-25 Mitchell light bombers and A-20 Havoc attack aircraft sported extra nose-mounted heavy machine guns to give close air support to ground troops and attack Japanese shipping trying to resupply their starving men. Through these efforts, the Allies continued to hold Port Moresby in southeastern New Guinea against repeated attacks and MacArthur's forces began to make headway. Though fighting continued in islands to the east including Bougainville, Allied armies began to wear down the 350,000 Japanese defending the region and inch their way west. By July 1944, at the expense of thousands of casualties, the Allies were within five hundred miles of Mindanao and MacArthur was making plans to recapture the Philippines. The efforts of the guerrillas ashore were becoming all the more crucial to this undertaking, while Japanese efforts to curb the insurgents became all the harsher targeting guerrillas and civilians alike. Stories of gruesome reprisals abound. These measures failed to deter the freedoms fighters and only served to incite their cause as numbers increased and territory controlled by the guerrillas expanded. Supply efforts by the Spyron missions continued to be crucial to these vital forces.

The weary *Nautilus* crew began loading cargo for another patrol soon after arrival at Darwin. A scheduled departure three days hence afforded the opportunity for minor repairs, though number one main engine would continue to be run on fourteen cylinders. On June 30, Lt. Cdr. George Rowe reported aboard with a party of twenty-two men for transportation to Mindoro. Four additional army enlisted men were received aboard for transportation to Leyte and Bohol. That evening, at 1835, the ship was underway for her eleventh war patrol and third Spyron mission.

She proceeded northwest on a now familiar route into the Timor Sea. On the morning of July 1, while proceeding on the surface not yet two hundred nautical miles from Darwin, radar reported a contact.

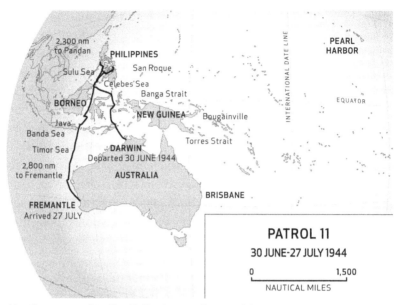

Nautilus returned to the Philippines on her third Spyron mission for her eleventh patrol. ILLUSTRATION BY BETHANY JOURDAN.

"Conn, radar. Contact dead ahead range five miles. Believe to be an aircraft."

"Very well," replied Lt. (jg) Charles Cummings who had just come on watch as officer of the deck. "Lookouts, radar has an aircraft ahead." This close to home it was presumed to be friendly, but *Nautilus* had been attacked by friendly forces before.

In moments the lookouts spotted it. "I see a single aircraft just off the starboard bow," reported one of the sharp-eyed sailors. Through binoculars he could see details of the plane four miles in the distance and headed across the bow. "It's a twin engine bomber."

"Probably a Beaufort," commented Cummings, referring to the British-built bomber. They watched as the plane zig-zagged away at two miles distant, then it suddenly turned and bore in at the submarine.

Cummings belatedly realized a submarine has no friends. "Dive, dive!" he yelled. Lookouts scrambled below as the young lieutenant watched a bomb tumble from the belly of the plane. The ship was just beginning to settle as the bomb hit the sea just ahead. The plane roared overhead as Cummings slammed the hatch.

"Last man down!" he rasped, breathing hard with fear and alarm in his voice. The lookout who first spotted the plane was already on the periscope. "He's coming around again!"

The aircraft reversed course and opened fire with wing-mounted guns. Luckily, his aim was no better as the rounds stitched the sea harmlessly about a hundred feet to starboard. Captain Sharp climbed into the conning tower.

"Report, Mr. Cummings!"

"Sir, we were attacked by a Beaufort bomber. A friendly." He detailed the incident. By then the submarine was safely below the waves.

"Are you sure it wasn't a Lily?" asked Sharp, which was the Allied code name for a Japanese Ki-48 light bomber, somewhat resembling the British Beaufort. The aircraft was widely used in the Philippines theater, but it would be quite a long way from home base this close to Australia.

"I don't believe so, Captain." Sharp made a point with the young officer to make no such assumptions in the future. They stayed submerged for an hour then surfaced and continued on. The next few days were uneventful, though many distant sails and other ships were seen. Nothing was deemed worthy of a chase and only once did an aircraft approach close enough to warrant another quick dive. On July 5, they completed transit of the Sibutu Passage and entered the Sulu Sea, this time continuing north along the coast of Panay to Mindoro, just one hundred miles south of enemy occupied Manila.

On July 8, *Nautilus* approached a pair of islands known as Pandan, just off the west coast of Mindoro. At 0230, three of commander Rowe's men paddled ashore in a rubber boat to reconnoiter the landing area. The submarine, submerged, lurked just offshore for the rest of the day, dodging sailboats and patrol craft, at one point rigging for depth charges, which thankfully, never appeared. In the late afternoon security signals were seen on the beach, indicating the coast was clear for landing the remaining troops and supplies. At 2052, *Nautilus* surfaced and came as close as 250 yards to shore as cargo was unloaded into rubber boats. By 0230, Commander Rowe and his twenty-two men were ashore, along with twelve tons of supplies to sustain their clandestine mission. *Nautilus* sped away at four engine speed, heading south to clear the area.

The crew's mission was far from complete as another rendezvous awaited them on the thirteenth. Circling the southern end of Negros Island, they entered the Mindanao Sea and spent a day patrolling the eastern end of the area, operating deep inside Japanese controlled territory in confined waters. No worthy targets were seen. The next evening, *Nautilus* transited Surigao Strait and entered Leyte Gulf, where the largest naval battle of the war would be fought in just a few months. On the morning of July 13, Sharp and his men scanned the beach off Lagoma but failed to see any signals, so they proceeded to an alternate site at San Roque the next day. This time signals were seen and that evening a flotilla of small boats led by Col. Ruperto Kangleón, a regular officer of the Filipino army. Kangleón had led an infantry regiment against the Japanese invasion but was captured and imprisoned. In December 1942 he managed to escape and returned to Leyte where he formed a guerrilla

Nautilus made deliveries at three locations and sent troops ashore during her eleventh patrol. ILLUSTRATION BY BETHANY JOURDAN.

movement. By early 1944 his forces were on the offensive, keeping the Japanese on the island at bay in fortified coastal towns. Kangleón and his men would provide a bridgehead for the Allied landings on Leyte in October when MacArthur would return as promised.

Cargo was quickly moved to the waiting boats. Sounds of fighting reached them from the jungle just a few miles away. Sharp reported that the colonel's men were well organized and disciplined, and that they had but one desire: "guns and ammunition." Regardless, *Nautilus* treated the guerrillas to additional items from the ship's stores, including over a half ton of corned beef, ham and bacon, powdered eggs, and sugar.[6] Soon after midnight on the fifteenth, the submarine headed back into Surigao Strait and west to Negros Island and the now familiar Balatong Point. On the evening of July 16, the ship made her third rendezvous of the patrol, this time reacquainting with Colonel Abcede, who turned over an unspecified "special cargo" of a box and two packages. Sharp returned the favor with two hundred pounds of food and ammunition. In just twenty minutes, *Nautilus* was on her way southwest to Sibutu Passage.

As the submarine proceeded through the Sulu Sea, many sails and a few planes were sighted. One dropped a depth bomb in their vicinity, to no effect. As the ship approached Sibutu, the crew received a welcome message.

"Did you hear the news?" Word had reached the crew, and John Sabbe was eager to share it.

"Yeah," replied Nick Bruck, dejectedly. "I heard we're almost out of coffee!"

"And we're out of flour," noted Foy Hester. "Five hundred pounds of it had to be ditched because of weevils. We gave the rest away to the guerillas. No more bread for us!"

"Oh, stop your bellyaching, that's not news. We're not going back to Darwin. We're headed to Fremantle for a refit and some R&R!"

"Really? On the level?" asked Bruck?

---

6. It is likely that three of the four US army men destined for Leyte and Bohol debarked here, but it is not mentioned in any report or log. *Nautilus* did not stop at Bohol. The fourth man accidentally shot himself in the leg with his .45 pistol, resulting in a compound fracture of his tibia. Sharp noted that he was treated and in good spirits, but his leg would have to be reset upon hospitalization ashore. Presumably he returned with the submarine.

"Yessirree Bob!" replied Sabbe with a grin. "Forget about bread and pastries, and even coffee! Bottled sunshine[7] awaits!"

Morale took a significant turn for the better as *Nautilus* continued south into the Makassar Strait heading for southwestern Australia. Entering the Java Sea, their progress was interrupted briefly by a rendezvous with USS *Ray* and an assignment to search for an enemy convoy spotted in the area. A day's search yielded nothing. The ship continued through the Lombok Strait east of Bali and on July 21 spent the better part of a week cruising south, short on coffee, pastries, and patience. Finally, on the morning of July 27, *Nautilus* docked at Fremantle having spent eighty-seven of the previous ninety-four days underway, covering more than twenty thousand nautical miles since the last maintenance refit.

Sharp commended Chiefs Goodman and Bruck for diligence in "maintaining an efficient main engineering plant in spite of chronic weakness and unreliability." He also singled out Lieutenant (jg) Winner's performance as diving officer and Ensign Porterfield's outstanding contribution to "the success and smartness of the execution of all special missions." Admiral Christie congratulated Sharp and his crew for the successful completion of the important missions, and though they did no direct damage to the enemy, the patrol was deemed a success. An additional measure of gratitude was offered by none other than Gen. Douglas MacArthur, who sent letters of commendation to the entire crew, stating:

> *The successful completion by the USS* Nautilus *of its assigned missions has been a most important contribution to the strengthening of our military forces and the sustaining of our operations. I desire to commend Commander George A. Sharp, USN, and his officers and men for the splendid manner in which this task has been undertaken and executed and express to them my grateful acknowledgement of service well done.*

Captain Sharp and the officers enjoyed a fifteen-day recuperation period at Fremantle's Majestic Hotel while the crew retired to the Ocean Beach Hotel. The respite was certainly "needed and enjoyed by all hands."

---

7. Beer.

CHAPTER NINE

Iuisan Shoal and Luzon

NICK BRUCK AND JOE GOODMAN STOOD DEJECTEDLY, ARMS CROSSED, glumly regarding the massive diesel engines. They had just returned from their two week break, leaving the engine room in the hands of the submarine tender mechanics who performed a complete overhaul on all four diesels. Expecting to find them in working order, they instead learned that all four were out of commission. *Nautilus* was far from ready for sea. Bruck addressed Sharp and the ship's engineer, Hal Winner, as he ticked off the major issues.

"Well, sirs, it seems that the main engine housings are pitted and corroded. They used a kind of iron cement to patch them. We'll have serious problems with that within months. The bearings we ordered for number one came in the wrong size, so we're still on fourteen cylinders. The tender ginks ground the journal bearings too thin and so after running a battery charge they were all wiped. The rings on number two are shot. They should have replaced them, now we'll have to do it." He continued detailing the deficiencies as the captain patiently listened. Finally finished, he looked at Goodman. "Did I about cover it, Chief?"

Goodman nodded, with nothing more to say.

Winner jumped in. "Can you and your men fix all this?"

Bruck sighed. "Yes sir. We know these engines. Just keep those jerks from the tender out of our hair!"

"I'll promise you that," agreed Sharp. "Also, give me a detailed writeup of these problems. I'll put them in my next patrol report. Command needs to know what we're dealing with."

Bruck, Goodman, and the other machinists got to work. Two weeks and six hundred man hours of labor later, the main engines were hammering away on all cylinders, ready for action.

Besides the engine work, *Nautilus* received new radar equipment and an overhaul of all sea valves. The ship was fumigated, though apparently not to the captain's satisfaction. Torpedo and gunnery training helped the twenty-five new crewmen adjust to their surroundings and duties. On August 16, 1944, the crew assembled for a brief ceremony honoring Lt. Cdr. Ben Jarvis, Chief Foy Hester, Chief Joe Goodman, and Gunner's Mate Myles Banbury for "heroic and meritorious services . . . in the transporting of a Marine detachment to Japanese-occupied Apamama [Abemama] Island." The men were awarded Bronze Star medals, and forty other crewmen received letters of commendation, notably for performance during the friendly fire incident when *Nautilus* was hit by gunfire from the destroyer *Ringgold*. On August 27, the ship got underway, leaving Fremantle behind. Nine days later vessel and crew arrived at Darwin and began loading cargo for yet another Spyron mission. Frustratingly, problems with engine clutches needed further repair, which required an extended stay in port, and more toil and sweat by the machinists. Before getting underway, a new officer came on board with the unusual name of Willard de Los Michael. Lieutenant Commander Michael would shadow Ben Jarvis to learn the art of navigating the treacherous waters around the Philippines archipelago, and was slated to eventually relieve Sharp as commanding officer. Also joining the wardroom was none other than John Sabbe, the third *Nautilus* crewman to be promoted to ensign and remain on board.

Finally, on September 17, 1944, *Nautilus* got underway for her twelfth war patrol, carrying 106 tons of cargo bound for several locations and two US Army enlisted men aiming to rendezvous with guerrilla units. Over the next week the submarine followed her former tracks, wending her way through narrow passages to enter the Sulu Sea and turn west into the Bohol Sea. This time Sharp directed the ship into the Cebu Strait, aiming for a location on the coast of the island of Cebu called Iuisan Point. Seeing proper security signals on the evening of September 25, they surfaced and saw a small boat waving an American flag, occupants

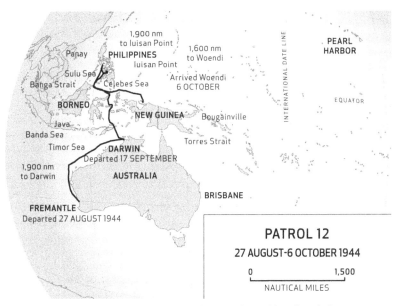

After a short period of crew R&R, *Nautilus* conducted her fourth Spyron mission for her twelfth patrol. ILLUSTRATION BY BETHANY JOURDAN.

"displaying length of hair to demonstrate their nationality" (that is, not Japanese). Soon a flotilla of twenty-five small boats was alongside receiving cargo. Just before 2100, forty tons of cargo was on its way to the beach and Sharp was waiting for passengers. Minutes passed, an hour passed, and no passengers appeared. One native officer explained the delays were due to "filipinitis." Finally, out of the darkness, boats set out from shore bringing eleven evacuees and their baggage including mail and captured documents. The crew fetched them quickly, got them on board, and the ship was immediately underway, engines ahead standard speed.

The submarine swung around with full rudder, its speed increasing. Suddenly, with a grinding, screeching crunch the ship came to an abrupt stop. Unsecured baggage flew about the spaces and men staggered forward. The hull was hard aground on Iuisan Shoal, stuck on a sand and coral reef.

"Damage report!" called Hal Winner, officer of the deck. No damage was noted in any compartments, other than a few bumps, bruises, and broken coffee cups. Sharp and Porterfield were still on the bridge having just supervised the loading of passengers. Sharp took over. "Back her off, Mr. Winner." He ordered full astern, then emergency power, but the ship did not budge. "Blow forward main ballast tanks and pump all forward ballast to sea," ordered the captain, hoping to lift the bow off the bottom. As the pumps began their work, Porterfield spoke up.

"Captain, I suggest we sally ship."

"Good call, Mr. Porterfield. Make it happen!" Red set about organizing the crew and passengers to head topside and move in coordination from side to side across the large deck. This time-honored method of freeing a grounded ship involves using the weight of the crew to rock the vessel and try to break suction with the bottom. Altogether, the crew tallied nearly eight tons of weight, but the trick was to get them moving in coordination. Red did his best to set the hull in motion while the engines ran furiously, the screws churning the sea, but all efforts were futile. *Nautilus* was stuck fast.

Sharp called a halt to efforts and gathered his officers to discuss what to do. Jarvis pointed out the high tide would come at 0400. Dawn would creep in two hours later, with sunrise at 0702. Already a dozen air contacts had been logged since leaving Darwin, and as soon as they were discovered aground the Japanese air force would be on top of them. Ground troops would follow. It was critical to get off the reef before dawn.

Porterfield recommended they lighten the ship, not just forward but overall. They discussed what ballast and other weight could be offloaded. For starters, the eleven evacuees and their baggage were sent back to shore, along with the captured documents they brought on board and about forty additional tons of cargo meant for another location. Sadly, the civilians would have to wait for another opportunity to leave the island. Sharp also had all secret and confidential materials burned so none could fall into enemy hands if the ship was captured. All variable ballast was blown overboard, along with fifty-nine thousand gallons of reserve fuel amounting to two hundred tons, and all the gasoline they carried for the small boat engine. The crew jettisoned 190 rounds of six-inch ammunition amounting to ten tons. Nothing else came to mind. The tide continued to go out so that the boat was up a degree-and-a-half by the bow and listing twelve degrees to starboard. Porterfield suggested they flood the forward and middle main ballast tanks to hold the ship in place as the tide turned and flooded in, preventing her going higher up on the reef. By 0330, all excess weight was off the ship and the tide was rising quickly. It was time to go.

"Blow all main ballast tanks!" Sharp commanded. High pressure air entered the large tanks forcing hundreds of tons of seawater out. The ship began to gently roll back to vertical.

"All back two-thirds!" called Sharp. The engines responded and the screws bit. The boat shuddered but did not move. "Back full!" The diesels rumbled and the sea churned. Still no movement.

"All back emergency!" ordered Sharp. The engines roared. Bruck and Goodman crossed their fingers, hoping the old diesels would not fail them. Suddenly, the ship lurched free and began to move rapidly astern. She was off! "All stop!" yelled Sharp over the din, relieved. It was 0400 and they were clear. Moving ahead, Sharp safely passed the shoals and headed to deep water.

They were free of the reef, but not yet out of danger. So much ballast had been cast overboard they could not submerge. The oil and gasoline tanks needed to be reflooded, a process normally taking five hours, but sunrise was just three hours away. Again, Red had an idea. At his direction, the crew removed manhole covers from the tanks and rigged fire hoses to quickly fill them with seawater. By 0611, dawn was upon them, and radar reported a contact at eleven thousand yards. Sharp hoped it was the submarine USS *Mingo*, sent to render assistance, and rescue the *Nautilus* crew if necessary. At 0637, a periscope was sighted. A few minutes later Sharp gave the order to dive. *Nautilus* started down and in short order was underwater, and sinking! Too much water ballast had been added and the submarine was now ninety thousand pounds heavy! Lieutenant Winner pumped furiously and eventually got the ship back in trim. That evening Sharp was able to contact *Mingo* and let them know that help was not needed.

Nautilus continued her mission, undeterred by the dramatic events off Cebu. She headed north to Panay Island and her second rendezvous point. On the morning of September 29, signals from the Coastwatchers

Nautilus ran aground at Iuisan Point but was able to refloat before morning.
ILLUSTRATION BY BETHANY JOURDAN.

were sighted and three large sailboats were observed, with much activity on the beach. Surfacing that evening, the submarine nudged near shore and began striking cargo topside. By 0144 the next morning, forty tons of supplies plus a thousand pounds of ship's dry stores were ashore, and forty-seven evacuees including twenty-two women, nine children, and sixteen men came aboard. *Nautilus* was on her way. A third rendezvous was cancelled as the supplies meant for that spot had been offloaded to lighten ship, and so much fuel had been pumped overboard they were running low. The submarine headed to Sibutu Passage and into the Celebes Sea, and from there continued east toward New Guinea. A new base was operational at Mios Woendi, with the submarine tender USS *Orion* (AS-18) serving as an impromptu submarine repair depot.

At noon on October 6, forty-seven evacuees plus one stowaway discovered shortly after departure from Panay, were transferred to a waiting vessel. Also departing were the two army enlisted men destined for the third rendezvous that was cancelled. Their names were not recorded, but the crew was sorry to see them go. Sharp reported, "They did more than their share of ship's work and during the unloading periods they worked as hard as anyone on board. They were good shipmates." At 1236, *Nautilus* moored in Woendi, completing her fourth Spyron mission. The commander of Task Force 72, Capt. John Haines, was pleased with the patrol, stating, "It was only through the coolness and good judgement of the commanding officer and the determined efforts of all hands that the *Nautilus* was saved to fight again."

In spite of all evidence to the contrary, many of the Japanese high command subscribed to the fiction that America would give up the war in the face on one major decisive defeat. Allied navy and Marine forces led by Admiral Nimitz had pushed through the Mariana Islands, breaching Japan's strategic defensive ring, and threatening the home islands. Army forces, supported by the navy and led by General MacArthur, gained ground in New Guinea. An invasion of the Philippines was imminent, and the dwindling power of the Japanese Combined Fleet prepared to meet it yet another decisive engagement code named Shō-Gō.

Though weakened by successive defeats, Japan still possessed significant land-based air power in the region, numbering some 1,500 planes operating from airfields in Luzon and the islands to the north, Formosa (now Taiwan) and Ryukyu. In a surprise move ahead of the invasion, Adm. William "Bull" Halsey led his fast carrier task force with seventeen aircraft carriers and more than a thousand aircraft on a series of raids against air bases on the northern islands from October 12–16. The Japanese counterattacked, striving to sink Halsey's carriers, but attrition had sapped Japan of her experienced pilots while well-trained American airmen flew newer aircraft. In three days of aerial combat the enemy forces were routed, losing six hundred planes, knocking the northern air forces out of the coming battles.

Thanks in large part to the successful guerrilla activity on the southern Philippine islands, MacArthur decided to bypass Mindanao and invade at the eastern beaches of Leyte, where *Nautilus* and other Spyron missions had regularly rendezvoused with guerrilla leaders. If the landing forces could quickly capture an airfield, then planes from Australia could move in and help Halsey's carrier-based aircraft to defend the beachhead. As the invasion forces landed on October 17, Japanese high command, with unfounded optimism, set operation Shō-Gō in motion. The Combined Fleet no longer had an air force, as its few remaining carriers had only a handful of planes left and few crew to fly them. However, they retained a powerful force of warships including the super battleships *Yamato* and *Musashi*, each sporting eighteen-inch naval guns, the largest ever floated, as well as five other battleships, twenty cruisers, and dozens of destroyers. With hope of air cover from land-based planes in Luzon, their mission was to approach the invasion beaches from the north through San Bernadino Straight and from the south through Surigao Strait and crush the Allied landings. To have any real chance of this they needed to neutralize Halsey's carrier force. To this end, a decoy fleet designated the Northern Force, built around the few remaining Japanese aircraft carriers, was stationed east of Luzon, about five hundred miles northeast of Leyte, hoping to lure the US fast carrier force away from the battle.

On October 23, the most powerful squadron, designated the Center Force, was heading from its base in Borneo toward Mindoro aiming to enter the Sibuyan Sea and emerge through the San Bernadino Strait, counting on the Northern Force to do its decoy job and take Halsey's carriers out of the fight. Consisting of five battleships (including *Yamato* and *Musashi*), plus ten heavy cruisers and other ships, the Center Force was detected in a narrow passage near Palawan Island by the submarines USS *Dace* and USS *Darter*. Gaining a favorable position and attacking at first light, the submarines were able to hit three of the heavy cruisers sinking two, including the commanding admiral's flagship. The formation sped on after fishing their admiral out of the sea. While following the crippled cruiser, *Darter* ran aground at Bombay Shoal and could not be refloated. Her crew was rescued by *Dace*.

The Center Force continued to Mindoro and passed its southern point into the Sibuyan Sea. Though Halsey remained unaware of the decoy fleet, many of his ships were rearming after the Formosa raids or

Major movement of forces during the Battle of Leyte Gulf. ILLUSTRATION BY
BETHANY JOURDAN.

supporting the landings on Leyte and were not in position to counter
the threat. One element of his task force was nearby and moved to block
the Japanese. Three waves of land-based aircraft attacked the American
ships and managed to sink the light carrier USS *Princeton*, but aircraft
from the remaining carriers fell on the Japanese in the Sibuyan Sea and
began scoring hits, focusing on *Musashi*. At least seventeen bombs and
nineteen torpedoes struck the heavily armored battleship in a series of
attacks, and she finally capsized and sank. One cruiser was also crippled,
but as the Center Force retreated, it was largely intact. Halsey assumed
this force was defeated, and having belatedly discovered the Northern
Force with its attractive, though impotent, carriers, he gathered his ships
and sent them to the north in pursuit. That evening the still powerful
Center Force reversed course and headed back to the now unguarded
San Bernadino Strait.

Meanwhile, the Southern Force, joined by a force of cruisers from
a base in Formosa, had sailed through the Sulu Sea past Negros Island

and into the Bohol Sea, following the same route taken by *Nautilus* on her eleventh and twelfth patrols. This fleet included two older battleships, four cruisers, and several destroyers. They aimed to time their arrival into Leyte Gulf with the Northern Force and make short work of the transports and landing craft there. But first they would have to negotiate the narrow thirty-five-mile-long Surigao Strait. It was a trap. Rear Adm. Jesse Olendorf of the US Seventh Fleet commanded a task force of six aging battleships (five of them sunk or damaged during the Pearl Harbor attack and subsequently refloated and repaired) that had led the preinvasion bombardment of the beachhead. Though low on ammunition (particularly of armor-piercing rounds used on ships), they formed a battle line at the head of the strait. In front of them were eight cruisers with smaller guns, and farther ahead were squadrons of fast destroyers with deadly torpedoes. At the entrance to the strait were several dozen PT boats. As the Southern Force entered the area in the predawn darkness, they swept past the little PT boats but ran into a fusillade of destroyer torpedoes from both flanks. Both Japanese battleships were hit along with several destroyers. As the crippled ships continued to press on to the head of the strait, they came under fire from the guns of USS *West Virginia* followed by the other American vessels in what was the last engagement ever to be fought between battleships. Both Japanese battleships were sunk, and the remaining vessels retired in disarray, two of them colliding in the confusion. The Southern Force was no longer a threat to the Leyte beachhead.

As the action in Surigao proceeded, the Center Force passed through the San Bernadino Strait unmolested and was bearing down on Leyte, steaming along the east cost of the island of Samar. Only fifty miles from the entrance to Leyte Gulf, *Yamato* and her eighteen-inch guns would be in range within the hour. Standing in the path were three US escort carrier units totaling sixteen small carriers with a screen of antisubmarine escort destroyers. Four battleships, eight cruisers, and eleven destroyers surprised this meager US force as it approached the beachhead. The carriers immediately launched their planes and ran for cover under a rain squall to the east, while the escort destroyers made a smoke screen to conceal their retreat. The Japanese commander, unaware that the decoy force's deception had succeeded, assumed he had encountered Halsey's fleet and prepared for air attack. He was not disappointed as the escort carriers' 450 planes fell upon the Japanese ships, unopposed by enemy fighters. These aircraft were equipped for antisubmarine operations and many had only machine guns, of little threat to the well-armored battleships and cruisers. Regardless, their attacks were relentless and certainly reinforced the impression that Halsey was afoot.

The small, unarmored destroyers steamed into the Japanese formation at flank speed, wildly maneuvering to avoid large caliber gunfire and launching torpedoes as soon as they were within range. Rather than retreating after expending their torpedoes, the little ships opened fire on the cruisers and battleships with their five-inch guns, to be joined by the single gun on each escort carrier as the Japanese continued to approach and come within range. The torpedoes did some damage, as did the five-inch fire and the air attacks. But soon the larger caliber Japanese guns began to take a toll with several destroyers and the carrier *Gambier Bay* taking fatal hits. The Japanese were in position to sweep through the opposition and take Leyte Gulf under fire. The old battleships that repelled the Southern Force were out of position and nearly out of ammunition, in any case outgunned by the larger enemy vessels. Halsey was hundreds of miles away. MacArthur's return to the Philippines hung in the balance.

At that crucial moment, the Japanese fleet reversed course and headed north in retreat. The ferocity of the near suicidal American resistance and the assumption that they were facing Halsey's carrier force discouraged the attackers. Fearing further losses, the flotilla steamed north and back into San Bernadino Strait. The liberation of the Philippines would continue.

Nautilus ended her twelfth patrol at Mios Woendi, a small atoll just off the northwest coast of New Guinea. This site was selected as a PT boat supply and repair base, and construction began in early June despite ongoing fighting in the region. In a few weeks' time, Seabees[1] built pier and base facilities with acres of Quonset huts covering the tiny island. With more than two thousand feet of navigable beachfront adjacent to a deep water lagoon, the island would become the largest PT boat facility in the Pacific. The torpedo boats began operating from the base in late June as the camp continued to expand. A three hundred bed naval hospital, torpedo dump, dry-docking facilities, a seaplane base, and a mobile amphibious repair base for landing craft were eventually built there. Roads crisscrossed the island serving rows of tents, warehouses, stores, offices, living quarters, docks, ramps, parking areas for planes, and radio stations. The facility also served submarines and became a base for the Combined Field Intelligence Service in support of guerrillas and Coastwatchers. The submarine tender USS *Orion* was moved there, and many Spyron missions originated from that location. It was declared useable for submarines on August 7, 1944, just sixty days before *Nautilus* arrived.

The crew was disappointed to miss a visit by a USO troupe on August 11, including Bob Hope, singer Frances Langford, and dancer Patty Thomas. The Seabees built a stage in short order and the visit featured a short cruise for the entertainers on a PT boat. *Nautilus* was in Mios Woendi only four days loading for the next mission as *Orion* machinists helped with minor repairs and the ship was again fumigated, this time to Sharp's satisfaction. Some of the crew relaxed at "Club Plonk," a Quonset hut set on a barge anchored off shore that provided libations to thirsty submarine sailors. Visitors were given an official guest member card conferring mock prestige to the spartan establishment.

While *Nautilus* and her crew were enjoying a few days' respite at Woendi, submarine command was becoming increasingly worried about fellow Spyron boat USS *Seawolf* (SS-197). *Seawolf* was on her fifteenth war patrol, having departed Brisbane on September 21, assigned to deliver supplies and army personnel to the east coast of the island of Samar. In command was Lt. Cdr. Albert Bontier, who had just relieved *Nautilus* veteran Ozzie Lynch. She exchanged recognition signals with *Narwhal* along the way on October 3, but failed to report the next day when

---

1. The acronym CB (or Seabee) refers to a naval construction battalion.

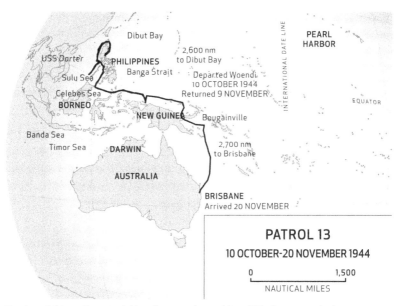

For her thirteenth patrol *Nautilus* conducted her fifth Spyron mission. ILLUSTRATION BY BETHANY JOURDAN.

directed and was never heard from again. Eventually, she was declared lost along with eighty-three crewmen and seventeen army passengers. It was later surmised that she was sunk by the American destroyer USS *Rowell*, believing her to be an enemy submarine. The tragic loss of *Seawolf* underscored the maxim, "A submarine has no friends," and brought home the danger that *Nautilus* and other Spyron boats regularly faced.

On the afternoon of October, 10, 1944, *Nautilus* got underway for her thirteenth war patrol. The departing crew was much the same as sailed on the previous mission but for two notable exceptions. Departing was Lt. Cdr. Ben Jarvis, who turned over executive officer and navigator duties to Lieutenant Commander Michael. Then there was the curious case of Juan Locquiao Echanes, a junior Filipino steward. The ship's official muster roll of September 30, records that Echanes "Deserted in enemy held territory," and went on to note, "Pay due $181.88. Report forwarded to BuPers."[2] It seems he accompanied the eleven evacuees returned ashore when the ship

---

2. Bureau of [Naval] Personnel.

was aground near Iuisan Point, though no mention of his departure was found in the ship's log or patrol report. Minor cases of AWOL sailors returning late from liberty were duly noted and punishments were documented in the deck logs, so the absence of any mention in the daily log of desertion in enemy held territory, a very serious offense that in wartime could merit the death penalty, is more than puzzling.

Regardless, *Nautilus* had a Spyron mission to fulfill. With the Leyte invasion imminent and the southeastern coasts of the Philippine islands teeming with ships and aircraft, Sharp and his crew were routed along the west side of the archipelago, past Manila, through the Ryukyu Islands, and all the way around to the east coast of Luzon. Much of the eleven-day, 2,500-nautical mile transit was in view of enemy held territory, and a number of ships and aircraft were sighted. MacArthur's troops landed during this voyage and the Japanese ships of the Shō-Gō operation crossed the submarine's path just a few days later. On October 21, security signals were observed at a prearranged spot in Dibut Bay on the east coast of Luzon near Manila, but when *Nautilus* surfaced that evening no boat was seen. An hour later a series of unreadable signals were seen about a half mile from the designated spot, including a red light waving in the darkness. Sharp concluded that the shore party was ambushed, yet they bravely took the chance to warn the submarine. Sharp turned tail and sped out of Dibut Bay.

Heading farther south along the coast on October 23, *Nautilus* approached a second designated location, this one just fifty miles east of Japanese-occupied Manila. Though visibility was poor, security signals were confirmed, and that evening cargo and an unrecorded number of passengers were transferred to shore. These resistance fighters were willingly braving the most dangerous territory in the backyard of the Manila enemy garrison. MacArthur's forces would not land in Luzon to relieve them until January. Meanwhile, cargo continued to be offloaded until dawn when the submarine had to move offshore and submerge. She returned the next evening and by around midnight the job was finished. *Nautilus* bid farewell to the shore party and headed back up the coast to reconnoiter Dibut Bay. All day they scanned the shore for signals, peering through the periscopes, seeing nothing. Finally giving up, Sharp was heading out to sea when lookouts spotted a signal. *Nautilus* reversed course and headed back into the bay. At 1910, Capt. Robert Lapham came aboard.

Lapham was a legend among the Philippines resistance. A US Army officer who was not keen to surrender when the Japanese took the islands in 1942, he helped organize a raiding party that slipped through the Japanese lines and gathered intelligence to support future operations. He so hated the prospect of surrender that he reasoned it was his duty to continue to fight the war as best he could.[3] After the fall of Bataan, he organized a guerrilla regiment in the central plains of the northern island of Luzon, and by 1944 he commanded more than thirteen thousand men, mostly Filipino. Among his command were several Coastwatcher units. Besides intelligence collection and sabotage, Lapham's forces were credited with helping to liberate 513 prisoners of war who were about to be executed as MacArthur's forces were approaching. Promoted to major by war's end, Lapham was awarded the Distinguished Service Cross by General MacArthur and was the third American to receive the Philippine Legion of Honor, the others being MacArthur and President Roosevelt. One of the *Narwhal* Spyron missions delivered thirty tons of supplies to Lapham in August 1944. *Nautilus* had another twenty tons of vital cargo to offload.

To assist the unloading operation and with the beachhead secure, *Nautilus* took the unusual step of anchoring in the bay and sending a line ashore, tying the ship to a tree to stabilize its mooring. By these means the job was finished in a few hours. At 2315, the submarine weighed anchor and was underway, headed north to retrace the path around the north of Luzon and down the west coast of the archipelago. As they pulled away from the rendezvous, Japanese ships were retreating in defeat from the Battle of Leyte Gulf, as operation Shō-Gō had been thwarted.

A few days later, as the submarine was cruising south along the west coast of Luzon, Sharp received unusual orders from Task Force 72. He called his executive officer and navigator Lieutenant Commander Michael and his gunnery officer Lt. (jg) Bob Gustafson into the wardroom.

Sharp, with orders from command in hand on a clipboard, said, "Mr. Gustafson, how would you like to fire those six-inchers?" The big guns

---

3. Lapham and Norling (1996).

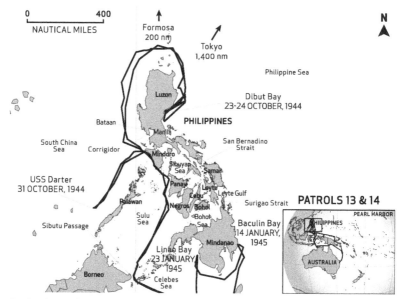

During her thirteenth patrol, *Nautilus* delivered supplies within fifty miles of Manila and was tasked to destroy the grounded submarine USS *Darter*. On her fourteenth and final patrol she delivered supplies to Mindanao Island.
ILLUSTRATION BY BETHANY JOURDAN.

had not seen action except for training since Gustafson had come aboard as a young ensign on the tenth patrol.

"Yes sir!" he said eagerly. "The men have been itching for a chance!" Then he paused, perplexed. No targets had been sighted and with so many Allied ships now operating in the area the rules of engagement had changed requiring a vessel to be confirmed an enemy ship before attacking. "What are we shooting, sir?"

Sharp tapped the message board. "Says here the task force commander wants us to sink one of our own subs!"

"What?" blurted out the other officers in unison. "That can't be right!" said Michael.

Sharp chuckled. "It's true!" He scanned the message and paraphrased. "Seems as though USS *Darter* ran herself aground while chasing a Jap cruiser four days ago and could not get off. Fortunately, *Dace* was with her and took on the crew, but *Darter* is not worth salvaging."

"So what are we supposed to do?" asked Gustafson. "Why the guns?" "Command is concerned that the Japs will try to salvage it. We don't want them to get a hold of one of our new *Gato*-class boats. They want us to wreck it best we can." He again looked down at the message. "Says here it's on Bombay Shoals, southwest of here."

Michael consulted his chart. "That's about three hundred miles from here." He noted a spot on the chart just west of Mindoro Island. "We're about here, and will be passing through the strait in a few hours. We need to head southwest now."

"Plot a course and make it happen." Sharp got up. "Mr. Gustafson, get your men ready for surface action. We'll be there morning after next."

"They're ready now, sir!" replied Gustafson as Michael headed up to the control room to plot a course. In a few minutes, *Nautilus* turned right and headed down the coast of Palawan toward Bombay Shoals.

When *Darter* ran aground just after midnight on October 25, the area was thick with Japanese ships and aircraft supporting (and eventually retreating) from Shō-Gō. As she tried to extricate herself with the help of *Dace*, a Japanese destroyer approached, but did not engage the helpless submarine. The enemy ship inexplicably sailed away. With the tide falling and danger lurking, it became clear that the ship could not be freed without a full salvage effort. With dawn approaching, the captain, Cdr. David McClintock, gave the order to abandon ship. Secret materials and equipment were destroyed, and scuttling charges were set inside the hull. *Dace* stood by and was able to take off the entire crew. The explosives failed to destroy the ship, so *Dace* fired several torpedoes at her erstwhile companion. The torpedoes hit the reef and exploded before reaching the submarine. *Dace* then opened up with her three-inch deck gun and managed to score twenty-one hits, but did not make much of an impression on the tough hull.

On October 27, the submarine USS *Rock* was sent to try to finish off *Darter*. Nine torpedoes (six of which spent their charges on the reef) failed to do the job. Hence the orders to *Nautilus*, with hopes that her cruiser gun battery could succeed. At 0921 on October 31, the submarine wreck was spotted off Bombay Shoals. An hour and a half later they were within range.

"Man battle stations, battle surface!" called Hal Winner, officer of the deck. *Nautilus* came to the surface and gunner's mates scrambled to ready their weapons. By 1113 all was ready. "Commence firing!" came the order. The guns erupted as the 105-pound projectiles flew to the target. After a few salvos the gunners began to score hits. As they zeroed in on the target, the men first focused on the conning tower and control room area, smashing through the hull with armor-piercing shells and setting the ship afire. Switching to high-capacity rounds, the crew worked fore and aft of the doomed ship, setting off large explosions from one end to the other. Crewmen hauled the heavy rounds up from the magazine by hand, the balky mechanical hoists having long since been removed. After forty salvoes the forward gun went quiet, the breech plug having failed, but the aft gun kept up the barrage. Dense yellow smoke poured out of *Darter's* control room and a huge oil fire started aft. After eighty-eight rounds the captain called a cease-fire. Sharp recorded at least fifty-five hits, and commented, "It is very doubtful that any equipment on *Darter* will be useful to Japan—except as scrap."

Nautilus secured from battle stations, reversed course, and headed northwest along Palawan Island to pass through Mondoro Strait and resumed her transit back to Mios Woendi. The route was thick with contacts, Sharp finding thirty-one vessels and fifty-six aircraft worth logging in his patrol report. Most of the sightings were Allied craft or unidentified. At one point he commenced an approach on a vessel "hoping for a ship which would conform with the limited targets allowed us." Identifying the contact as a large power-driven sailing vessel, he let it go for reasons unexplained.

On the morning of November 9, *Nautilus* arrived at Woendi Lagoon and moored alongside the tender USS *Orion*. She only stayed long enough for the crew to refuel, load several tons of spare parts for delivery to the submarine base at Brisbane, and make a brief appearance at Club Plonk. Early afternoon the next day she set sail for eastern Australia, arriving in Brisbane without incident on November 20, ending her thirteenth patrol.

Brisbane offered a welcome opportunity for fifteen days R&R and a short refit including yet another main engine overhaul. On December 11, George Sharp detached, turning over command to his executive officer, Willard de Los Michael, who became the fourth and final wartime captain of *Nautilus*. Sharp served after the war bringing captured German submarines to the United States, and was one of the commanders in charge of atomic bomb testing in the Marshall Islands, eventually making the rank of rear admiral before retirement.

A turnover of crew saw the departure of recently promoted Lt. (jg) Floyd "Red" Porterfield who after the war commanded the submarine USS *Redfish* (SS-395), and later a destroyer. He served in the Mediterranean, including tours in Lebanon and Vietnam, and was awarded two Silver Stars, a Bronze Star, and Navy and Marine Corps medals for his service. Among the more unusual events in Porterfield's long career were opportunities to help make movies. While he was commanding officer in the spring of 1954, *Redfish* was fitted with a dummy rear fin, and played the part of Jules Verne's *Nautilus* in the Walt Disney film *20,000 Leagues Under the Sea*. Later, in 1957, *Redfish* played the part of the fictional submarine USS *Nerka* in the 1958 motion picture *Run Silent, Run Deep*, based on the Edward Beach novel. Porterfield retired as a commander after a thirty-year naval career.

Another departure was Chief Electrician Foy Hester, like Porterfield, veteran of thirteen *Nautilus* war patrols. He first reported in 1936 and with eight years on board was one of the longest tenured men on the ship. After bidding farewell to his shipmates, Foy was transferred to the submarine repair unit in Brisbane and eventually made his way stateside. He was recommended for advancement to warrant officer and remained in the navy until he retired in 1947, having served nearly twenty-one years. While on board *Nautilus* he received a Bronze Star, the Presidential Unit Commendation, and the Philippine Presidential Unit Citation among many other awards. Foy meticulously kept his dive log for the duration of his time on board *Nautilus*, showing that from April 1942 through November 1944 the submarine made 881 dives for a total submerged time of 3,070 hours—more than 127 days under water.

An unexpected arrival was Petty Officer Juan Locquiao Echanes, "deserter" of patrol twelve. It seems that Echanes was picked up by sister submarine *Narwhal* on September 17 during her recent Spyron patrol along with refugees including six adults, fourteen children, and five Filipinos who wanted to become steward's mates in the navy. Echanes was dropped in Brisbane and awaited his own ship's return. On November 20 upon arrival in Brisbane, the *Nautilus* muster roll remarked, "Deserter returned. Reported on board for duty." The ship's deck log remained silent on the matter.

On December 15, Allied troops landed on the Philippine island of Mindoro just south of Luzon, but the southern island of Mindanao still harbored Japanese forces and the guerrillas needed supplies. *Nautilus* got underway for her fourteenth patrol and sixth Spyron mission on January 3, 1945, after loading ninety-five tons of cargo. Just days later on January 9, landings on Luzon, the island of Manila, began the culminating drive to recapture the Philippines. The ship made Darwin on January 13, refueled, and after minor repairs headed north the next day.

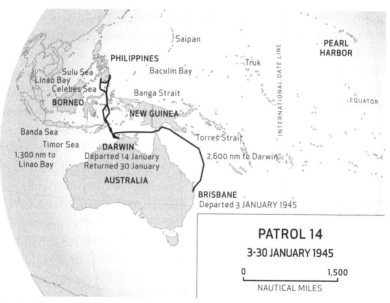

For her fourteenth and final patrol *Nautilus* conducted her sixth Spyron mission. ILLUSTRATION BY BETHANY JOURDAN.

Nautilus followed similar routes to earlier patrols and made her way into the Celebes Sea and the west coast of Mindanao without incident, though many aircraft were sighted. Entering Moro Gulf on January 20, Captain Michael sighted security signals at a spot off Linao Bay, and that evening saw a motor whaleboat standing offshore with "Old Glory" hoisted. The submarine surfaced, and though the danger of Japanese attack was waning, Michael took no chances. He had the crew make ready four 20-mm machine guns and trained out both six-inch guns with five rounds for each on hand. He commented, "Should be able to return the average surprise with dividends." Before midnight, all forty-five tons of cargo was ashore and a single evacuee was taken on, a soldier who was sick and malnourished, having subsisted on rice and fish for the last three years.

Departing the area, *Nautilus* continued around the south of Mindanao, sighting wave after wave of American aircraft, mainly flights of B-24 Liberator heavy bombers. Over the course of the patrol thirty-one air contacts were logged, in groups of as many as sixteen planes. From time to time recognition flares were fired if an aircraft seemed threatening, and on a few occasions a quick dive was in order. By this time, sea and air spaces were well under control by Allied forces, so ships and aircraft were to engage targets only after verifying they were enemy. Still caution was in order, as submarines have no friends.

On January 23, the ship made the east coast of the island and sighted signals at Baculin Bay. That evening, a banca flying the American flag came alongside and the crew began transferring cargo. As few boats were available from shore, Michael had the ship's rubber boats broken out and shortly after midnight all remaining supplies were ashore. The progress of Allied forces in the theater was such that the thousand pounds of dry stores provided by the submarine included such nonmilitary items as books, magazines, and office supplies.

Nautilus proceeded south returning to Darwin late morning on January 30, completing her fourteenth and final war patrol. The task group commander congratulated Captain Michael, officers, and crew upon the "expeditious completion of another hazardous assignment." Adm. James Fife, Seventh Fleet Commander of Submarines had the following to say:

It is noted that this fourteenth patrol of the Nautilus *terminates the active patrol duty of this gallant ship, during which several hazardous special missions were successfully completed in the SOWESPAC[4] area. Her departure from this force is met with regret and pride in a job well done.*

Seven men made all fourteen *Nautilus* war patrols: Ens. John Sabbe, Chiefs Myles Banbury, Nick Bruck, Peter Freitas, and Joe Goodman, and First Class Mates Colin Campbell and Robert Hyde.

Veterans of thirteen war patrols pose with the *Nautilus* battle flag. Pictured standing from left: Floyd "Red" Porterfield, Nick Bruck and Foy Hester (holding flag), and John Sabbe. Crouching from left: Myles Banbury, Joseph Goodman, Peter Freitas, and Robert Hyde. Not pictured: Colin Campbell. U.S. NAVY.

4. South West Pacific.

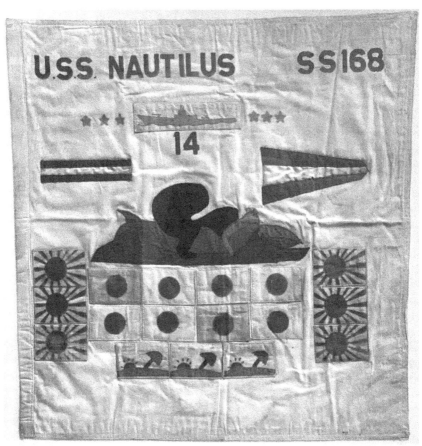

USS *Nautilus* battle flag updated after her fourteenth and final patrol. The banner depicts the submarine combat patrol pin flanked by six stars (two silver representing five patrols each and four gold) for a total of fourteen patrols. The ribbon and pennant are for the Presidential Unit Citation award. Below the "14" is a cartoon of a sailor in a chambered nautilus shell riding a torpedo. The Japanese flags tally six warships and eight merchant ships sunk, and the three islands represent Makin, Attu, and Abemama. COURTESY LARRY BROCKMAN.

Supported mainly by *Nautilus* and *Narwhal,* but with other submarines as well, Spyron missions delivered 1,325 tons of supplies, sent ashore 331 military personnel, and evacuated 472 people, most of them civilians, many women and children. A 1948 assessment[5] of Spyron said, "The practical importance of this efficient supply service by cargo submarine can scarcely be overestimated. It became the life-line of the guerrilla resistance movement." The Spyron program was ended after *Nautilus* completed her special mission at Baculin Bay with Allied forces on the ground and the battle for the Philippines well in hand, though it would be weeks before Manila was captured, and pockets of resistance continued through the end of the war. The Philippines campaign cost the US Army nearly fourteen thousand lives lost against more than three hundred thousand Japanese. It is estimated that some nine hundred thousand civilians perished over the course of the invasion, occupation, and retaking of the islands.

---

5. Assessment by Gen. Douglas MacArthur's Southwest Pacific Area headquarters.

Epilogue

With the US Army on the ground in the Philippines, B-29 Superfortress bombers attacking the Japanese homeland, and hundreds of new submarines patrolling enemy coastal waters, the illustrious *Nautilus* was slated for retirement. On February 3, 1945, she got underway from Darwin, her destination the Philadelphia Naval Shipyard, with Captain Michael commanding. Cruising along the north coast of Australia, she traveled south of New Guinea where fighting was yet ongoing, and entered the Coral Sea. The ship arrived at Espiritu Santo Naval Base on February 13 for refueling and a few days' rest for the crew. Departing on the sixteenth, *Nautilus* headed east for the seven thousand nautical mile voyage across the Pacific.

World War II, of course, was far from over. On February 19, US Marines landed on Iwo Jima and engaged in what would be the bloodiest battle in the Pacific since the taking of Attu, near the war's beginning. More than 6,800 American troops lost their lives in fierce fighting, which was symbolized in the iconic photograph of six Marines raising the Stars and Stripes atop Mount Suribachi on February 23. The battle saw extensive use of kamikaze air attacks hitting eighteen US ships and sinking the aircraft carrier USS *Bismarck Sea*, the last American carrier to be lost to enemy action. On March 3, 1,300 miles to the southwest, US Army troops recaptured Manila, relieving the city from its three-year occupation.

On March 12, *Nautilus* arrived in Balboa, Panama, at the west end of the Panama Canal. The next few days provided a welcome opportunity for sightseeing as the ship cruised along the canal, entering the Atlantic

Ocean on the afternoon of March 16. Heading north, the ship passed west of Cuba, cruised along the Florida Keys, and sailed up the Eastern Seaboard before entering the Delaware Bay, arriving in Philadelphia on March 25. She berthed alongside sister ship *Narwhal*, also slated for decommissioning. The three-year wartime voyage of *Nautilus* came to a well-deserved end.

Back in the Pacific, the largest amphibious assault of the war took place on April 1 as the US Tenth Army, with more than 180,000 Marines and army troops, landed on the Japanese home island of Okinawa, barely three hundred miles from the mainland. Fighting would continue for many weeks with prodigious casualty counts. The Imperial Navy made yet another last-ditch effort to oppose the landings with Operation Ten-Go. Led by the super battleship *Yamato*, ten warships forged a suicide attack, hoping to beach the flagship and use her battery as coastal artillery and her crew as ground troops. The huge ship and most of her escorts were sunk long before reaching Okinawa. Days later, on April 12, came news that stunned America. President Franklin Delano Roosevelt, who had served in office since 1933 and led the country through the war, had died.

The *Nautilus* crew learned of these events as they prepared the ship for decommissioning, which included dry-docking and removing of weapons, stores, and equipment. All celebrated Victory in Europe Day on May 8, though the war yet raged in the Pacific. The Allies made plans for an all-out assault on the Japanese mainland with Operation Downfall, which was scheduled to launch in November. It was to involve some six million Allied soldiers, sailors, and airmen, many arriving fresh from the German battlefields.

Many *Nautilus* men were detached to return to wartime duties, but forty-seven crewmen and seven officers were present at decommissioning on June 30. Presiding over the ceremony, Lt. Cdr. Willard de Los Michael, her last commanding officer, addressed the crew stating, "Well men, I guess that's about all for the *Nautilus*. She's been a grand ship. . . . I can't say much else." He then handed a bottle of champagne to Ens. John Sabbe, veteran of all fourteen war patrols, who smashed the bottle over the breech of the forward six-inch gun, proclaiming, "*Nautilus*, I decommission thee!"

Nautilus at the Philadelphia Naval Shipyard for decommissioning. The officers and crew salute colors for the last time. Capt. M. Mathewson, Commanding Officer of the Navy Yard, stands next to Lt. Cdr. Willard de Los Michael, *Nautilus* Commanding Officer (facing at right). June 30, 1945. U.S. NAVY.

Nautilus in drydock at the Philadelphia Naval Shipyard. Officers and crew assemble for the ship's decommissioning ceremony on June 30, 1945. U.S. NAVY.

Ex-*Nautilus* in drydock at the Philadelphia Naval Shipyard being prepared for scrapping, January 26, 1946. U.S. NAVY.

Nautilus was stricken from the Navy Register on July 25, 1945. Just days later, on August 6, the American B-29 *Enola Gay* dropped an atomic bomb on the city of Hiroshima. On August 9, a similar weapon destroyed Nagasaki. Russia declared war on Japan and in days routed Japanese forces that were occupying Manchuria. Victory in Japan was declared on August 15. The war was ended.

Though the venerable ship was sold to the American Smelting Company for scrap, the legacy of *Nautilus* lives on with her namesake, USS *Nautilus* (SSN-571), the world's first nuclear powered submarine. Launched in 1954, she was the first vessel to complete a submerged transit of the North Pole on August 3, 1958. The nuclear *Nautilus* was decommissioned in 1980 and designated a National Historic Landmark in 1982. The submarine has been preserved as a museum ship in Groton, Connecticut, near the New London submarine base.

Over the course of her service, USS *Nautilus* (SS-168) won fourteen battle stars, the Philippine Presidential Unit Citation, and the US Presidential Unit Citation for "outstanding performance in combat." She received wartime credit for sinking seventeen enemy vessels totaling more than forty-nine thousand tons, and Capt. William Brockman ranked sixty-ninth among the top submarine commanders of the war by JANAC's more conservative tally. As a testament to Brockman's leadership, five of the six officers who sailed on his first patrol went on to captain their own subs—the only exception being Joe Defrees, who was killed in action as a lieutenant on *Sculpin*. Tom Hogan and Roy Benson also ranked among the top seventy-five submarine skippers during their commands. At least one of Brockman's senior enlisted crewmen, Red Porterfield, also commanded a submarine later in his career. Brockman, Roy Benson, Ozzie Lynch, William Irvin, and George Sharp advanced to flag rank, all retiring as rear admirals.

Over the course of her service in World War II, *Nautilus* traveled nearly 125,000 nautical miles, over forty thousand leagues under the sea.

Buzz Lee said of the men who served with him: "I am convinced that every man on the *Nautilus* put his life behind him and came of age on June 4, 1942, when the fury of war came down upon us. It was a moment when we knew the enemy had every intention of destroying us, our families, and taking our land—it was never more evident."[1] Lee and most of his shipmates have since departed on "eternal patrol," but their legacy lives in every submariner who serves today. May their service and sacrifices never be forgotten.

---

1. Interview with Harold "Buzz" Lee, March 2005.

APPENDIX

The following lists are drawn from a number of sources. Officer rosters are compiled from the Navy Directory, the Navy Register, Deck Logs, and other lists. Enlisted rosters are drawn exclusively from muster rolls that were published quarterly and at sailing. Occasionally, there is disagreement among sources as to spelling, and of course errors may be present in the source material. Multiple sources were used whenever available.

COMMANDING OFFICERS OF USS *NAUTILUS* (SS-168)

Name	Rank*	From	To	Days in Command
Doyle, Thomas John, Jr.	Lt. Cdr.	7/1/30	6/4/32	704
Glutting, Paul R.	Lt. Cdr.	6/4/32	6/5/35	1,096
Fife, James, Jr.	Lt. Cdr.	6/5/35	12/30/37	939
Bergesen, Alf Ole Ruh	Lt. Cdr.	12/30/37	7/1/40	914
Follmer, Lloyd Dallas	Lt. Cdr.	7/1/40	6/3/41	337
Thew, Joseph Phillip	Lt. Cdr.	6/3/41	3/3/42	273
Brockman, William Herman, Jr.	Lt. Cdr.	3/3/42	8/26/43	541
Irvin, William Davis	Cdr.	8/26/43	4/19/44	237
Sharp, George Arthur	Cdr.	4/19/44	12/17/44	242
Michael, Willard de Los	Lt. Cdr.	12/17/44	6/30/45	195

* Rank shown at time of detachment.

NAUTILUS OFFICERS SERVING ON WAR PATROLS

Name	Rank*	Position	Patrol
Bedell, Donald Warner	Lt. (jg)	Radar	14
Beebe, William Frater	Lt. (jg)	Communications	12–14
Benson, Roy Stanley	Lt. Cdr.	Executive Officer	1
Berman, Leonard Stanley	Lt. (jg)	Radar	9–12
Bowell, John Howard	Lt. Cdr.	Executive Officer	14
Bowman, Clingmon E.**	WO1		1–2
Brockman, William Herman, Jr.	Lt. Cdr.	Commanding Officer	1–5
Cummings, Charles Read, Jr.	Lt. (jg)		7–11
Davis, George Stebbins, Jr.	Lt.		4–11
Davis, Hugh B.	Ens.		3–4
Defrees, Joseph Rollie, Jr.	Ens.	Commissary	1–2
Eckert, Philip Frederick	Lt.	Torpedo & Gunnery	3–8
Foster, Milton M.	Lt. Cdr.		4–6
Gibson, Scott K.	Lt. Cdr.		2–4
Gustafson, Robert Bergstrom	Lt. (jg)	Gunnery	9–14
Henning, Donald Anton	Lt.	Executive Officer	14
Hess, Franklin Grant	Lt.	Communications	1
Hogan, Thomas Wesley, Jr.	Lt. Cdr.	Engineer, Electrical	1–3
Holloway, Robert Allen	Ens.		8
Irvin, William Davis	Cdr.	Commanding Officer	6–8
Jarvis, Benjamin Campbell	Lt. Cdr.	Executive Officer	7–12
Knoepfler, Robert J.	Lt. (jg)		5

Name	Rank*	Position	Patrol
Lynch, Richard Barr (Ozzie)	Lt. Cdr.	Executive Officer	1–7
Mason, Wilbur J.	Lt.		6
McCain, Walter Moffatt	Ens.	Asst. Communications	13–14
Michael, Willard de Los	Lt. Cdr.	Commanding Officer	12–14
Peirano, James Henry**	Ens.	Asst. Navigator	4–14
Porterfield, Floyd Robert**	Lt. (jg)	1st Lieutenant	1–13
Ray, Sherry Buford	Lt. (jg)		2–3
Rooney, Roderick Shanahan (Pat)	Lt. Cdr.	Executive Officer	1–3
Sabbe, John**	Ens.	Torpedo & Gunnery	1–14
Sharp, George Arthur	Cdr.	Commanding Officer	9–13
Slawsky, Stanley Martin	Ens.		8
Smith, Norman Sherrill	Lt. (jg)	Commissary	9–12
Strong, George R.	Lt. (jg)		7
Welch, Raymond Vincent	Lt.		5
Whitcher, Ruel Rustin	Lt. (jg)	Asst. Engineer	8–13
Winner, Hal "M."	Lt.	Engineer	4–14
Woolridge, Frank Austin	Lt. (jg)	Commissary	13–14

* Rank and position shown at time of detachment.
** Promoted from enlisted crew.

NAUTILUS ENLISTED CREW SERVING ON WAR PATROLS

Crew Member		Rating when Detached*	Patrol
Adamos, Apilonio	CS1	Commissary Steward	4
Adams, Joseph Lee, Jr.	SC3	Ship's Cook	3–4
Agustin, Cepriano Luzano	St3	Steward	4–8
Aldridge, John Ernest	GM1	Gunner's Mate	8–11
Alvord, Claude Oran	F1	Fireman	12–14
Anderson, Ardmoure LeRoy	MoMM1	Motor Machinist's Mate	6–13
Anderson, Francis Harold	CRT (AA)	Chief Radio Technician	7–14
Anderson, Marshall Victor, Jr.	F1	Fireman	14
Anderson, Victor John	TM2	Torpedoman	2–5
Anunciacion, Teofilo	CC1	Chief Commissary Steward	1–2
Arruiza, Joaquin Adolincia	Ck2	Cook	5–14
Bacon, Floyd Thomas	TM3	Torpedoman	1–2
Baker, Howard Lee	MoMM3	Motor Machinist's Mate	7–13
Baker, James Lee	MoMM1	Motor Machinist's Mate	9–14
Balduc, Albert William	CCStd (AA)	Chief Steward	4–5
Banbury, Myles Raymond**	CGM (AA)	Chief Gunner's Mate	1–14
Barcoozy, John, Jr.	QM3	Quartermaster	4–5
Barrett, Roy Dallas	RM3	Radioman	2
Becker, William Robert	FC1	Fire Controlman	8–14
Berg, Roy Edward	EM2	Electrician's Mate	7–14

Crew Member	Rating when Detached*		Patrol
Berganio, Fermin Roquero	StM1	Steward's Mate	2–11
Bergman, Julius John	Bkr3	Baker	2
Billig, Robert William	GM3	Gunner's Mate	12–13
Bishop, Vernon Arley	GM3	Gunner's Mate	3–4
Bodenburg, Gerard Louis, Jr.	MoMM2	Motor Machinist's Mate	9–14
Bowman, Clingmon E.	CEM (PA)	Chief Electrician's Mate	1–2
Braun, Claude	CQM (PA)	Chief Quartermaster	12–14
Bright, John William	CSM (PA)	Chief Signalman	1
Brocklesby, Albert Fremont	SM1	Signalman	1–6
Brodbeck, Cyril Allen	Cox	Coxswain	6–13
Brown, Raymond Franklin	MoMM2	Motor Machinist's Mate	4–11
Bruce, Jackson Howard	MoMM2	Motor Machinist's Mate	5–14
Bruck, Nicholas Anthony**	CMoMM (PA)	Chief Motor Machinist's Mate	1–14
Bueckner, John Earnest	EM3	Electrician's Mate	8–11
Burke, Henry Earl	TM3	Torpedoman	6–11
Burrell, Robert Anthony	Y1	Yeoman	3–7
Campbell, Colin**	MoMM1	Motor Machinist's Mate	1–14
Campbell, Everett Wane	TM2	Torpedoman	1–6
Campuzano, Raymond Thomas	MoMM2	Motor Machinist's Mate	6–11
Carlson, Harold Frederick	RM2	Radioman	5–11

Crew Member	Rating when Detached*		Patrol
Carroll, Charles Arthur, Jr.	GM3	Gunner's Mate	4
Catlin, Clarence Barton, Jr.	MoMM2	Motor Machinist's Mate	9–14
Chapman, John Robert	EM3	Electrician's Mate	14
Cherry, John Sherwood	SM3	Signalman	12–13
Clauder, Authur Hugh	Bkr3	Baker	7–14
Cofield, Perry C.	CP (AA)	Chief Photographer	2
Colantonio, Paul Joseph	EM2	Electrician's Mate	9–14
Conlan, William Andrew	QM2	Quartermaster	5–14
Corduan, Malcolm Mandeville	EM1	Electrician's Mate	4–14
Cote, Lewis Henry	Sea2	Seaman	1
Creech, Thomas Truxton	TM2	Torpedoman	2–3
Currie, Frank, Jr.	MoMM1	Motor Machinist's Mate	2–11
Damico, Samuel Phillip	GM3	Gunner's Mate	14
Dawson, Kenneth Dee	RM3	Radioman	7–8
De Courcey, John Joseph	MoMM3	Motor Machinist's Mate	9
Denholm, John Patrick	SM1	Signalman	2–5
DePaul, Arthur Anthony	GM1	Gunner's Mate	1
Diehm, Willard David	SC2	Ship's Cook	8–14
Doll, Lambert Charles	MoMM1	Motor Machinist's Mate	5–11
Donovan, Fred William	CMoMM (PA)	Chief Motor Machinist's Mate	1–3
Dougherty, Joseph John	Cox	Coxswain	14
Draper, Earl August	SC3	Ship's Cook	2–4

Crew Member	Rating when Detached*		Patrol
Drew, Wesley Arthur	EM2	Electrician's Mate	1–6
Dryke, Richard Henry	F1	Fireman	9–13
Echanes, Juan Locquiao	St3	Steward	6–12, 14
Eggers, Walter Earl	GM3	Gunner's Mate	6–14
Elkins, Willis Watson	RM2	Radioman	9-14
Engleman, Albert Thomas	CRM (PA)	Chief Radioman	8–13
Epps, Louis L.	Matt2	Mess Attendant	1
Evans, Jerry W.	EM3	Electrician's Mate	12–14
Everton, Lonnie James, Jr.	EM2	Electrician's Mate	2–4
Fernandez, Manuel Aquino	CS1	Commissary Steward	1–5
Filkoff, Joseph Solomon	Sea1	Seaman	12–13
Fisher, Raymond Rex	Bkr1	Baker	6–14
Fitzwater, John Addison	Sea1	Seaman	14
Fong, Daniel	MoMM3	Motor Machinist's Mate	14
Fox, Bruce Carlton	RT1	Radio Technician	4–8
Fox, John William	Cox	Coxswain	12–14
Freitas, Peter Raphael**	CMoMM (AA)	Chief Motor Machinist's Mate	1–14
French, John Marrion	CCStd (AA)	Chief Steward	6–14
Galli, Walter Oswald	TM3	Torpedoman	1–4
Gentry, Ross Cardwell	BM1	Bos'n's Mate	3–14
Gillespie, Harold Aden, Jr.	Sea1	Seaman	12–14
Glover, Lelian Eugene	RM3	Radioman	12

Crew Member	Rating when Detached*		Patrol
Goebel, Clyde Marcel	CMoMM (AA)	Chief Motor Machinist's Mate	6–14
Golden, William	SC2	Ship's Cook	9–11
Gomil, James Patrick	MM1	Machinist's Mate	1–6
Gonzales, Joe	EM2	Electrician's Mate	6–14
Goodman, Joseph Vernal**	CMoMM (PA)	Chief Motor Machinist's Mate	1–14
Gourley, Kelly	F1	Fireman	5
Graham, Preston "C."	MoMM2	Motor Machinist's Mate	1–5
Grasham, William Paul	Cox	Coxswain	5–8
Greene, James Richard	F1	Fireman	1–4
Gregorich, Anthony	Sc3	Ship's Cook	5
Griebel, Arthur Henry, Jr.	RT2	Radio Technician	9–14
Gross, Jerome Simmon	CMoMM (AA)	Chief Motor Machinist's Mate	1–6
Grove, Spurgeon	CTM (PA)	Chief Torpedoman	1–4
Hafner, James Joseph	SC2	Ship's Cook	6–14
Hansen, Asger, Jr.	MoMM3	Motor Machinist's Mate	9–14
Harmon, Elwood Carlyle	Sea1	Seaman	9–11
Harrington, Robert Lee	SC3	Ship's Cook	2–3
Harrison, Albert John	MoMM2	Motor Machinist's Mate	5–14
Harrison, William O.	SC3	Ship's Cook	2
Hartman, Robert Marcus	EM1	Electrician's Mate	14

Crew Member	Rating when Detached*		Patrol
Hedderman, Raymond William, Jr.	F1	Fireman	3–5
Hester, Foy Benton	CEM (PA)	Chief Electrician's Mate	1–13
Holcomb, LeRoy Francis, Jr.	GM2	Gunner's Mate	6–14
Holihan, Joseph John, Jr.	RM2	Radioman	2–14
Holman, John Eldie	Sea2	Seaman	9–11
Holmes, Joseph Clyde	EM2	Electrician's Mate	7–14
Holtz, Paul K.	Sea1	Seaman	1–2
Hood, Walter Lee, Jr.	TM3	Torpedoman	9–14
Hornby, William E.	CMM (PA)	Chief Machinist's Mate	1
Houser, Robert Armand	RM3	Radioman	5–7
Howell, Joe Oliver	EM1	Electrician's Mate	1–8
Hudson, Joseph Sidney	CPhM (AA)	Chief Pharmacist's Mate	1
Hunter, Milton Louis	TM3	Torpedoman	2–3
Hyde, Robert Lincoln**	EM1	Electrician's Mate	1–14
Irwin, Grover Virgil	CMoMM (AA)	Chief Motor Machinist's Mate	1–5
Jones, John Joseph	StM1	Steward's Mate	12–14
Kaplan, Max	RM1	Radioman	1
Keirs, Robert William	MoMM1	Motor Machinist's Mate	7–14
Kelley, Bernard James	GM1	Gunner's Mate	1–5
Kelley, Leslie Vernon	CCStd (PA)	Chief Steward	1–2

Crew Member	Rating when Detached*		Patrol
Kemp, Joseph Vincent	F2	Fireman	2–3
Kesecker, Donald Dayton	RM3	Radioman	12–14
Kile, Kenneth Halsey	CRM	Chief Radioman	14
Killgore, Ross Smith	CMoMM (PA)	Chief Motor Machinist's Mate	1–4, 6–8
Killian, Donald L.	EM3	Electrician's Mate	1
King, William James	SM3	Signalman	9–11
Kinsler, Cedric Clae	MoMM2	Motor Machinist's Mate	4–8
Kirkland, James	SM3	Signalman	3–4
Klein, William Christopher	Y3	Yeoman	6–8
Krambeck, Stanley Louis	F1	Fireman	3–5
Krivy, Andy John	MoMM2	Motor Machinist's Mate	2–6
Kudzik, Henry Stanley	GM2	Gunner's Mate	5–8
Kurtz, Leslie Ray	Sea1	Seaman	4
Landers, Buddy Boyd	RM2	Radioman	3–4
Lange, Walter Charles	CEM (PA)	Chief Electrician's Mate	1–8
Leabo, Jack Duane	Sea1	Seaman	9–14
Lee, Harold Gordon	CRM (AA)	Chief Radioman	1–6
Lee, Robert "E."	TM3	Torpedoman	3
Leedom, Wilbur Lee	GM3	Gunner's Mate	9–13
Lewis, Lester Beale	TM1	Torpedoman	1–7
Likert, Gilbert Roland	BM1	Bos'n's Mate	1–8
Liles, Ray Darrell	MoMM2	Motor Machinist's Mate	6–14

Crew Member	Rating when Detached*		Patrol
Lindell, Earl Ernest	F1	Fireman	4
Lindley, Vernon "Z.," Jr.	TM1	Torpedoman	6–14
Loomis, Robert Louis	Sea1	Seaman	5
Loosli, Leo Daniel	TM2	Torpedoman	8–11
Lynch, Owen Francis	GM1	Gunner's Mate	4
Maelhorn, Luther Eugene	Cox	Coxswain	5–14
Mangloss, Kenneth Wayne	TM3	Torpedoman	12–13
Marshall, Leland R.	Sea2	Seaman	1
Matthews, James Arnold	MoMM1	Motor Machinist's Mate	1–8
McAhren, Lawrence Emmet	MoMM2	Motor Machinist's Mate	7–8
McCall, Gus Armstrong	Matt2	Mess Attendant	1–3
McClellan, James Mitchell	Y3	Yeoman	14
McConnell, Arthur LeRoy	MoMM2	Motor Machinist's Mate	1–8
McCoy, Wendell Gail	SM3	Signalman	13–14
McGrath, Robert Eugene	F1	Fireman	1–3
McKenney, Floyd, Jr.	SC3	Ship's Cook	1
McKinley, William	TM2	Torpedoman	1–3
McLauren, Warren F.	BM1	Bos'n's Mate	1
Messner, Van Arthur	EM3	Electrician's Mate	5–7
Middleton, John Raymond	Y2	Yeoman	1–3
Mielke, Harold Raymond	FC1	Fire Controlman	2–3
Miller, James Robert	MoMM2	Motor Machinist's Mate	7–14

Crew Member		Rating when Detached*	Patrol
Milnes, Walter Floyd	FC1	Fire Controlman	4–7
Milstead, James B., Jr.	Sea2	Seaman	1
Molek, Jerome Stanley	GM2	Gunner's Mate	6–14
Morast, William Don	SM2	Signalman	1–3
Morgan, Orville A.	CMM (AA)	Chief Machinist's Mate	1–2
Mosby, Clifford Warren, Jr.	Sea1	Seaman	12
Moss, Paul	Sea1	Seaman	14
Mueller, James Frank	MoMM2	Motor Machinist's Mate	7–14
Mullan, John William, Jr.	QM3	Quartermaster	14
Munski, Walter Leo	GM3	Gunner's Mate	5
Murphy, Edwin Fabian	EM3	Electrician's Mate	6–8
Murphy, Ernest James	QM3	Quartermaster	1–4
Nagle, John Joseph, Jr.	RM3	Radioman	12–14
Navratil, Edward Joseph	TM1	Torpedoman	1, 4–14
Neely, Bernard	QM1	Quartermaster	1–3
Novak, Frank Louis	MoMM2	Motor Machinist's Mate	2–6
Oakley, Otho Lee	Sea1	Seaman	12–14
O'Brien, Patrick Anthony	TM1	Torpedoman	1, 4–7
Okerblom, Victor John	SM3	Signalman	14
Ollman, LaVeen John	Sea1	Seaman	14
Olsen, Bertle Berdell	TM3	Torpedoman	5–8
Olsen, Stanley R.	MM1	Machinist's Mate	1

Crew Member		Rating when Detached*	Patrol
Orr, Richard Raymond	MoMM2	Motor Machinist's Mate	4–8
Owens, Earl Malvi	EM1	Electrician's Mate	5–14
Pace, John Ray	TM2	Torpedoman	4–14
Patrick, James W., Jr.	Sea2	Seaman	2
Peek, Clovis	GM1	Gunner's Mate	5–13
Peirano, James Henry	Ens.	former Signalman	4–14
Pettebone, Nelson Streater	MoMM1	Motor Machinist's Mate	1–7
Petty, Garland Moore	CMoMM (AA)	Chief Motor Machinist's Mate	5–11
Platia, Salvatore George	RM1	Radioman	6–14
Pleu, Harry Calvin	F1	Fireman	12–14
Porter, Loran R.	TM1	Torpedoman	1
Porterfield, Floyd Robert	Lt. (jg)	former Bos'n's Mate	1–13
Potts, Joseph Neil	CPhM (AA)	Chief Pharmacist's Mate	2–14
Prairie, Gordon Boyd	QM2	Quartermaster	6–14
Price, Robert	F1	Fireman	12–14
Prinz, Henry G.	Sea1	Seaman	1
Privitt, Leonard Arnold	MoMM2	Motor Machinist's Mate	6–14
Ramey, Curtis Sylvester	Sea1	Seaman	9–11
Randall, James Leonard	Y2	Yeoman	8–13
Reibel, Kenneth Edward	GM1	Gunner's Mate	1–3

Crew Member	Rating when Detached*		Patrol
Reichert, Louis Pious	Cox	Coxswain	1–5
Renck, Robert Bryce	F1	Fireman	9–14
Richardson, Charles McKinley	Ck1	Cook	13–14
Roe, Samuel Arnold	MoMM2	Motor Machinist's Mate	1–3
Rossi, Lawrence Guy	Y2	Yeoman	4
Roth, Robert Charles	MoMM1	Motor Machinist's Mate	6–14
Rovge, Melvin Joseph	Sea1	Seaman	9–14
Sabbe, John**	Ens.	former Torpedoman	1–14
Sagaser, William Daniel	RT1	Radio Technician	8–14
Sangster William Greer	SC1	Ship's Cook	1–3
Santarelli, Silvano William	MoMM2	Motor Machinist's Mate	6–11
Sciotto, Phillip Anthony	CMoMM (AA)	Chief Motor Machinist's Mate	1–6, 9–14
Sheiner, Bernard	MoMM3	Motor Machinist's Mate	12–14
Sidars, Leslie Oliver	CMoMM (PA)	Chief Motor Machinist's Mate	5
Skeldon, James Adam	Sea1	Seaman	7
Skipper, Frank Abraham	CCStd (PA)	Chief Steward	3–8
Slyter, Gilbert Gordon	EM3	Electrician's Mate	9–11
Smith, Arthur John	MoMM1	Motor Machinist's Mate	1–11
Smith, Clarence Otto	EM3	Electrician's Mate	12–14
Smith, Joseph	EM1	Electrician's Mate	12–14

Crew Member	Rating when Detached*		Patrol
Smith, Leo William	Sea2	Seaman	3
Smith, Robert Lowell	RM2	Radioman	1–3
Snyder, Victor Glenn	F1	Fireman	14
Spalding, Luther	MoMM1	Motor Machinist's Mate	6–14
Stanton, Robert Waldo	F2	Fireman	1, 3
Starks, Walter Boney	Sea1	Seaman	8
Staton, Guy Osbon	CBM (PA)	Chief Bos'n's Mate	6–13
Stenberg, Charles Russell	Bkr2	Baker	1–5
Stenger, Leo Joseph	BM1	Bos'n's Mate	2–6
Sterling, Dale George	MoMM1	Motor Machinist's Mate	4–14
Stevens, William Wallace	Y1	Yeoman	9–14
Stewart, Charles Monteith	TM2	Torpedoman	4–8
Stocker, Garth Basil St. Maur	QM3	Quartermaster	2–4
Strait, Warren Alexander	EM3	Electrician's Mate	12–13
Stull, Wiliam Gene	MoMM1	Motor Machinist's Mate	1–5
Sullivan, James Frederick	TM3	Torpedoman	7–8
Taylor, Lawrence Edward	F1	Fireman	12–14
Thomas, John Cornielous	MoMM2	Motor Machinist's Mate	4–7
Thompson, Donald "B"	Sea1	Seaman	12–14
Ticknor, George O.	CEM (AA)	Chief Electrician's Mate	1
Tidd, Russell Ellis	TM2	Torpedoman	12–14
Trosclair, Lester Joseph	Y3	Yeoman	5

Crew Member	Rating when Detached*		Patrol
Troutman, William F., Jr.	Sea1	Seaman	1
Turner, Ralph Charles	SC2	Ship's Cook	6–8
Ussin, Reno	GM2	Gunner's Mate	1–7
Valentine, Elliott Harry	CMoMM (AA)	Chief Motor Machinist's Mate	1–11
Van Dyke, Joseph Conrad	Sea1	Seaman	7–11
Wagner, Charles Oscar	MoMM3	Motor Machinist's Mate	9–14
Wagner, Earle Jentoft	F1	Fireman	1
Walls, Carl H.	TM2	Torpedoman	1
Walters, John Lewis	TM3	Torpedoman	9–14
Warford, Raymond Paul	CMoMM (PA)	Chief Motor Machinist's Mate	1–
Waterhouse, John Wellington	SC2	Ship's Cook	5
Watson, Leon, Jr.	EM2	Electrician's Mate	1–6
West, Albert Lee	TM1	Torpedoman	8–14
Wetmore, Irving Earl	CRM (AA)	Chief Radioman	1–3
White, Charles Louis	CRM (AA)	Chief Radioman	7
White, Joseph Rodney	SC3	Ship's Cook	13–14
Whiteley, Grady	F1	Fireman	1–4
Williams, Earl J.	Matt2	Mess Attendant	1–2
Wills, Robert William, Jr.	MoMM2	Motor Machinist's Mate	12–14
Wilson, Thomas Doak	SM1	Signalman	4–11

Crew Member	Rating when Detached*		Patrol
Wines, Lawrence Giffing	SoM2	Sonarman	8–11
Wood, Lester M.	Y3	Yeoman	1
Wurster, Ralph Bernard	EM1	Electrician's Mate	1–11
Yaryan, Charles Leon	EM2	Electrician's Mate	2–3
Ylinen, Arthur	Sea2	Seaman	7
Young, Jefferson T.	MM2	Machinist's Mate	1

*"AA" = Acting Appointment; "PA" = Permanent Appointment
** These men served on all fourteen *Nautilus* war patrols.

REFERENCES

BOOKS

Alden, John D. 1979. *The Fleet Submarine in the US Navy*. Annapolis, MD: Naval Institute Press.

Bagnasco, Erminio. 1978. *Submarines of World War Two*. Annapolis, MD: Naval Institute Press.

Beach, Edward L. 1983. *Run Silent, Run Deep*. Annapolis, MD: Naval Institute Press.

Blair, Clay, Jr. 1975. *Silent Victory: The U.S. Submarine War against Japan*. Philadelphia: J. B. Lippincott.

Bruning, John. 2017. *Indestructible*. New York: Hachette Books.

Campbell, Douglas, *Save Our Souls*. Self-published.

Fluckey, Eugene. 1992. *Thunder Below! The USS Barb Revolutionizes Submarine Warfare in World War II*. Urbana: University of Illinois Press.

Gross, Jerome S. 2007. *Silently We Served: U.S. Submarines in WWII*. Bellmore, NY: Sheron Enterprises, Inc.

Jourdan, David W. 2015. *The Search for the Japanese Fleet: USS Nautilus and the Battle of Midway*. Lincoln: Potomac Books, University of Nebraska.

Keegan, John. 1989. *The Second World War*. New York: Penguin.

Lapham, Robert and Bernard Norling. 1996. *Lapham's Raiders: Guerrillas in the Philippines, 1942–45*. Lexington: University Press of Kentucky.

Lord, Walter. 1977. *Lonely Vigil*. New York: Viking.

McNerney, Eileen, and Maureen McNerney Habel, eds. 2016. *Trapped in Paradise*. Newport Beach, CA: Dockside Sailing Press.

Michener, James. 1946. *Tales of the South Pacific*. New York: The Curtis Publishing Company.

Mitchell, Robert, Sewell Tying, and Nelson Drummond. 1944. *The Capture of Attu*. Washington, DC: Infantry Journal, Inc.

O'Kane, Richard. 1977. *Clear the Bridge! The War Patrols of the USS Tang*. Chicago: Rand McNally & Company.

Peatross, Oscar. 2006. *Bless 'Em All: The Raider Marines of World War II*. Tampa, FL: Raider Publishing.

Roscoe, Theodore. 1949. *United States Submarine Operations in World War II*. Menasha, WI: George Banta.

Rottman, Gordon L. 2005. *U.S. Special Warfare Units in the Pacific Theater 1941–45: Scouts, Raiders, Rangers and Reconnaissance Units.* New York: Osprey Publishing.
———. 2014. *Carlson's Marine Raiders.* New York: Osprey Publishing.
Smith, George W. 2001. *Carlson's Raid.* Novato, CA: Presidio Press.
Tully, Anthony P. 2009. *Battle of Surigao Strait.* Bloomington: Indiana University Press.

INTERVIEWS AND PRIVATE CORRESPONDENCE

Beach, Edward L. Letters to Jeff Palshook, October 2000 and February 2001.
Burrell, Robert. Phone interviews with Jeff Palshook, December 2000.
———. Video interview with Liv Schad, *Texas Veterans Remember WWII*, May 2004.
Hester, Foy, Jr. *75 Years Ago Today.* Series of posts detailing *Nautilus* activities based on diaries and memorabilia from Chief Electrician's Mate Foy Hester, June 2017–November 2019.
King, Spence. Phone interviews with Michele Cooper, August 2006.
Lee, Harold Gordon. Letters to Jeff Palshook, December 2001–April 2005.
———. Memoir. San Diego, 2001.
———. Phone interview with Michele Cooper, March 2007.
———. Phone interviews with Jeff Palshook, November–December 2001, March 2005.
O'Brien, Patrick Anthony. Phone interviews with Jeff Palshook, February 2000.
Palshook, Jeffrey. Phone interview with Michele Cooper, August 2006.
Peirano, James Henry. *Collection, Veterans History Project.* American Folklife Center, Library of Congress, 2007.
Porterfield, Floyd Robert. Letter to Jeff Palshook, March 2002.
———. Phone interviews with Michele Cooper, August 2006.
———. Phone interviews with Jeff Palshook, February 2000, August 2006.

OFFICIAL MILITARY DOCUMENTS

American Prisoners of War in the Philippines. Office of the Provost Marshal General Report November 19, 1945.
Deck Logs: USS *Nautilus* (SS-168). December 1941–June 1945.
The Fleet Type Submarine, NavPers 16160–69, Bureau of Naval Personnel. June 1946. Made available by the San Francisco Maritime National Park Association.
History of Ships Named Nautilus. Office of the Chief of Naval Operations, Naval History Division, August 1962.
Patrol Report of USS *Nautilus* (SS-168). Patrols 1–14, July 16, 1942–1930, January, 1945.
Tooke, Lamar. *Infantry Operations in the Aleutians: The Battle for Attu.* U. S. Army War College, 1990.
United States Submarine Losses, World War II. NAVPERS 15784, 1949.
U.S. Hydrographic Office. *Submarine Report: Depth Charge, Bomb, Mine, Torpedo, and Gunfire Damage, Including Losses in Action, 7 December 1941 to 15 August 1945, War Damage Report No. 58.* Bureau of Ships, Navy Department, January 1949.

Articles and Websites

Benson, Roy S. 1984. *The Reminiscences of Rear Admiral Roy S. Benson, U.S. Navy (Ret.)*. Annapolis, MD: U.S. Naval Institute.

Dwyer, John B. 2005. *Remembering the Alaska Scouts*. American Thinker, https://www.americanthinker.com/articles/2005/11/remembering_the_alaska_scouts.html.

Eckert, Philip F. 1987. *Still on Patrol. Shipmate* (September).

———. 1989. *Left Overboard from a Diving Submarine. Shipmate* (June).

Hackett, Bob. *IJA Hospital Ship/IJN Transport America Maru: Tabular Record of Movement*. Imperial Japanese Navy Page. http://www.combinedfleet.com/America_t.htm.

Hall, Harry. 2004. *The Diesel Boat Era*. U.S. Submarine Veterans World War II, Connecticut chapter.

Helgason, Guðmundur. *George Arthur Sharp, USN*. U-boat.net. https://uboat.net/allies/commanders/3338.html.

Hemingway, Al. 2018. *Bitter Cold, Bitter War: The Aleutian Islands in WWII*. Warfare History Network. https://nationalinterest.org/blog/reboot/bitter-cold-bitter-war-battle-alaskas-aleutian-islands-world-war-ii-176549.

Hogan, Tom. 1980. *Memories. . . . Thirty-Eight Years Later*. VFW Newsletter USS *Argonaut* Ship #1928.

Horazdovsky, Kortnie. 2018. *Alaska's Forgotten War*. Anchorage, AK: KTUU-TV May 17.

Howard, Ed. *Spyron: The Submarine Spy Squadron*. http://www.subsowespac.org/.

Huber, Thomas M. 1991. *The American Bataan Campaign December 1941 to April 1942*. Army History, no. 21, 1–13. JSTOR, www.jstor.org/stable/26302928.

Irvin, William D. 1980. *Reminiscences of Rear Admiral William D. Irvin, U.S. Navy (Ret.)*, Annapolis, MD: U.S. Naval Institute.

Mason, Rachel. *Attu Prehistory and History (with Prehistory section adapted from Corbett et al. 2010*. National Park Service. https://www.nps.gov/aleu/learn/historyculture/index.htm

United States Marine Corps Amphibious Reconnaissance Battalion Wikipedia page. https://en.wikipedia.org/wiki/United_States_Marine_Corps_Amphibious_Reconnaissance_Battalion.

Other Material

Historic Naval Ships Association. Audio recordings including World War II training recordings with shipboard calls and commands; actual recordings of the sounds of depth charges exploding at various distances, inside and outside a submarine hull; JP sonar training records; and even a unique recording made in the conning tower of USS *Sealion* (SS-315) during the attack and sinking of the Japanese battleship *Kongō* on November 21, 1944. Smithfield, VA. www.hnsa.org.

Lynch, Richard Barr. 16-mm films (converted to VHS tape). Pacific theater including periscope images, 1942–1946.

Index